The Ohio Presidents

ALSO BY QUENTIN R. SKRABEC, JR.
AND FROM MCFARLAND

*Benevolent Barons: American Worker-Centered
Industrialists, 1850–1910* (2015)

Rubber: An American Industrial History (2014)

*The Green Vision of Henry Ford and George Washington Carver:
Two Collaborators in the Cause of Clean Industry* (2013)

*The Carnegie Boys: The Lieutenants of Andrew
Carnegie That Changed America* (2012)

Edward Drummond Libbey, American Glassmaker (2011)

Henry Clay Frick: The Life of the Perfect Capitalist (2010)

H.J. Heinz: A Biography (2009)

*The Metallurgic Age: The Victorian Flowering of
Invention and Industrial Science* (2006)

The Ohio Presidents

Eight Men and a Binding Political Philosophy in the White House, 1841–1923

QUENTIN R. SKRABEC, JR.

McFarland & Company, Inc., Publishers
Jefferson, North Carolina

LIBRARY OF CONGRESS CATALOGUING-IN-PUBLICATION DATA

Names: Skrabec, Quentin R., author.
Title: The Ohio Presidents : eight men and a binding political philosophy in the White House, 1841–1923 / Quentin R. Skrabec, Jr.
Description: Jefferson, North Carolina : McFarland & Company, Inc., Publishers, 2018 | Includes bibliographical references and index.
Identifiers: LCCN 2018032820 | ISBN 9781476669304 (softcover : acid free paper) ∞
Subjects: LCSH: Presidents—United States—History. | Presidents—Ohio—History. | Republicanism—Ohio—History. | Populism—Ohio—History. | Republican Party (Ohio)—History. | Ohio—Politics and government—1865–1950.
Classification: LCC E176.1 .S6144 2018 | DDC 973.09/9 [B] —dc23
LC record available at https://lccn.loc.gov/2018032820

BRITISH LIBRARY CATALOGUING DATA ARE AVAILABLE

ISBN (print) 978-1-4766-6930-4
ISBN (ebook) 978-1-4766-3334-3

© 2018 Quentin R. Skrabec, Jr. All rights reserved

No part of this book may be reproduced or transmitted in any form or by any means, electronic or mechanical, including photocopying or recording, or by any information storage and retrieval system, without permission in writing from the publisher.

The front cover images are (left to right, from the top) of William Henry Harrison, Ulysses S. Grant, Rutherford B. Hayes, James A. Garfield, Benjamin Harrison, William McKinley, William Howard Taft and Warren G. Harding (Library of Congress)

Printed in the United States of America

McFarland & Company, Inc., Publishers
  Box 611, Jefferson, North Carolina 28640
  www.mcfarlandpub.com

To Our Lady of Covadonga and
my granddaughter Anna Elizabeth Shamrock

Acknowledgments

The William McKinley Presidential Library and Museum in Canton and the McKinley Birthplace Home and Research Center in Niles are wonderful resources for research on President McKinley as well as the congressional papers. I would particularly like to credit the help and vast knowledge of Janet Metzger at the William McKinley Presidential Library and Museum. The staffs at are outstanding and passionate. Special thanks also to the outstanding research of the Stark Historical Society. Another important resource is the Hayes Presidential Center archives. At the Hayes, I would like to thank Nan Card, the chief archivist, and Merv Nall. Background research is critical to the success of a focused biography, and I wish to highlight several excellent organizations that helped me. These include the Benson Ford Research Center in Dearborn; the Clement Library of American History at the University of Michigan; the Ohio Historical Museum in Columbus; the William Holmes McGuffey Museum in Oxford, Ohio; the Library of Congress (Presidential Papers Collection); and the Heinz Historical Center in Pittsburgh. I would like to give special thanks to Julie McMasters of the Toledo Museum of Art and Kimberly Brownie, Ann Bowers, and Barbara Floyd of the Ward M. Canaday Center at the University of Toledo. These women are local treasures of knowledge and professional help and have published on Ohio history extensively.

There are also several key Ohio presidential resources I would like to thank: the James A. Garfield National Historic Site in Mentor; the Warren Harding Home in Marion; the Rutherford Hayes Presidential Library in Fremont; the William Taft National Historic Site in Cincinnati; and National First Ladies Library in Canton.

Table of Contents

Acknowledgments	vi
Preface	1
ONE—Death at the Summit	11
TWO—Roots of Ohio Republicanism: Ohio Whigs, Temperance, Abolition and Common Schools	30
THREE—Birth of the Republican Party	44
FOUR—The Civil War in Ohio and the Republican Party	49
FIVE—President Grant and the Foundation of Republicanism	58
SIX—Ohio Republicanism and the American Empire—Rutherford Hayes	70
SEVEN—The Rise of National Capitalism versus Internationalism	80
EIGHT—Ohio Republicanism in the Wilderness	91
NINE—Benjamin Harrison	103
TEN—Congressman McKinley and the Rise of Ohio Republicanism as a National Movement	112
ELEVEN—Ohio Republicanism Challenged	129
TWELVE—Ohio Republicanism at the Summit	139
THIRTEEN—McKinley's Final Days and the Setting of a Vision	151
FOURTEEN—Progressivism's Back Door	159
FIFTEEN—Ohio Republicanism Reformed and Adapted for the Times	171

SIXTEEN—The Republican Party in Rebellion and
  the Election of 1912 — 181
SEVENTEEN—Twilight of Ohio Republicanism — 186
EIGHTEEN—A Renaissance of Ohio Republicanism — 194
NINETEEN—Is There a Ghost of Ohio Republicanism? — 202

Chapter Notes — 207
Bibliography — 215
Index — 219

Preface

Ohio claims eight presidents (one Whig and seven Republicans) who served during the period from 1841 to 1923: William Harrison (1841), Ulysses S. Grant (1869–1877), Rutherford Hayes (1877–1881), James Garfield (1881), Benjamin Harrison (1889–1893), William McKinley (1897–1901), William Taft (1909–1913), and Warren Harding (1921–1923). Colonial Virginia claimed most of the lands in southern Ohio at the time of William Harrison's birth so he is often claimed by Virginia. Of the five presidents that fought in the Civil War, all were from Ohio. Four died in office—Garfield and McKinley were assassinated by terrorists, William Harrison died of pneumonia after one month in office, and Warren Harding died of a heart attack. They were all bound by the evolving frontier philosophy of Ohio republicanism.

Historians' viewpoint is as follows: "No Ohio-born president enjoys such a strong [compared to those from Virginia] reputation as a custodian of the executive office. Of the seven Ohio born presidents [excluding William Harrison, who was born in Virginia], only Hayes and McKinley are rated average or slightly better by students of the presidency; indeed, Ohio presidents are often perceived as a rather dull and colorless lot."[1] In C-Span's extensive 2017 survey of presidential historians, only William McKinley (at 16) was in the top half of presidents ranked. The C-Span survey reflects the opinion of most polls in regard to the Ohio presidents. Two of these leaders, William Harrison and James Garfield, were in office too short a time for a complete critical evaluation but received low rankings. Two others, Warren Harding and Benjamin Harrison, are often considered among the worst. A recent historian says of Benjamin Harrison: "No one even bothered to type up his Civil War letters, most of them written in pencil are now fading away in the stacks at the Library of Congress."[2]

This view of the individual Ohio presidents may be valid, but as a group, these men represented a political movement best called Ohio republicanism that dominated America from 1850 to 1929. All of these Ohio presidents shared a similar culture and educational experience. The period from the first to last administration of an Ohio president saw a farming nation become the world's leading industrial power. America would achieve world leadership in every segment of industry and business. The nation's technology changed the world. On the social front, America ended slavery and started on the long process of granting full civil rights to all citizens.

I have spent more than forty years researching and documenting America's pantheon of industrial leaders. Before I can close the project, there remains one section of that pantheon to be completed. A theme appeared throughout my research: the industrial, governmental, and economic policies born in Ohio that dominated our nation for many decades. Examining this subject required a study of the presidents from Ohio. These men represented a movement and philosophy born on America's frontier. Their viewpoint resulted from a confluence of nationalism, populism, economic growth, public education, civil rights, and social values best represented by the cultural roots of Ohio. There indeed was a strong philosophical bond among Ohio presidents rooted in their common experience. This philosophical link is still reflected in Ohio voters.

What is unique about the Ohio presidents is that their industrial policies and social beliefs formed a legacy that spanned over 100 years. From 1860 to 1930, Ohio republicanism dominated politics across the nation. The simple definition of that legacy might be called Ohio republicanism (small *r*), which referred to the American republic versus a political party. While this belief system was integral to the Republican Party of the period, it cannot be viewed through the eyes of the Republican Party of today. Ohio republicanism was an alliance of social, Christian, and conservative economics. Initially, the philosophy was populism in search of a party, including elements from the Whig, Democrat, and Republican parties. At times it even embraced Democrats such as President Grover Cleveland. Ohio republicanism formed party politics. Evolving from Harrison to Harding, this viewpoint shaped presidents rather than being their product. It was a philosophy based on the frontier beliefs of Ohio and the American Midwest. We shall see that while Ohio republicanism is remembered for protectionism and economic growth, its foundation included social values such as abolition and temperance. Ohio republicanism would not fit perfectly in either of today's political parties. It was, however, a perfect reflection of American frontier values and culture in the Victorian age. Ohio republicanism embodied the nationalism and frontier movement away from big government, with two exceptions—federal control of international trade and national defense, which are clearly delineated in the Constitution as part of the federal government.

The term *republicanism* is derived from Article IV, Section 4, of the Constitution: "The United States shall guarantee to every State in this Union a Republican Form of Government, and shall protect each of them against Invasion; and on Application of the Legislature, or of the Executive (when the Legislature cannot be convened), against domestic Violence." The Founders had a clear view of a republic as a government in which supreme power was vested in the people, who exercised it directly or indirectly through a system of representation. Still, a republic limited federal power to the assurance of basic rights, defense, and trade, referring most other issues to the states. Ohio republicanism in many ways completed the vision of the Founders. The philosophy was on the forefront of the resolution of slavery on bloody American battlegrounds. In its American application, the idea of a republic came to mean a limited form of government and regulation, but also one where the government was responsive to the will of the people and protective of their rights. The reader should not try to define Ohio republicanism as a political system, but more correctly as a frontier populist movement. The movement was not defined or even created by the legacy of Ohio presidents. Instead, it came of the people. While Ohio republicanism can be viewed as an ideology, it had a flexibility from its populist base. Often it was the movement that changed the Ohio presidents, rather than the presidents changing it.

The ideal of Ohio republicanism was rooted in nationalism and Christian morals. Basic Christian morals of the time were believed to be universal and consistent with all religions. Government existed strictly for all the American people. Out of this belief came the idea that it was the government's duty to protect American jobs first. On the moral level, Ohio republicanism meant civil rights for all the people, thus providing the deep roots of abolition. Like any other philosophy, it extended beyond its vision at times, as in its inclusion of the temperance movement. We will see that Ohio republicanism was bigger than any political party, although for the time frame it was embodied in the Republican Party of the 1800s, the home of the presidents from Ohio. The reader can assume that the legacy of these presidents is reflected in the term *Ohio republicanism*. The reader should also not look at the dominance of Ohio presidencies as some lockstep allegiance to a philosophy these leaders modified, rebuffed, and lost elections for. A type of America- and Constitution-first philosophy remained the core of Ohio republicanism. The lifetime of the movement matches that of liberal progressivism since the 1930s, but it did ebb and wane over time. Ohio republicanism ended not so much in failure as in a shift in society and environment.

On the economic front, guided by belief in American prosperity first, Ohio republicanism proved flexible to the times. The economic policy evolved, as did American industry and trade. The philosophy's frontier social roots of morals, civil rights, women's rights, education for all, and at least a limited spread of alcohol remained constant. It was a unique relationship of economic and social issues that gave Ohio republicanism its strength as a political movement. Its successful economic results allowed it to maintain a very conservative social agenda against a progressive trend of the times. While 20th-century progressivism would eventually replace it as the national view, Ohio republicanism's midwestern roots still exist to this day.

Ohio republicanism had a distinct and constitutional approach to government. Ohio had been populated by those running from government control, and thus the state's republicanism supported a limited role for government, particularly at the federal level. Government regulation should come through the legislative branch and be open to judicial review. This variation of federalism accepted federal authority over state authority when necessary, but it preferred such jurisdiction to be driven by the legislative branch versus the executive. Ohio republicanism saw the president as an enforcer of laws made in Congress, not as an active regulator of society.

There are roots of Ohio republicanism in both parties of today, but it is best for the reader to look at the parties of the 1800s and early 1900s as distinct entities. Indeed, we shall see that Ohio republicanism evolved from the whole spectrum of political factions driven by populism. This political ideology and the Ohio presidents' legacy constituted a frontier movement, a cocktail of nationalism, state loyalty, populism, moralism, patriotism, technology, and capitalism. Ohio republicanism's policies varied, but it was an America-first philosophy. It was the result of environment rather than an academic viewpoint or policy. It was not a top-driven ideology, instead reflecting the beliefs of Ohio's people, but it proved adaptable to all Americans. The presidents from Ohio all held these beliefs to a lesser or greater degree and brought this ideal to the nation. It was reinforced by the public school system, religious ethics, and the people's capitalistic drive. Most of these factors, such as the public school system, abolition, temperance, and economic expansion, were birthed or deeply rooted in Ohio.

The old roots of Ohio republicanism have surfaced from time to time in the legacy of nationalism, protectionism, and moral principles. These beliefs often caused voters to cross political lines as the Reagan Democrats did. More recently, the protectionist-voter vein surfaced with Donald Trump, as neither party offered a protectionist platform. The geography of these voters followed the historical roots of Ohio republicanism, as did the voters' unusual focus on jobs, nationalism, and ethical principles. Ohio republicanism demanded high morals, Christian sourced, but not requiring allegiance to any denomination or sect. Of the Ohio presidents, Garfield and William Harrison were Christian with no affiliation, Benjamin Harrison and Hayes were Presbyterian, McKinley was Methodist, Harding was Baptist, and Taft was a Unitarian.

Ohio republicanism is and always has been a populist reflection of voter trends changing with the events and the times. That populism often confounds political analysts. Theodore Roosevelt noted: "I think there is only one thing in the world I can't understand, and that is Ohio politics."[3] And yet the Ohio voter is often the harbinger of political success. Ohio presidents embraced the populism without trying to lead or form it, and that is their real legacy.

Ohio's presidential legacy is unique in that it embraces more than any one president. It represents a common theme and a philosophy. The Ohio presidents were not a monolithic group in religion or politics, but they clearly were sons of Ohio. Ohio republicanism was not always in lockstep with the initial views of Ohio's presidents, but it would change those leaders. The state's presidential legacy evolved into a national view of moral and economic direction best categorized as Ohio republicanism. One fact that always struck me as odd as I grew up in Pittsburgh and managed in the steel industry was the existence of a loyal remnant of Republicans in Democratic burghs. A few Republican steelworkers, such as my grandfather, traced their party allegiance to the days of William McKinley and William Taft. Such loyalty was highly unusual for union members, who were often strict Democrats in a Democratic town and industry. Even more amazingly, these Republican steelworkers were also Catholic. These remnant Republicans seemed more politically aligned with the Democrats of the time based on demographics. The steelworkers of my day looked to the Republican Party as the party of the bosses. It would be thirty years before I gave the matter much further thought. I never understood this historical oddity until I researched William McKinley. The latent votes of Ohio republicanism arose from time to time, as seen in the allegiances of the Reagan Democrats, the Blue Dog Democrats, the Sanders movement, and the Trump populists in Ohio and the Midwest.

The Republican remnant of steelworkers was part of a great political alliance built on American manufacturing in the 1800s by a line of Republican presidents from Ohio. President McKinley solidified this alliance into a political force. William McKinley had come from a middle-class family of ironworkers. He believed that a strong American industry was the beating heart of our democracy, and he had fought for protective tariffs from the beginning of his political career. No matter how hard the criticism, he never wavered from his position on such tariffs. McKinley found few allies in colleges, the merchant class, bankers, and some farming areas, but he built new alliances in the middle and working classes and with manufacturing owners. He politically united labor and the bosses for the good of industry and America, and he struck a moral chord in the middle class as well. Regions of the old Ohio republicanism surfaced again in 2016 in the industrial Midwest. Ohio republicanism was a conservative movement rooted in populism, and the origin of that legacy is the subject of this book.

For many, tariffs and protectionism were the hallmark of Ohio republicanism, and they might have seemed to be an expansion of government or of a strong central government. However, the reader should note that such tariffs were set through Congress, not the executive. Ohio republicanism demanded a legislative approach, and it rationalized, based on the Constitution, that defense, civil rights, and control of interstate trade were the only matters where a strong federal government was required.

Ohio republicanism supported states' rights with the glaring exception of civil rights. The school of thought did not support state authority in the case of such freedoms before or after the Civil War. In fact, Ohio republicanism had deep roots in the abolition movement, maintaining even after the Civil War that the federal government should maintain the rights of former slaves. Moralism was the only factor that trumped the economic and political views, and this circumstance often made the Ohio voter unpredictable.

The Ohio republicanism and presidential legacy embraced the missing implementations of the nation's Founders, such as abolition, radical equality for all, and a moral compass for the nation. Ohio republicanism would supply the patch in our Constitution for issues the Founders passed on, such as slavery. At times, including during the temperance movement, that moral compass pointed in too extreme a direction for the nation. This Ohio legacy of moralism was infused into America through the famous *McGuffey Readers*, which were born in the heart of Ohio and used as the nation's textbooks for almost a hundred years. It was with the didactic and patriotic *McGuffey Readers* that Ohio presidents began their education.[4] Maybe more importantly, the *McGuffey Readers* became a standardized text for the nation's youth, spreading the philosophy of Ohio republicanism across the country. Ohio's presidential legacy defined American exceptionalism in a moralistic view. Exceptionalism was not seen as national pride but as national humility; in fact, our success was not so much an achievement as a blessing. Of course, this belief in a Manifest Destiny was at times viewed as arrogance. But in terms of the Ohio legacy, this direction and blessing was natural and God given.

While their moral legacy reflected the agrarian society of Jefferson, the Ohio presidents' economic philosophy was Hamiltonian, believing industrial growth was part of America's Manifest Destiny. They proved to all to be early adopters of technology. The Ohio presidents also believed in American-led internationalism versus today's globalization. Most of them were involved in the expansion of the canal system that brought economic prosperity to Ohio. Later, Presidents Grant, Hayes, Garfield, Harrison, and McKinley would play key roles in the building of the Panama Canal. Four of the men even worked on the canal system in their youth. All Ohio presidents supported and promoted some of America's greatest world's fairs, such as those in 1876 in Philadelphia, in 1896 in Chicago, in 1901 in Buffalo, and in 1904 in St. Louis.

Rutherford Hayes was the first president to install telephones in the White House. As President Garfield struggled for weeks after being shot, Alexander Bell tried an electric induction coil to help doctors find the bullet that had wounded him. McKinley was the first president to drive an automobile, and Taft created a national automobile club shortly thereafter. McKinley was also the first president to ride in an electric car (it would be the ambulance used after he was shot). A worried McKinley aide asked inventor Thomas Edison to rush an X-ray machine to Buffalo to find the stray bullet in the president's body. The machine arrived but wasn't used. Warren Harding often joined Thomas Edison and Henry Ford in their famous cross-country Model T trips. Harding signed the Federal Highway Act of 1921, and from 1921 to 1923, the federal government spent $162 million on America's highway system. Harding was the first to have his speeches carried by radio, and he was the first to have radios installed in the White House.

The Ohio presidents reflected the early immigration into Ohio from the original thirteen states. These immigrants and their views formed the foundation of Ohio republicanism. This immigration was driven by a desire for even more freedom from government regulations and taxes. The state's new residents included early religious migrants fleeing the strict rules of New England's churches. Many others came in the 1790s, fleeing the whiskey taxes of the new federal government. Not surprisingly, Ohio republicanism was deeply based on individual rights over government. Originally, Virginia, Pennsylvania, and Connecticut claimed Ohio. In 1780, Congress incorporated the area into federal land known as the Northwest Territory. After the American Revolution, Ohio was a true frontier, and it would be contested by the Native American tribes. Early settlers were fur trappers, traders, and those seeking the true freedom of government offered by the frontier. Many were seeking freedom from taxes, such as the aforementioned federal tax on whiskey making. Others looked for cheap land. New England immigrants were deeply religious and of English stock. From Pennsylvania came government-hating and freedom-loving Scotch-Irish. German farmers looking for more land also came from Pennsylvania. Virginia was a source of prospectors, retired military, and politicians. From Connecticut came those wanting to form new congregational churches of their own. New Yorkers came searching for new business opportunities.

The first major wave of immigration in the 20th century came from New England. Connecticut had called northeast Ohio the Western Reserve, and immigrants of Puritan stock were seeking new congregations of more free-thinking Calvinist philosophy. Many of the Ohio presidents, including Grant and Garfield, could trace their families back to the Puritans of the 1600s. Others from New England poured in to Ohio in the 1810s while looking for better economic conditions. Politically, these early immigrants were antislavery

Federalists, and they formed the early roots of the temperance movement. The families of Presidents Grant, Hayes, Taft, Harding, and Garfield came from this group. Amazingly, the vote from Ohio's Western Reserve still tracks closely with that of Connecticut.[5]

In the 1790s, Ohio received a steady influx of Pennsylvania Scotch-Irish seeking freedom from the federal taxes on whiskey and iron. These immigrants fiercely opposed government authority and taxes, yet on the local level they imposed taxes or community service to ensure education for all. Here again, we see social values trumping political beliefs. Politically, these early immigrants were initially Jeffersonian, but they would eventually become Whigs supporting economic and industrial growth. President William McKinley's family came from this stream of settlers.

Virginia supplied many immigrants to southern Ohio. Presidents William and Benjamin Harrison's family came from Virginia, which tended to be Jeffersonian. Settlers from Virginia tended to be ambivalent about slavery but were willing to listen to the people. They integrated well into Ohio and often married into abolitionist families in the Cincinnati area, as did members of the Harrison family. This stream of immigrants tended to find a place in the emerging Whig Party of the 1820s. The Whig value of economic growth was a core value of all of Ohio presidents and the movement of Ohio republicanism.

Most of the Ohio presidents came from strongly abolitionist roots and old national Whig Party roots. It would be the Ohio Whigs with their abolition and temperance views that fractured the Whig Party and formed its replacement, the Republican Party. The glue that unified Ohioans in the Republican Party was abolition and antislavery sentiment. Abolition pulled in the majority of former Whigs, but it also pulled in Jeffersonian Democrats, Quakers, and the Shakers of central Ohio. Still, the Republican Party remained committed to economic growth. Even with the shortages of the Civil War, Lincoln demanded a buy-American-first policy.

Ohio developed its own America-first economic approach, but the plan did not involve isolationism. The state was accommodating to international trade, from which its farmers had prospered. As a voting bloc and nation within a nation, Ohio was its own mix of agriculture and manufacturing. The canal system and road building of the 1820s had made Ohio an international player. In fact, the economic drive for the canal was to open up eastern and European markets to the state's farmers. By the 1850s, Ohio was a leading manufacturing state, iron producer, and agricultural exporter.

Presidents McKinley and Taft were descendants of iron-making industrial families. The most enduring legacy of the Ohio presidents' latent Founding ideals was the creation of Alexander Hamilton's vision of a manufacturing empire. The Whigs' roots were deep, following the progressive industrialism of Henry Clay. The Whig Party had come to national prominence by its support of the United States Bank, a national canal system, and a scientific approach to pro–American trade policies. The United States Bank had been the source of credit and capital for regional economic growth, particularly in the West. Ohio republicanism evolved into the world's most successful approach to manufacturing and trade. It would be an economic strategy that guided the United States from 1860 to 1930 and created a golden age of American business. The foundation of Ohio manufacturing policy for the nation was one of scientifically managed trade built on the core principles of nationalism, job protection, protection of critical and basic industry, congressional oversight of profiteering, reciprocity in trade agreements, and an acceptance of internationalism, not isolationism. Ohio presidents Ulysses S. Grant, Rutherford Hayes, James Garfield, Benjamin Harrison, and William McKinley developed a balanced trade system far more complex than the narrow historical view of extreme tariffs. This scientific approach to tariffs would fund national economic projects and protect American industries. The policy brought Ohio industries such as steel, glass, iron, and heavy manufacturing into international dominance. Protection of American industry and laborers would become a core value of Ohio republicanism.

President Grant improved on Lincoln's protectionist policy to strengthen American industry in areas of critical needs through tariffs. President Hayes expanded civil rights while continuing Lincoln's and Grant's economic policies. Garfield, Harrison, and McKinley fully developed the Hamiltonian policy to protect infant and job-creating businesses, manufacturing everything from steel beams to Heinz pickles. Garfield and McKinley applied scientific rates to tariffs with reciprocity agreements that expanded American markets while protecting home industries. McKinley's fully evolved system created a permanent congressional Tariff Commission to ensure capitalists were not pocketing the profits but investing in jobs and plant expansion. Annual reviews could result in reduced tariff rates for profiteering. Finally, Presidents McKinley and Taft applied reciprocity requirements to international trade agreements, which limited the possibility of trade wars. This nationalistic approach respected the global nature of the market. Presidents Hayes, Harrison, McKinley, Taft and Harding maintained the industrial home market while investing in import growth through the building of the Panama Canal, the merchant marine, and world's fairs.

To the modern conservative, the use of tariffs would appear to be an extension of government regulation, not a move inherent to the roots of less government and Ohio republicanism. However, the initial Whig thinking was that the only rightful government regulation was in international trade and defense. The use of tariffs was based on the Commerce Clause of the U.S. Constitution, which describes an enumerated power listed in Article I,

Section 8, Clause 3. The passage states that the United States Congress shall have power "To regulate Commerce with foreign Nations, and among the several States, and with the Indian Tribes." Early Americans were more familiar with the use of trade as an economic weapon. England had used it against the colonists for decades. In the years after the War of Independence, England used dumping to successfully destroy the American iron industry. Iron makers in western Pennsylvania, Ohio, Kentucky, Connecticut, and New Jersey never forgot the economic destruction leveled against them by trade. Thus popular support for tariffs rose, peaking with the McKinley administration.

No Ohio president represented the story of Ohio and Ohio republicanism better than William McKinley (1897–1901). His family emigrated from the eastern states to avoid government regulation and taxes. The son of an iron furnace manager who lost his job to a wave of deindustrialization caused by cheap imports, McKinley was a Civil War veteran and a civil rights advocate. He believed the role of the American government was to ensure American workers' prosperity before pursuing geopolitical goals. McKinley was one of a few presidents whom factory workers and owners admired. At his untimely death, his popularity and that of Ohio republicanism had reached a peak.

The deep roots of Ohio republicanism and the economic Whig foundation can still be seen in elections of today. These metaphysical ruins of great political parties and politicians can still be felt in Ohio. The ghosts of Ohio presidents are real, and they often haunt politics today. These ghosts are apolitical but anchored in a belief in American manufacturing and traditional values. Ohioans have voted for both of today's political parties over the years. It is not surprising, however, that the regional results of the 2016 election reflect these ghosts. In fact, both parties' latent views on trade in 2016 echo the Ohio presidents and their vision of Ohio republicanism.

Since 1993, I have traveled routinely through the heart of Ohio from Toledo to my family in Pittsburgh by back roads that take me through the center of Whig and Ohio republicanism. For years in election season, I counted political signs, but never did they augur a trend till 2016. In 2016, there was an explosion of Trump signs, most handmade. They increased to a peak in the Youngstown area. "Make America great again" had clearly hit a nerve, and I knew something was very different this time. This change was about the hope of industrial greatness.

Chapter One

Death at the Summit

"Am I shot?" These were the simple words of one of America's most popular presidents after the second bullet entered his body.[1] The blood on his hands answered the question before anyone could respond. Only seconds before, he had given his lapel carnation to a little girl, since she had waited so long in the receiving line at the Buffalo World's Fair (Pan-American Exposition) of 1901. The audience at President McKinley's speech that day numbered over 50,000, a huge crowd for the times. As President McKinley fell into the arms of a secret service agent, a black waiter quickly struck the shooter, knocking him to the floor. Within moments, the assassin came under attack from both soldiers and police.[2] Though mortally wounded, McKinley would not join his friend and fellow Ohio president James Garfield in the pantheon of dead presidents for several more days. It had been only twenty years ago in September that President James Garfield died in office from an assassin's bullet. More than any other Ohio president, McKinley represented the ideology of a movement known as Ohio republicanism.

As the electric ambulance rushed the conscious president to the Exposition Hospital near the fairgrounds, he expressed several concerns. First, he worried about his wife and how she might take the news. Second, he did not want the assassin beaten or even lynched as the crowd wanted. Third, he expressed regret for the trouble his shooting would cause the Pan-American Exposition. The event was to highlight America's debut as a world power, and McKinley had been looking forward to it for years. The Pan-American Exposition World's Fair was to introduce the American empire to the world as the Great Exposition had done for England in 1851. Even more, the fair would be the triumph of the earlier philosophy of Ohio presidents Grant, Benjamin Harrison, Hayes and Garfield, who had envisioned a South American canal to reduce travel time from the West Coast to the East Coast. Moreover, the festivities would celebrate the opening of the Panama Canal, which

Artist's rendering of Czolgosz shooting President William McKinley with a concealed revolver at Pan-American Exposition reception, September 6, 1901. Library of Congress.

cut weeks of travel time and added more muscle to America's industrial might. These were the type of economic improvements rooted in the philosophy of Ohio republicanism.

The Panama Canal had been the personal dream of an earlier Ohio president, James Garfield, who had organized a canal conference in 1881. In the 1840s, a teenage Garfield had worked on the Ohio and Erie Canal as a mule boy. Mules pulled the canal boats. Garfield knew firsthand the economic prosperity the canals had brought to Ohio—no other American state had prospered on that scale. Similarly, Garfield had believed that the Panama Canal would bring prosperity to America. In 1877, he had become minority leader for the Rutherford Hayes administration and had first talked of building a canal to cut the time of shipping from the East Coast to the West Coast of America. President Hayes and Ohio congressman Garfield would help position a young congressman, William McKinley, as their expert on trade and industrialization. This Ohio troika of politicians and their ideas would become the foundation of an industrial policy for the United States for decades.

McKinley had been James Garfield's apostle on the canal when they had served together in Congress on the Ways and Means Committee. McKinley's legacy dated to the 1880s, when as chair of the Ways and Means Committee, he had initiated the era of expansion for American industry and American trade. The September 5, 1901, speech in Buffalo was to mark the final phase of a vision that had built an American industrial empire. The bulldog of protectionism had just completed that notable address at the Buffalo Pan-American Exposition, heralding a significant change in America's view of industry's role. The McKinley trade tariffs had brought an unheard-of level of prosperity to American industry in the last quarter of the 19th century. The problem now was the American market alone could not drive the industrial growth of the past 30 years into the future. That development was the result of a long line of Ohio politicians' determination to protect, expand, and build a lasting legacy for American industry.

From his youth, William McKinley had championed Henry Clay's belief in industrial republicanism, which blended Jeffersonian creativity, Emersonian self-reliance, and Hamiltonian finance with Washingtonian patriotism. The American industry knew no rival and accepted no competitor under the McKinley Tariff. The American steel industry overtook the production and productivity of British steel, which was the symbol of Victorian industrial might, by the late 1890s. McKinley's protectionism was unabashed Americanism, which he viewed more as an economic Monroe Doctrine. His protectionism was a political alliance of big business and the American workingman to secure the country's industrial destiny. He believed the next world empire would not be one of militaristic strength, but one of industrial might. Thus the president's plan reflected a global, economic Manifest Destiny. To the cheers of the American public that day in Buffalo, McKinley prepared to launch the final phase of industrial conquest—world markets.

He took the grand platform that September Thursday to note the success of his belief in protectionism and Ohio Industrialism. McKinley roared with pride:

> My fellow citizens, trade statistics indicate that this country is in a state-of unexampled prosperity ... they show that we are utilizing our fields and forests and mines that we are furnishing profitable employment to the millions of working men throughout the United States, bringing comfort and happiness to their homes and making it possible to lay by savings for old age and disability.... Our capacity to produce has developed so enormously and our products have so multiplied that the problem of more markets requires our urgent and immediate attention.... By sensible trade arrangements which will not interrupt our home production we shall extend the outlets for our increasing surplus.... Reciprocity is the natural outgrowth of our wonderful industrial development under the domestic policy now firmly established.... Reciprocity treaties are in harmony with the spirit of the times; measures of retaliation are not.[3]

Garfield, as a member of the Ways and Means Committee, and then McKinley, as its chairman, had designed American manufacturing policy based on Ohio republicanism. McKinley had passed his famous Tariff Act of 1890 under the presidency of Ohioan Benjamin Harrison. Both men were committed to protecting American jobs and industry, yet the eastern blue-blood banking wing of the party objected to high tariffs. Bankers such as J. P. Morgan were making millions from international trade. Morgan would lead an internal break with the Harrison and McKinley wing in the 1890 congressional and 1892 presidential elections. Morgan's support of Democrat Grover Cleveland would lead to a defeat of William McKinley in the congressional election and of Benjamin Harrison in the presidential election in 1892. For McKinley, it was the only major election he ever lost. The defeat would, however, stiffen McKinley's support for a scientific approach to fair trade. He added the concepts of reciprocity and increased exports to his balanced trade approach. At Buffalo, McKinley was ready to open a new door to international trade, but his policy was still rooted in nationalism.

In the fair speech, McKinley proposed a rebuilding of the U.S. merchant marine, which had been one of the few casualties of McKinley protectionism. With an expanded merchant marine, he hoped to increase American exports to new levels. He had argued for the building of the Panama Canal (called the Isthmian Canal, as Panama was not a country at the time), which was now the foundation of his new trade policy. McKinley had also created a vision for a Pacific cable for communications. He had defined the concept of reciprocity in trade as follows: "By sensible trade arrangements which will not interrupt our home production, we shall extend the outlets for our increasing surplus."[4] Reciprocity allowed an "America First" economic philosophy. McKinley's trade agreements were economic based, and they represented the ultimate of the Whig economic and the Hamiltonian manufacturing view for America.

After McKinley's death, trade reciprocity became an international political tool until the 1930s. The new approach would fracture the Republican Party along old fault lines. Nations such as Germany would try to emulate McKinley's nationalist approach to industry. The new breed of Republicans, the old-line Democrats, and the Edwardian industrialists saw American manufacturing and business as a trading chip in international politics. America therefore moved its focus from a home economy to an international political center. That economic boom had built great new industrial cities such as Buffalo, Cleveland, Cincinnati, Pittsburgh, and Chicago. Ohio McKinley Republicans, however, hoped to maintain the domestic manufacturing growth. The East Coast Republicans with their bankers wanted all-out trade and had little feeling for protecting domestic manufacturing.

McKinley had chosen the jewel of America's manufacturing cities to highlight his industrial philosophy. In 1901, Buffalo was the eighth-largest city in the United States and had some of the largest office buildings in the world.

Buffalo and Niagara Falls represented America's greatest industrial achievement, supplying the power that would light the country. McKinley had visited Niagara Falls the day before his fatal speech at the World's Fair. Only three years earlier, in 1897, the world's greatest inventors had gathered at Buffalo's exclusive Ellicott Club to celebrate the yoking of Niagara Falls to become America's power source. Niagara Falls was supplying more electrical power than the world had ever known. German electrical engineer Professor Siemens estimated in 1888 that "the amount of water falling over Niagara is equal to 100,000,000 tons [of coal] an hour." Sir William Siemens calculated that "if steam boilers could be erected vast enough to exhaust daily the whole coal output of the earth, the steam generated would barely suffice to pump back again the water flowing over Niagara Falls."[5] The power of waterfalls throughout the world remains preeminent in electrical generation, even today accounting for 25 percent of all power generated. McKinley's visit that September focused on the great hydroelectric generators built by his friend George Westinghouse at his huge new factory. The Pan-American Exposition was a celebration of American technology exemplified by Buffalo's industrial might. Its focus was to be the use of technology in everyday life. Ironically, the Exposition Hospital lacked electric lighting, and the X-ray machine from Thomas Edison's laboratory on exhibition, which might have saved McKinley's life, was never used.

McKinley had been a proponent of American technology from his earliest days in Congress. Ohio president Rutherford Hayes had encouraged him to study technology and business for his political base.[6] President Hayes had been very close to the young congressman and often invited McKinley and his wife over to the White House to talk of the latest scientific developments. Hayes and McKinley had also been leaders of the temperance movement, a status that limited their social circles with the Washington elite and often made them look anti-progress. However, they were both supporters of high technology projects over the years. As governor of Ohio in 1775, Rutherford Hayes had promoted a major role for Ohio in the 1876 Centennial Exhibition, officially named the International Exhibition of Arts, Manufactures, and Products of the Soil and Mine (Philadelphia World's Fair). That fair had been the effort of another Ohio president—Ulysses S. Grant. As president, Hayes opened the Exposition of 1876, and Congressman McKinley joined in its praise. Hayes would first use many of the featured inventions, such as the telephone, in the White House and his Ohio home. McKinley had looked forward to the Pan-American Exposition in Buffalo as a highlight of his presidency. The fair would also feature the motion picture technology of Kodak and Edison. The first motion pictures of an American presidents were made at McKinley's swearing in and funeral.

McKinley's exposition speech at Buffalo had linked former Ohio presidents Rutherford Hayes and James Garfield to future Ohio presidents William Taft and Warren Harding. The address expressed a philosophy of midwestern morals anchored to the regulation of national capitalism and the advancement of technology. These concepts would be the foundation of the Republican Party for years to come. However, this philosophy would also split the Republican Party until this day. The division centered on nationalistic capitalism versus global capitalism, and it also stemmed from midwestern moral values such as abolition, temperance, and civil rights promoted by early Ohio politicians. These socially conservative views did not sit well with the East Coast party elite. The party split also represented the divide between East Coast bankers and Midwest industrialists. America's great New York banker J. P. Morgan had opposed McKinley's nationalistic approach to trade to build American industry. Financiers such as Morgan loved free, borderless trade and made their money on total trade volume like a modern casino. Midwest industrialists preferred regional banks focused on domestic growth. Ohio politics and McKinley saw trade as building America, as did the great midwestern industrialists.

The problem in the Republican Party of the 1800s was that it needed compromise between east and west factions to win elections. Ohio and the Midwest industrial belt represented the party base and critical votes. The East Coast Republicans, however, held the necessary money to win. Starting with the presidency of Ulysses S. Grant, presidential tickets reflected the necessary accommodation of the two elements. McKinley, however, had created an industrial alliance of workers and wealthy business owners such as Mark Hanna, and this coalition required less compromise with eastern money and bankers. William McKinley had the backing to move forward on a policy that attracted immigrant blue-collar Democrats for the first time. Overall, big bankers represented the Washington elite and free trade. McKinley became the first president since Andrew Jackson to take on the Washington establishment. He would be one of a growing number of populists in both political parties.

McKinley had envisioned a new type of international trade, as trade relations would be based on reciprocity, not "free" trade. He would not trade high-paying American jobs, which he believed were the right of the nation's democratic success, for cheap consumer goods. Those jobs had been made with American blood. Thus this philosophy clearly promoted American industrial expansion without any apologies. McKinley based his model on that of his friend and supporter, George Westinghouse, whose Pittsburgh workshops and workers supplied over 90 countries with railroad brakes and equipment. Such a model required the maintenance of a fragile alliance of business and labor. In his cerebration of free enterprise, McKinley realized that "the problem with capitalism is capitalists."[7] He had used his enormous popularity to hold the coalition between business and labor together in the face of the capitalists' abuses. Yet McKinley also espoused a simple philosophy based on the voters of his industrial hometown of Canton, Ohio. Simply put, the best things for American workers were high-paying long-term jobs, and the only way to secure and create jobs was through the expansion of business. It was this campaign slogan of "dinner-pail Republicanism" that was at the root of McKinley's popularity, America's industrial growth, and the Republican Party's political success. McKinley's vision of the great capitalistic alliance of labor and owners monitored by government sunk with his life signs that day in September. In fact, within a year after McKinley's death, the breakdown of that alliance ushered in the great era of trust-busting.

McKinley's death did not come quickly. An emergency operation took place at the Exposition Hospital after the shooting, and when it was completed, McKinley was moved to the large home of the exposition's president, John Milburn. The president would struggle for days with intermittent recoveries. By September 13, it was clear he would not survive. Urgent word was sent to Vice President Roosevelt, who was in the Adirondack wilderness in New York; a park ranger was sent to find him, since he was miles from any telegraph or telephone. Roosevelt's vice presidency reflected internal party compromises. He had little in common with the philosophy of Ohio republicanism.

Future president Teddy Roosevelt was of the East Coast money wing of the Republican Party represented by Henry Cabot Lodge. Roosevelt saw McKinley as a type of Ohio middle-class hillbilly. In a visit in 1899 to the McKinleys' summer "White House" in Canton, Ohio, Roosevelt, then the vice president, looked down his nose at the simple house. McKinley had taken years to save enough money to buy his old, middle-class home on Canton's Market Avenue. Though the president was very proud of his purchase, Teddy Roosevelt thought it was below the dignity of the office. McKinley appeared happier than ever at his Canton home as he planned improvements and gardens. He noted: "I am happy as a child to have it back. It's a fine old place."[8] Canton always had a restorative effect on McKinley's wife, Ida, and that alone helped him relax. He loved to get up and walk, then have breakfast while reading the local newspaper. The evening could be spent on the front porch. The summer home was a reminder of McKinley's middle-class roots and simple pleasures. The McKinleys made a few day trips for picnics and relaxation, enjoying the nearby small lakes and rural towns such as Zoar, Ohio. Often, the president and First Lady talked of their eventual retirement in Canton. These modest enjoyments stood in stark contrast to the globe-trotting of Roosevelt.

While the East Coast Republicans opposed McKinley, his acceptance of Roosevelt as vice president had temporarily healed the split. The main opponents of McKinley's "dinner-pail republicanism" were a rising majority of socialists, labor reformers, muckraking journalists, politically oriented immigrants, and neo–Luddites. However, the real problem was the capitalists themselves, and reporters, political reformers, and socialists played to an undercurrent of discontent with corruption. McKinley's assassin in many ways was the edge of that underground discontent with capitalism. Now Roosevelt would be in a position to move closer to progressivism and socialism.

European socialists following Karl Marx had for decades created a reign of terror throughout Europe, and by the 1880s they had made inroads into America. At the time the term for the politics of Marx's followers was *socialist*. But there was a more radical version of these beliefs pushed by anarchists promoting the use of terror and violence. These terrorists were driven by the Marxist philosophy and anti-capitalism stance. The poor economic conditions in the 1880s and early 1890s fueled the movement. Peaceful proponents of socialism had some success in elections, but individual terrorist cells were still operating in most industrial cities. These cells had a national and an international network but were often stirred to violence at the local level. McKinley believed regulated capitalism was the solution to the unrest.

Leon Czolgosz, McKinley's assassin, was a socialist and an anarchist, but more importantly, he expressed the emotion of a broader underground movement. In Czolgosz's own words, "what started the craze to kill was a lecture I heard some time ago by Emma Goldman." Goldman was a Russian socialist and professed anarchist who was the leader of an American socialist movement. Her followers had been problematic; her ex-lover had shot industrialist Henry Clay Frick after the 1892 Homestead Strike. Goldman's thinking represented the antithesis of McKinley's view of America's industrial opportunity. Leon Czolgosz fed off the setbacks of laborers in Detroit, Cleveland, and Chicago. The socialist movement found allies in the muckraking press and in the abuses of the capitalists. McKinley's success was in forming a voting alliance of workers and capitalist owners, as well as in addressing abuses centering on pay and the eight-hour day.

Anarchists such as Czolgosz did not so much represent the oppressed factory worker as an international political movement. Anarchists raged against the economic distribution of wealth in capitalist countries. They found allies in the world's socialist parties, including those in America. Anarchists and socialists appeared whenever there were labor problems, but the American labor movement managed to remain above such political indoctrination. McKinley and labor leaders such as Samuel Gompers, father of the AFL-CIO, forged a unique and cooperative environment for labor resolution by 1901. It was the type of alliance that McKinley had tried so hard to foster. McKinley had grown up with ironworkers and knew their greatest fear was unemployment. He believed the American laborer would never support the socialist platform if the factories kept working. When McKinley did pass away on September 14, this great labor alliance was visible—industrial workers filed by his casket in Buffalo at the rate of 10,000 an hour.

The capitalists, to a large degree, had profited by the use of cheap immigrant labor. The abuses of labor were just starting to make the headlines during the McKinley administration. Exploitation had given rise to the unions, but unions came with abuses of their own. Organized labor at the time discriminated against blacks and unskilled workers. McKinley had moved on both labor and capital as needed to hold up his ideal of capitalism. He had won over a large following of workers with his approach and had overcome the anti-labor brand of the Republican Party in the 1870s. McKinley had adeptly remedied the image rooted in the use of federal troops during strikes.

The 1870s had brought labor unrest to America's shores. In July 1877, America's first general strike was called against the Pennsylvania Railroad and East Coast railroads over a 10 percent wage reduction. Two days of rioting in Pittsburgh alone left over 20 dead, hundreds wounded, and over $5 million worth of damage. The strike spread across America with similar violence. The Great Railroad Strike of 1877 began to lose momentum when President Hayes sent federal troops from city to city. Hayes, however, had damaged the Republican brand with workers for over a decade.

The 1880s brought further unrest in the coalfields of Pennsylvania and the workhouses of Chicago. In 1892, the Homestead Strike at the Carnegie Steel mills resulted in deaths and news coverage, and this time Ohio Republican William Harrison sent troops to the picket lines. During all the unrest, the excessive lifestyles of the "robber barons" were making headlines as well. News outlets covered the great banking trusts of J. P. Morgan and August Belmont that seemed to have given the ownership of America's industrial assets to a handful of businessmen.

Since he was never personally close to the big bankers of New York who had crushed his industrial friend George Westinghouse, McKinley had united owners and labor in the need for a protective tariff. However, McKinley needed these businessmen's money. Getting the bankers' funds required some compromises, such as the selection of Theodore Roosevelt as vice president. Still, McKinley won over a weary working class with his protection of American industries. In 1901, 65 percent of America's wealth was controlled by the banking trusts, but the industrialists remained nationalistic. The industrialists wanted protection as much as labor, and this desire was the common ground used for McKinley's voting bloc. Using these labor votes, McKinley built a new coalition and brought in traditional Democratic voters.

McKinley's trade policies did attract one Democratic stronghold. The traditionally Democratic immigrant Irish of the Northeast believed that free trade had ruined Ireland. All immigrants were reminded of the great Satan of free trade—England. The Irish knew the free traders and international bankers of London that promised more jobs but delivered economic devastation. Working-class immigrants well understood the relationship between free trade and employment. They realized it was better to endure the abuse of the business owners than the hunger pains of not working. By today's standards, the McKinley voting bloc was an unusual alliance of labor and capitalists. These Irish immigrants came to America to work, not to be sold out again by free traders. Abuses could be addressed later. The barbaric 12-hour day in the steel industry actually found labor union support because no one wanted the pay cut of an eight-hour day. Unions in the glass industry ignored child labor while pursuing higher wages for skilled workers. Even labor disputes were exclusively over wages, not conditions.

Like his first election victory in 1896, McKinley would win by a landslide in 1900. McKinley bested the popular vote record of Ohio president Ulysses S. Grant, and he won the electoral vote 292–155 (21 votes higher than his 1896 results). McKinley's coattails were extremely long; the Republicans increased their House majority from 151 to 197 members, and their Senate majority from 35 to 55 members. The president-elect gained in all economic classes of voters as well in the large ethnic groups. Still, socialists and anarchists fueled a growing unrest aimed at McKinley. Eugene Debs, a Socialist Party candidate, garnered almost a million votes in the election.

Yet with all the unrest, America prospered in 1901. Immigrants who were jobless in Europe found work plentiful in the United States. America's poor were well-off compared to the poor of Europe and Asia. While Czolgosz and Goldman saw limited upward mobility, others read of the rags-to-riches dreams daily. Carnegie, Westinghouse, Schwab, Pullman, Edison, and even McKinley had come from poor-to-modest means. Even America's old money, including the blue-blood Adams and Roosevelt families, was amazed by the rise of new capitalists. But members of the old-money elite looked down their noses at those with newly found riches. This mixed view was the nature of the era that allowed countercurrents of discontent to flourish in good times. McKinley struggled to hold his alliance of business and labor together within these crosscurrents. He had supported better wages for Ohio coal workers, warned the trusts of their abuse, and protected jobs with tariffs. McKinley also befriended the more progressive capitalists such as George Westinghouse and H. J. Heinz. Westinghouse paid fairly and built family values among his employees. The new president feared that if his manufacturing alliance of business and labor failed, the international movement of socialism would fill the void. The owner and labor alliance was holding in 1901 and seemed to have a bright future based on the popularity of President McKinley and Ohio republicanism.

Historian John Kasson chronicles the movement of republicanism:

Republicanism developed into a dynamic ideology consonant with rapid technological innovation and expansion. The older moral imperatives of eighteenth-century republicanism were modified to suit a new age of industrial capitalism. As technological progress offered new stability for republican institutions, luxury lost its taint. For its part, the ideology of republicanism helped to provide a repetitive climate for technological adaptation and innovation. The promise of laborsaving devices strongly appealed to a nation concerned with establishing economic independence, safeguarding moral purity, and promising industry and thrift among her people. So too did the hope that increased production, improved transportation and communications would centralize a country that continued to fear regional fragmentation. Yet the union of technology and republicanism, while settling some issues, raised others. Particularly pressing was the question whether the new centers of American production, her manufacturing towns, could avoid the blight and degradation of their English counterparts and achieve a new standard as model republican communities. If not, then Jefferson's worst fears might stand confirmed.[9]

The gunshot of September 6, 1901, in many ways ended this heroic view of American industrialism and Ohio republicanism. McKinley's deathbed ordeal would be far shorter than the 80 days James Garfield had suffered after being shot. After struggling for days at a private home in Buffalo, McKinley's end came on September 14, 1901, the 39th anniversary of the Battle of South Mountain, where he had distinguished himself for bravery in the Civil War. The president's last words were representative of his life—"Good-by, all; good-by. It is God's way. His will be done." He died a man of great faith and deep love for his country. He saw the best in people to a fault and was often let down. While a socialist's bullet ended his life, McKinley believed that America was a nation destined to lead the world with its capitalism. Unlike those who would follow him, he never feared socialism as a fundamental alternative to the American System, but as a plague of those who put greed above nation. McKinley even saw his assassin as a misguided man versus an enemy.

Few realize that McKinley was one of America's most popular presidents, as he was often being overshadowed by the flamboyance of his successor, Teddy Roosevelt. Appropriately, a workingman and his family were the first of thousands to visit McKinley's body at a public viewing in Buffalo. The mourners passed at a rate of 60 per minute, with the city's immigrant working class making up the majority. Buffalo had in many ways been the product of McKinley industrialism. The slain president was also popular with America's youth. Many such as Howard Heinz, the son of H. J. Heinz, used newly imported automobiles to travel hundreds of miles to Buffalo for the ten-hour visitation. The funeral train left Buffalo on the morning of September 17 headed for Washington. As the train approached the Capitol that evening, bonfires lit the way along the railroad tracks. The crowds in Washington pressing to see McKinley's body were almost unmanageable. What reporters noted was the large proportion of women in the multitudes at a time when

"The Funeral of President McKinley—Crowd Waiting for a Last Look at the Beloved Remains, Washington, D.C." Library of Congress.

they could not vote and often paid little attention to presidents. McKinley had, however, been the first president to support women's suffrage. As governor, he had helped secure women's right to vote in school board elections in his Canton district.

On September 18 in the early morning, the body started its sad journey from the Capitol to Canton, Ohio. Pennsylvania Railroad tracks were packed with people in Maryland that had held a night vigil awaiting a glance at the funeral train. In Maryland, the train passed near the battlefields of South Mountain and Antietam, where McKinley had led a group of soldiers to deliver food to trapped Union forces. The late president loved to visit this battlefield to recall those honorable times and remember those who had fallen. Veterans of the Grand Army of the Republic lined the tracks—McKinley had remained active in veteran organizations and veteran affairs his whole life. A humble man, McKinley had stopped an appeal to give him the Congressional Medal of Honor in the 1880s for his efforts during the Civil War. Two years after this funeral train had passed Antietam, a 33-foot monument was erected near Burnside Bridge to commemorate the heroism of the slain president.

Still in the early darkness, the train passed through Pennsylvania coalfields, where thousands of miners came out of the shafts with their lanterns to pay tribute to a friend. Others built large bonfires in the hills over the Pennsylvania Railroad tracks. Earlier in his law career, McKinley had represented poor miners against abuses by the mineowners. The defense would lead him to an upset victory in Canton (then a Democratic town) as prosecuting attorney to start his political career. The coal miners never forgot McKinley's work, and they delivered massive Republican votes in national elections, which normally went Democratic. Southwestern Pennsylvania was always McKinley country, being true to its Whig roots and the Republican Party's birthplace.

As the funeral train was entering Allegheny County, with Pittsburgh at its heart, crowds increased. McKinley in Congress had become the protégé of Pennsylvania's William "Pig Iron" Kelley. Kelley had left the Democratic Party over slavery and tariffs. He would become a founder of the Republican Party, making freedom for the slaves and protection for American industry its core principles. The first Republican organizational meeting was in Pittsburgh in 1856. In 1860, Allegheny County delivered massive votes for the Republican candidate, Abraham Lincoln, giving him Pennsylvania and the Electoral College victory. Kelley would be Lincoln's whip in Congress for the application of protective tariffs, and protectionist politicians were financially backed by Ohio iron producers. McKinley and Ohio presidents Hayes and Garfield learned about trade law directly from Kelley on the Ways and Means Committee. The old Henry Clay and Whig Party industrial voting base in western Pennsylvania and eastern Ohio would continue to deliver for Ohio presidents. McKinley would even surpass Lincoln's majority in this industrial corridor.

The first large crowd for the funeral train in western Pennsylvania was at Pitcairn, a major center for the Pennsylvania Railroad in the Monongahela River Valley. A large group of women were there waiting to see the train before they took their rail connection to the valley's Westinghouse plants, where they were employed. Westinghouse had pioneered the workingwoman in industrial plants. Marshall Everett, a friend and writer, noted from the train: "In railroad cars at Pitcairn, hundreds of factory girls lined up. It was 8:35 a.m. when the train passed through Pitcairn, so most of the girls with their lunch boxes under their arms must have been quite late to work, all for the sake of a few seconds' look at the train."[10] The train continued on to Pittsburgh with crowds growing.

The funeral train passed through Wilmerding, a town that Westinghouse had developed and that McKinley hoped would be America's industrial future of labor peace. One of McKinley's closest supporters in industry was George Westinghouse. As the funeral train passed the large Westinghouse town clock atop the Westinghouse-built YMCA, many gathered to honor the former president of the Canton YMCA. Throughout their careers, both McKinley and Westinghouse had been promoters of the YMCA. McKinley had been chairman of the Ways and Means Committee in Congress, and he and Westinghouse had worked together on railroad safety in the 1880s. The businessman had shown that capitalism could have a heart, and he had built a workingman's town for Westinghouse Air Brake and Westinghouse Electric. McKinley had often pointed to Westinghouse as the model industrial baron. Westinghouse respected the worker, but unlike the industrial barons of the time, he did not see himself as a distributor of the wealth. He gave his money to create jobs, work, and loans for family development. He believed the best philanthropy to be giving someone employment. Westinghouse built no large art museums or music halls, instead creating workplaces that respected laborers and paid them fairly. His factories were not paternal industrial plantations, but examples of industrial democracy in the workplace. Wilmerding was a town that would have changed Jefferson's heart on the evils of industry. Leaders the world over had visited it to see a model industrial city.

This beautiful town of worker homes and community centers stood in stark contrast to the next rail station for the funeral train, Carnegie's Braddock. The smoke of the Braddock and Pittsburgh steel mills blocked the autumn sun at this point, but that smoke and sulfuric odor was itself symbolic of the great prosperity that McKinley had brought to the valley. Before entering the Braddock train tunnel, a large group of brightly dressed young girls waved flags before the dark passage. Exiting the tunnel, the funeral train passed the great slums of Braddock's First Ward at the gate of America's largest steel mill. McKinley had struggled with the contrast between Braddock and Wilmerding, yet he understood these ironworkers, having been one in his youth. They made a living through hot and dirty labor, and they breathed smoke and sulfurous fumes all the time. The streets and rails were covered with thick mill dust, as the many Bessemer steel converters had been running flat out through the night. Still, the workers in both towns lined the rails to honor the man that had retained high wages, increased jobs, and kept the mills at capacity. Thousands of these men had traveled by special train to Canton to shake hands with McKinley in 1896. Braddock, a town of poor immigrant steelworkers, had consistently supported McKinley in his presidential campaigns. Particularly notable was the huge salute of the Irish Catholic crews as the funeral train passed the blast furnaces. The group rarely gave tribute to Methodists, let alone a Mason and a Republican.

Prior to Pittsburgh, the train passed the village of Swissvale, the home of Union Switch and Signal. Union Switch and Signal was a special Westinghouse company that manufactured safety controls for railroad tracks. These devices came about through the overview and legislation of Congressman McKinley and with the help of industrialist George Westinghouse, and they reduced rail accidents by almost 90 percent. This legislation had launched the careers of both men, and they had remained friends. Across the Monongahela River from Swissvale was United States Steel's Homestead plant, site of the bloody steel strike of 1892, which had helped McKinley gain the White House. A few miles away was the home of McKinley's attorney general, Philander Knox, who was on the train that day and traveling in the cabinet car with President Teddy Roosevelt. McKinley had appointed Knox on the request of Andrew Carnegie and Henry Clay Frick.

The train rolled slowly past the home of George Westinghouse, where a special private train station had been built. Nearby also was the home of Henry Clay Frick, who was believed responsible for the Homestead Strike. There, cabinet member Philander Knox (on the funeral train) often played poker with Frick, Carnegie, Westinghouse, and Andrew Mellon. Henry Clay Frick (Andrew Carnegie's old partner) and McKinley were different men, but they shared a belief in capitalism, nationalism, and the American steel industry. One of America's richest industrialists, Frick had supported the protectionist policies against the advice of his banking partner J. P. Morgan, and of many international bankers. For all his faults, Frick was a strict believer in nationalistic capitalism. It had been Henry Clay Frick that had purchased a new suit for the then bankrupt McKinley to wear to his first swearing in as president. Later, Frick would build the McKinley Presidential Library in Niles, Ohio. Frick would lead a group of donators to build a memorial for McKinley in the town as well. The slain president's association with these men was often used to criticize his protection of big business, but on this day it was steelworkers who honored a man they considered their friend too. McKinley stood for steel and industrial jobs against the international bankers in his own party.

It may seem strange to the modern reader that the Democratic steel valleys of today were strongly Republican in 1901, but these political leanings were the result of the alliance McKinley had forged. He had even won over the leadership of the Knights of Labor union and the Amalgamated Association of Iron and Steel Workers. In addition, these laborers and industrialists of the steel valleys had formed a campaign fund for McKinley known as the workingman's tariff club. Of course, these Pennsylvania valleys were still dominated by Scotch-Irish like the late president. No president until John F. Kennedy would command so much loyalty in these steel valleys.

As the train approached the steel mills of Homestead and Pittsburgh in late morning, thousands of steelworkers carrying their dinner pails lined the tracks. Again it was noted that about a hundred girls stood on railcars, making "a most picturesque appearance."[11] The train passed in view of the Monongahela House, where presidents from Lincoln to McKinley had stayed. It was at the Monongahela House that Lincoln had stopped to thank the voters of this area while on his way to be sworn in. Allegheny County's surplus of 10,000 votes had given Lincoln the election. At Pittsburgh's Second Avenue, the train passed the exact location where the railroad air brake had been tested successfully, saving the life of a peddler. McKinley would pass legislation over the years that would make air brakes required on American trains. Also in the crowd at the Pittsburgh station was M. M. Garland, who was president of the Amalgamated Association of Iron, Steel, and Tin Workers during the Homestead Strike. Garland had become a McKinley supporter and was working with him for labor peace. Garland, like Samuel Gompers, had come to realize that prosperity meant union membership as well as corporate profits, and both men had worked on presidential committees on labor. Amazingly, union membership quadrupled during the McKinley administration because of the prosperity.

The train entered McKinley's beloved Ohio around 10 o'clock a.m., moving close to his boyhood home of Niles in northeast Ohio. The crowds were large even in these rural areas. Many trains were halted to allow the funeral procession to pass through America's highest concentrations of tracks in industrial northeast Ohio. This was the heart of Ohio republicanism. The Mahoning Valley had been the bastion of support for protective tariffs since the days of Henry Clay and the emerging Whig Party. It was here that William McKinley, Sr. (father of the president) teamed up with the famous ironmaster, Joseph Butler, Sr., to build a furnace across the state border in Mercer County, Pennsylvania, in 1838. Joseph Butler, Jr., would lead the area's "Iron Whigs" that financed many McKinley projects. The furnace was later named "Harry of the West" in honor of Henry "Harry" Clay. The area would become the stronghold of Republican presidents. The Iron Whigs and the "Pig Iron Aristocracy" of this region would become the Oracle of Delphi for Republican industrial policy for a century.[12] The train passed another furnace (Fremont Furnace) that had employed a young future President McKinley. This eastern Whig stronghold and its counterpart in the Cincinnati area would deliver Republican victories for candidates ranging from Abe Lincoln to George W. Bush.

Years after this train passed, the McKinley Presidential Library would be built in Niles with the help of Butler and his Iron Whigs. The Iron Whigs would be immortalized there with over 20 bronze busts. Henry Clay Frick would supply most of the money for the library, and the pantheon of busts would depict McKinley cabinet members who were on the train that day.

Outside Niles, the train entered Ohio coal country. It moved past some of the districts where the young lawyer McKinley had helped coal miners with their struggle for better working conditions. It was a sunny autumn day, and the crowds grew as the train approached Canton, Ohio. The number of flags among the onlookers increased as veterans of the Civil War amassed along the tracks to honor "the major." They were also mustering at Canton for the funeral.

The track over which the train passed in Alliance, Ohio, was strewn with carnations. Alliance was located at the Union Depot at the crossing of the Pennsylvania Railroad Lines; the Pittsburgh, Fort Wayne and Chicago; and the Cleveland and Pittsburgh. The banner hanging from the viaduct read "We mourn for our nation's dead. His life's work is our heritage." Alliance is known as the "Carnation City" because of McKinley. In 1876, Levi L. Lamborn ran against William McKinley for the congressional seat from this district. The two men were personal friends, although they were political opponents. McKinley had expressed his admiration for Lamborn's carnations; so before each of their political debates, Lamborn gave McKinley a carnation to wear on his lapel. McKinley won the election and associated the carnation with his success, and he wore carnations during his successful campaigns for governor of Ohio and then president of the United States.

The train reached Canton around noon. At Canton, over 100,000 flooded the streets of this industrial town—their industrial son had finally come home. The train approached in dead silence, sounding no whistles or bells. After this solemn arrival at the Canton train station, the band played the hymn "Nearer, My God, to Thee," which was McKinley's favorite and quoted some of his last words.[13] Hotels were packed to capacity, with four to five per room. This little industrial town and sun dog of industrial Pittsburgh in the center of Ohio best represented William McKinley. His casket came down the National Road (Route 30) from the station, which was the root of Canton's industrial growth. McKinley's idol, Henry Clay, had appropriated funds for the National Road in the 1820s from tariff revenues. This industrial burgh was the place McKinley called home. Now the world and the nation crowded in to Canton to pay final respects to him. Admiral Dewey led the color guard down Market Street to the courthouse for a public showing. Canton was filled with America's greatest leaders, industrialists, and bankers; but maybe the largest part of the crowd featured veterans of the Civil War, including members of McKinley's 23rd Ohio, who camped out by the thousands at his funeral.

Probably no greater assembly of American government was ever held in an U.S. city outside Washington. The day of the burial, mourners at the First Methodist Church of Canton overflowed into the streets. In the front rows were President Roosevelt, Roosevelt's cabinet, former president Grover Cleveland, future president Howard Taft, the Speaker of the House, 40 senators,

120 representatives, most members of the U.S. Supreme Court, most members of Ohio's state government, and an endless array of officials from other state governments.

The whole country honored McKinley on his burial day. Chicago factories declared a holiday, as did other industrial towns. Irish workers at the steel furnaces of Pittsburgh paused for a prayer during their 24–7 operation. New York City closed completely for the day. A national tribute halted America's workers for five minutes as McKinley was laid to rest. Every train, factory, steel mill, mine, and activity stopped for five minutes. Even the nation's entire telegraph system was shut down for five minutes. Foreign capitals also paused to praise McKinley. London, in particular, hailed the president that two years earlier had led American industry in overtaking that of Great Britain. The city was filled with pictures of McKinley, and Westminster Abbey held a special service. In many ways, McKinley represented the American version of Queen Victoria, who had died in early 1901. Like Victoria in 1840s Britain, McKinley had ushered in an industrial empire in 1890s America. One diplomat noted how the McKinley industrial era had changed things: "it is almost incredible that we should be sending cutlery to Sheffield, pig iron to Birmingham, silks to France, watchcases to Switzerland ... or building sixty locomotives for British railroads."[14]

The crowds and honors were a reflection of a man who had always been a bit naïve. McKinley really believed labor and capital could live in harmony. He trusted too much at times, but he held that all should benefit from being American. He shamelessly promoted American interests, believing in the supremacy of the nation's destiny. He trusted that capitalists would behave honorably, and he was disappointed in their failure to live up to his Christian standards. McKinley learned in his tariff legislation that regulation and oversight were needed to ensure ethical behavior in capitalistic societies. He saw no future in socialism because it limited dreams. As his wounds agonized him for days, McKinley also displayed that rare ability to forgive even his assassin. At McKinley's funeral in Canton, New York's Archbishop Corrigan of St. Patrick was so moved he could not deliver the sermon; a local priest read the archbishop's speech.

There were, of course, many eulogies given in Congress, but the one that McKinley would have liked best came from his friend Senator Chauncey Depew: "...with Washington and Hamilton, with Webster and Clay, he came, not alone, as they did, by the cold deductions of reason, but also by observation and experience, to the conclusion that the solution of our industrial problems and the salvation of our productive industries could only be had by the policy of a Protective Tariff. As Union and Liberty had been the inspiration of his courage and sacrifices as a soldier, so now America for Americans became an active principle of his efforts as a citizen."[15]

McKinley's passion for American industry was hailed. From his earliest days in industrial Ohio, "he witnessed and felt the seasons of employment and idleness which came to the workers in mills and factories ... his heart had been wrung by association with strong men suffering and seeking only work, and their sons no longer able to be at the district school."[16] McKinley's fight for protectionism had been the fight of the American worker whose wages remained high against those in free-trading Britain. McKinley believed that work was the key to the success of capitalism and America. It was a unifying vision that brought the capitalist and workingman together. With mourners' tears were concerns that free trade might again take laborers' jobs. The days of "dinner pail republicanism" were over, at least for a while.

Teddy Roosevelt never fully saw capitalism as heroic. Coming from the East Coast, Roosevelt saw business as money and banking, whereas McKinley saw it as industry and jobs. Republican Roosevelt would attack Ohio republicanism as successfully as any Democrat ever had. Roosevelt would fracture the foundation of the Republican Party, splitting it into progressives and the conservatives of Ohio republicanism. The east-west political fault line of old (going back to the Whig Party) would be opened. McKinley's Ohio industrialism would again resurface with the election of William Taft a decade later.

Chapter Two

Roots of Ohio Republicanism: Ohio Whigs, Temperance, Abolition and Common Schools

> *Take any individual ... separate him ... and look at him, apart and alone,— like some Robinson Crusoe in a far-off island of the ocean ... and, even in such a solitude, how authoritative over his actions, how decisive of his contemplations and of his condition, are the instructions he received and the habits he formed in early life!*
> —Horace Mann, "The Necessity of Education in a Republican Government"

The legacy and philosophy of Ohio Republicans such as William McKinley evolved out of what then was the American frontier. For decades, Ohio was part of our western frontier known as Transylvania. This area of southern Indiana, southern Ohio, and northern Kentucky was made up of Americans looking for even more freedom from government. The frontier was far from primitive, however, but a leading center of education and ideas. Transylvania was known as the center of America's western enlightenment. Scotch-Irish and German immigrants believed in education for all and built frontier schools as they pushed west. Their viewpoint was also part of a religious movement. Transylvania and its center, Cincinnati, Ohio, were the heart of the public-school moral education efforts of William McGuffey, as well the core of the abolition and temperance movements.

Politically, the area was Whig territory in the 1820s, reflecting its growing industry; but it was Ohio that left its mark on the future of the Whig Party. Ohio was predominantly Protestant and highly religious, and it promoted strict moral values. The state's Whigs also believed that the government should play a role in creating ethical citizens. Party members supported temperance, public education, and observance of the Sabbath. One branch of Ohio Whigs supported abolitionism. This fusion of morals, education, and industrialism would give birth to Ohio republicanism and a voter bloc that would give the state the American presidency for almost 80 years. Furthermore, Ohio was part of the manufacturing polygon of Transylvania, which consistently and overwhelmingly voted Whig and later Republican.

Early on, Transylvania birthed its own president in William Harrison, who took office in 1841. William Henry Harrison (1773–1841) was the ninth president of the United States (1841), an American military officer and Whig Party politician, and the last president born as a British subject. Because he was a resident of southern Ohio at the time of his election, he is considered Ohio's first U.S. president (although this status is still contested by his birth state of Virginia). William Harrison had personally known the ten previous presidents. He was also the first president to die in office, succumbing to pneumonia after serving only nine days. However, his grandson Benjamin Harrison would become a president from Ohio. The seed of the Whig economic policies had been built in the west by William Harrison. Transylvania Whigs believed in strong education, federal money for developing industry, and protection of American industry. Harrison was a son of the economic growth of Transylvania.

By connecting lines between Pittsburgh, Cleveland, Cincinnati, Louisville, Lexington, and Charleston, you can see the manufacturing polygon of Transylvania in the 1800s. This polygon included the Western Reserve of northeast Ohio, the Ohio Valley, Transylvania (northern Kentucky, southern Indiana, and southern Ohio) and Westsylvania (western Pennsylvania). This area has also been called the "Middle Border," and it makes up the heart of present-day Ohio and the Whig Party of the 1840s. Later in the 1860s, the Middle Border was the political heart of the new Republican Party. Still agricultural, this region was struggling for economic growth though it had more farm markets than manufacturing prior to the Civil War. While the Transylvanians had been known as refugees from the federal whiskey tax in the 1790s, they did not reject the need for a federal government. They were demanding better roads, canals, and river navigation. The National Road passed through the region, and canals were starting to emerge to support the growth of Transylvania and Ohio. The role of the federal government, in Transylvanians' view, was to ensure the mutual defense of the nation as well as foster economic growth.

Transylvania residents also believed in free quality education for all, which they deemed essential to a democracy. However, they saw education as basically a state government and a community issue. Lacking federal aid, Transylvanians used community funding and volunteers to ensure education for their children. Education would become the most cherished need of the frontier, and the region's efforts to obtain it led the way over those of many urban areas. Transylvanians' movement west was marked by a path of log cabin schoolhouses. The area's settlers would build colleges to rival those of the East.

The "Middle Border" included the home of the founder of the Whig Party, Henry Clay of today's Lexington, Kentucky. Transylvania to this day is rooted in Whig politics. It would be Whig politics that would form the foundation of Ohio republicanism and the future Republican Party. Southern Ohio and Ohio's Western Reserve would become the key to the national ambitions of the Whig Party in the 1830s. The Whigs' political core would be the Western Reserve of northeast Ohio and Cincinnati in southern Ohio. The election of Andrew Jackson in 1828 had posed a threat to commercial growth in the reserve. Jackson had opposed the federal canal building that was the reserve's economic foundation. Jackson had also shut down the National Bank that had financed economic growth in the West. Henry Clay formed the Whig Party in opposition to Andrew Jackson.

Young Ohio politician Joshua Giddings (who was also a future founder of the Republican Party), would become the force to establish the Whig Party in the Western Reserve of Ohio and later in all of Transylvania. He was able to cobble Henry Clay's first party, known as the National Republicans, into a political organization instead of an opposition movement. Giddings described building the National Republicans in this manner: "Reserve farmers depended on roads, canals, and well maintained harbors to ship their grain and dairy products to market. Henry Clay's 'American system' promised to help in such projects, while the laissez-faire Jacksonianism always seemed to stand athwart the Reserve's economic progress."[1] Ohio's Western Reserve was the heart of America's canal system.

The precursor to the Whig Party was Henry Clay's National Republican Party, under whose banner Clay ran for president in 1832. During the 1820s in Ohio, as well as Transylvania in general, frontier candidate General Andrew Jackson and his Democratic Party remained popular. However, the main political issues in Ohio were the development of the canal system in the Western Reserve, money for economic growth, and free schooling in the southern part of the state, none of which fit Jackson's Democratic national platform. Ohio became more supportive of the economic development and protective tariff policies of Henry Clay. The 1832 election saw Jackson win nationally, but the results were close in Ohio, with Jackson getting 81,246 votes and Clay getting 76,539. While Jackson won in a landslide, Ohio was signaling a shift in political alignment in Transylvania.

The new political alignment in Transylvania known as the Whig Party arose from an alliance of the National Republican Party and the Anti-Masonic Party. The negative views of Freemasonry among a large segment of the public gave rise to this single-issue party, which tended to attract anti–Jackson voters. This association between the parties centered in the Western Reserve, where the two natural allies resided. The formation was noted by politicians of the time: "National Republican coalition with Antimasons became the process through which the Whig Party in the Reserve had its genesis."[2] This alliance was typical of Ohio republicanism, merging moralism, economics, and nationalism. The partnership led to the rise of the Whigs and Transylvanian leader William Harrison.

William Harrison supported Whig economic policies but did not fully embrace the antislavery component of Ohio republicanism that had strong roots in the Ohio Whig Party. Joshua Giddings, leader of the Whig Party in the Western Reserve, opposed Harrison. For his part, Harrison started a campaign to remove Giddings from the party.[3] This internal Whig fight in Ohio would lead to the formation of the Republican Party.

Henry Clay at his Lexington, Kentucky, home. Painted by J. W. Dodge, 1843. Retrieved from the Library of Congress, https://www.loc.gov/item/2006676689/. (Accessed June 23, 2017.)

William Harrison was the first president from Transylvania. He made his name in the American Indian Wars of the 1700s and served under General Anthony Wayne during the War of 1812. After the Indian wars, from 1796 until the War of 1812, Harrison settled down to military frontier politics. He served as the first territorial congressional delegate from the Northwest Territory, then as governor of the Indiana Territory, and later as a U.S. representative and senator from Ohio. As governor of the Indiana territory, Harrison promoted the necessity of education, founding Jefferson University in Vincennes in 1801. The school was incorporated as Vincennes University in 1806. Vincennes University is one of only two U.S. colleges founded by a president of the United States; the other is the University of Virginia, founded by Thomas Jefferson. During his career, Harrison was committed to the Whig policy of seeing the United States grow in to an economic power driven by easy money, canals, roads, and education.

The political growth of William Harrison reflects the political formation of Ohio and Transylvania. Harrison had been born into a prominent Virginian family. His father had signed the Declaration of Independence and served as governor of Virginia. The Harrison family's famous Berkeley tobacco plantation used slave labor. After a decline of the family fortunes following the Revolutionary War, Harrison had to be sent to the rural Virginia college of Hampden-Sydney rather than William and Mary in Williamsburg. It was at college in the 1780s that Harrison became associated with the Humane Society, an abolitionist group. Like so many early southern Americans, he was torn between the moral dilemma of slavery and its economic necessity to the South. He never fully resolved this personal quandary. However, when Harrison eventually settled in Ohio, his views would be more tempered and tend toward Transylvania's strong abolitionist movement of southern Ohio and Indiana.

Harrison would have the same ambivalence toward politics in general. A military careerist, he did not grow up steeped in political views. He did blend political and military matters as the military governor of the Indiana Territory from 1800 to 1812. On economics, Harrison fit well into Henry Clay's Whig philosophy of federal support for economic development and regional banks to sustain growth. Throughout his career, Harrison would mold the Whig Party to suit Ohio and Indiana. He would unite the party platform concerning protection for American manufacturing through tariffs, canal expansion for economic growth in the West, and free schooling on a state level. Harrison would become a popular Whig leader and a follower of Henry Clay. Yet Harrison found a personal popularity that Clay had never been able to achieve—he made the Whig Party a national party.

The Whig Party roots had gone back to 1834 and Henry Clay's strong opposition to President Andrew Jackson, a Jeffersonian Democrat. Harrison, however, molded the frontier platform of the Whigs into a national vision. The Whig Party would have four presidents: William Henry Harrison (1841), John Tyler (1841–1845), Zachary Taylor (1849–1850), and Millard Fillmore (1850–1853). In an 1834 congressional speech, Henry Clay likened the opposition of President Jackson to the dictatorial policies of an American king.[4] Clay had initially run for president as a National Republican. His views and those of the Whigs had been revolutionary in the 1830s, supporting what would be called the "American System" of economic prosperity.[5] The Whigs had advocated an aggressive economic plan of government spending on canals, roads, and infrastructure. In addition, party members had championed a national bank with regional branches to make loans to businesses. To finance these ventures, Whigs had demanded a protective tariff to both safeguard American manufacturing and generate cash. Henry Clay was a hated politician because of his ego and personality. He had lost in the 1830s and early 1840s presidential elections, and he needed a candidate to front for his Whig Party principles. The Whigs had found a strong base in the Transylvanian states but could not fully unite. William Harrison had run as one of three Whigs in a divided party in 1836. Younger Whigs opposed another run by Henry Clay in 1844 with an "Anybody but Clay" campaign, which would make Harrison their candidate.[6]

The presidential campaign of 1844 was a bitter one with fierce opposition by the Jacksonians and the Democratic candidate, James Van Buren. Andrew Jackson feared the more likable personality of Harrison would give the Whig Party its first presidential victory. Interestingly, Harrison's family ties with slavery strengthened the Whigs in the South. Harrison's southern Whig support would lead to a progression of Whig presidents but would also be the seeds of the party's fall.

Harrison did win, but he was taken by pneumonia after his victory parade. He died one month into his term and was the first president to die in office. Andrew Jackson saw Harrison's death as a blessing: "A kind of overriding providence has interfered to prolong our glorious union and happy republican system which Gen. Harrison and his cabinet was preparing to destroy under the dictation of the profligate demagogue, Henry Clay."[7] Vice President John Tyler, a Whig, became president. Tyler had a loose relationship with the Whig Party and often supported pro–Jackson polices such as the close of the National Bank and a reduction in tariffs. A Virginian, he supported the southern Whigs and slavery while opposing tariffs that helped the manufacturing North at the expense of the southern cotton and tobacco farmers. Tyler's support of the economic system of slavery would divide the Ohio and New England Whigs from the southern Whigs. This division would eventually lead to the evolution of the Republican Party.

Despite his short presidency, William Harrison would put his own Transylvanian stamp on the Whigs via the 1844 election. Harrison brought frontier Transylvanian politics to the forefront and set the stage for the birth of the Republican Party. The heart of the Whig Party and ultimately the Republican Party came from the schooling, protective tariffs, abolition and temperance of the old Ohio frontier. These principles would become the cornerstone of the next hundred years of Ohio presidents.

The eastern Ohio and western Transylvania Whigs were the evangelicals of their time, blending the Whig pro–American conservativism with midwestern morals and progressive industrialism. The temperance and abolition of Transylvania would be injected into the Whiggery of the North. This combination would bring about the rise of the Methodist Church and split the Presbyterian Church on Calvinistic views. A strange alliance of moralism with economic principles would be the strength and the weakness of both the Whig and future Republican Party.

Many Whigs were Scots-Irish and had fled west to avoid government taxes and regulation. These Scots-Irish were often from iron-making families whose iron plantations in Pennsylvania, Maryland, and eastern Ohio had been destroyed by the dumping of cheap imported iron from England. Iron-making families such as the grandparents of President William McKinley fled to the East to build iron furnaces in the 1810s. Many other Scotch-Irish were from whiskey-making families of southwest Pennsylvania. These future families of Kentucky bourbon makers had been hurt by heavy federal excise taxes and had fled west after the Whiskey Rebellion of 1794. Such whiskey-making families moved to western Ohio. Those from Kentucky flax plantations also destroyed by cheap imports fled to southern Ohio. The aforementioned frontier settlers wanted federal protection from imports, as well as reduced federal taxes and regulation. Fleeing from government control of industry is a historical root of Ohio, and these economic migrants would become the core of Ohio republicanism.

On the local level, frontier Whigs demanded open and outstanding public education for all. Driven by the Scots-Irish, who had evolved out of Europe's great Scottish Enlightenment, the Ohio Scots-Irish gave us a frontier enlightenment and educators such as William McGuffey. By 1820, Transylvania College in Lexington, Kentucky, was one of the best in the nation, with 400 students and a 6,000-volume library. Henry Clay was one of the cofounders. In the 1820s, the institution graduated an average of 500 students a year. Transylvania College and Cincinnati College would become the Harvard-Yale of the West. Transylvania would become the center of a western enlightenment including the foundation of the public school and abolition movements. Not surprisingly, Ohio's first presidents U. S. Grant, Rutherford Hayes, Benjamin Harrison, James Garfield, and William McKinley came from Whig abolitionist families.

The Ohio Whig Party had become a special branch from the more aristocratic and shipping-oriented East Coast Whigs. The Ohio party had also grown more moralistic in supporting temperance and abolition than the southern party members. Ohio Whigs differed in giving social morals the same priority as economic needs. In particular, Ohio had become the center of the abolitionist movement as well as the temperance movement, which the state Whig Party readily incorporated in its platform. The political division on social issues between the East Coast, southern, and Transylvania Whigs was driven by the rising issue of abolition. Ohio would lead the effort to blend abolition into the economic policies that would morph Whigs into

Republicans in the 1860 election. Still, in political terms, that evolution took 40 years, with the Garden of Eden being Ohio. These new Ohio Republicans diverged from their eastern counterparts in that they were socially conservative, religious, populist, and nationalist. These qualities would create a fault line that can still be seen today.

The Ohio Republicans' political views would spread through the nation via the developing educational and public school system that was centered in Transylvania and Ohio, and later via the dominance of state politicians. Ohio's educational system become the model for the nation and thus would spread Ohio republicanism. This conservative, religious, and nationalistic schooling would educate not only future Ohio presidents but also a generation of like-minded voters across the nation. Ohio's social revolution and takeover of America's educational system started with the founding of Lane Theological Seminary. The school was established in the Walnut Hills section of Cincinnati, Ohio, in 1829 to educate student ministers. Lane took on national fame as its first president, Lyman Beecher, initiated debates on abolition and temperance. The seminary's approach quickly influenced other Ohio schools, such as Miami College, Cincinnati College, and Oberlin College. Antislavery and temperance debates pulled in churches and social organizations. Abolitionist ideas would become the core of the Transylvania educators known as the College of Teachers. The College of Teachers was a type of professional organization including social activists in the Transylvania area. More importantly, Cincinnati, and later Miami College, would become home to America's greatest schoolmaster and the moral muse for future presidents from Ohio. By the 1830s, William McGuffey's educational system would sweep the nation.

The decade of the 1830s was an extremely busy one for educator William McGuffey and his standardized textbooks for the nation's schools. These patriotic, nationalistic, and Christian-based *McGuffey Readers* would dominate the United States from 1840 to 1920. They reflected the Whig principles of Transylvania, where they were conceived. Transylvania was American culture in the making, and its views became those of McGuffey. McGuffey was much more the product of the manufacturing polygon than the area was a product of his molding. He was president of the struggling Cincinnati College while working on his textbooks, finishing his third and fourth *Readers* while working with the state for the establishment of public schools. The third and fourth *Readers* were aimed at today's high schoolers. These texts drew heavily on biblical readings as well as on the ideas of McGuffey's College of Teachers friends, such as Daniel Drake, Lyman Beecher, Catharine Beecher, and Edward Mansfield. A year later, in 1838, McGuffey published new revisions of the books. His lectures and Sunday Bible studies were extremely popular with the students. With the author's large network from the College of Teachers, the *McGuffey Readers* quickly took over the Cincinnati school system and Transylvania. By 1841, the first *Reader* had sold over 700,000 copies. Not surprisingly, all of Ohio's future presidents would be educated using *McGuffey Readers*. More importantly, the *Readers* were the common textbook of most American voters for over 70 years. President Truman often praised the works for "educating for ethics as well as intellect, building character along with vocabulary."[8] More than anything, the *McGuffey Readers* made the Ohio view of politics part of the national conversation.

Another Ohio-led part of the American educational system was the College of Teachers, which would spread Ohio republicanism, Whig economics, and temperance and abolition throughout the nation. The college represented a true galaxy of intellectuals in all fields on the then western frontier. One of these was Alexander Campbell (1788–1866), who was an early leader in the Second Great Awakening. A Scottish immigrant and initially a Presbyterian, Campbell was concerned with the direction of Christianity on the western frontier of Ohio and Indiana. This western religious movement came out of Transylvania (adjoining sections of Ohio, Kentucky, and Indiana) and promoted a more liberal Protestantism that favored the Methodists and Baptists. Campbell believed religion in the area should reflect western values such as abolition and temperance. He and Lyman Beecher came to share many ideas about the need for religious reform. Campbell found many allies in the College of Teachers, and he was featured in a number of debates by the organization. The college brought in major religious leaders, the most famous being Catholic archbishop Purcell of Cincinnati and textbook writer William McGuffey of Miami (Ohio) University. The College of Teachers would be the center of a cultural revolution that took the nation by storm and laid the groundwork for many Ohio presidential successes, for abolition, and, eventually, for the temperance movement.

The college took a very diverse approach to culture, embracing many facets of America. One of the most extreme members of the early College of Teachers was socialist James Dorsey, who was a follower of well-known industrialist and utopian socialist Robert Owen. Dorsey had served as a trustee of Miami University from 1809 to 1820. In 1816, he had formed the society of the "Rational Brethren of Oxford," which wanted to turn Oxford Township into a "socialistic community." Dorsey often had Robert Owen speak at Miami and the College of Teachers. Owen was the Scottish zealot who had transformed the mill town of New Lanark in Scotland into a happy socialistic manufacturing community and had started a similar community in New Harmony, Indiana, and in Kentucky. Ohio values would even leave their mark on this early socialistic movement. The Zora community in Ohio in the 1840s would apply Owen's principles to a manufacturing community that, while socially isolated, competed in the capitalistic structure of the state's economy. Conservatives such as McGuffey had rejected Owen's beliefs in socialism, but they had incorporated the morals and industrialism of Owen communities into their teachings.

The College of Teachers was the philosophical foundation of the emerging Whig Party in Ohio. Many members of the college were social reformers from the East, such as the Beecher family, thus strengthening the moral ties between Ohio and New England. Another social reformer was Sarah Peter of Cincinnati, who became an important member of the College of Teachers' inner circle. Peter was the daughter of Ohio's Governor Worthington. She had a long history of working with the city's underprivileged and had founded the Cincinnati Orphan Asylum and several homes for poor women. She was also active in the development of Sunday schools. Sarah Peter supported public common schools to address poverty, working with other members of the college to form proposals to send to the Ohio legislature. She argued often for including Catholics in common schools and textbooks. Peter subsequently moved to Philadelphia, where she opened the School of Design for Women in 1848, which is now known as the Moore College of Art and Design. Later in life, she joined the Catholic Church and served by helping the wounded on Civil War battlefields. In the 1870s, Peter traveled in Europe extensively while purchasing art for the Ladies' Academy of Fine Arts and the Art School of Cincinnati. She also left her mark on Ohio's educational system in regard to instruction for blacks and women.

The College of Teachers grew quickly in prestige and membership in the early 1830s. In 1832, Lyman Beecher and his daughter Catharine joined the group. Beecher, already America's most prominent preacher, had been persuaded to come to Lane Seminary in Ohio from Boston. He was a strict Calvinist who came to Cincinnati with his daughter to convert the West. Catharine Beecher was an accomplished educator who had started the Hartford Female Academy in New England, and she opened the Western Female Institute upon her arrival in Cincinnati. Catharine was also an accomplished poet and writer. She had published a book, *Suggestions on Education*. A few years later, another daughter of Lyman Beecher's, Harriet, came to Cincinnati and joined the College of Teachers. She would marry another member of the group, Professor Stowe of Lane Seminary. Harriett Beecher Stowe would become famous with the publication of *Uncle Tom's Cabin* in 1851, and she would also become a leader in black education.

The Beecher family also brought a passion for the temperance movement to the College of Teachers. Both Lyman Beecher and his son, Henry Ward Beecher, were leaders in the early temperance crusade of the 1820s. For the Beechers, sobriety was part of the social gospel, which was fundamental to the Great Awakening. In the 1820s, the temperance movement was concentrated in the Puritan New England states and was being resisted in the predominantly Scotch-Irish and German middle states. The Great Awakening of the 1820s and 1830s swept the middle states, and with it came the zeal for temperance. Alcohol was the drug problem of the day. In 1830, on average, Americans consumed 1.7 bottles of hard liquor per week, three times the amount consumed in 2010.[9] Ohio represented the frontline battlefield for temperance advocates, with progressives in the Transylvania area and New Englanders in the Western Reserve area of northeast Ohio. Liberal Presbyterians lost ground to the anti-drinking Methodists and Baptists in Ohio. The Beecher family found an ally in William McGuffey of the College of Teachers. Temperance, in return, became a prominent theme of the 1838 *McGuffey Readers*.

Daniel Drake became the lifeblood of the College of Teachers and created many subgroups that would meet daily and weekly. Initially, Drake held the meetings in his home's parlor. He was famous for his own brand of power breakfasts, and the fare at these informal meetings included his favorite baked apples with strong coffee. Maybe more important were his famous "Friday evenings." William McGuffey and his brother Alexander often attended these meetings in the 1830s, traveling 33 miles from Oxford. Drake did much at these gatherings to promote the use of "Buckeye" to refer to Ohioans. The meetings were held at Cincinnati's Buckeye Hall at Drake's Cincinnati College. For evening meetings, the large parlor contained a buckeye in a stone jar, and buckeyes were scattered around the room. Buckeye branches were also placed in hollowed-out pumpkins filled with earth. Another buckeye stump was used as a podium. In a connecting room, buckeye bowls were filled with popcorn and apples. Thus "Buckeye" would became synonymous with Ohio. It was here that education and Christianity were forged into Ohio politics. Daniel Drake would bring the idea of incorporating manual arts and skills into public education. In particular, President Rutherford Hayes would take up this point.

The College of Teachers was deeply religious but denominationally diverse. Members were unified on the need for public schools, a western textbook, professional status for teachers, discipline, and female education. Politically, the group had a Whig bias and antislavery views. It was the ideal platform for William McGuffey to test his ideas. There were many arguments between "Old School" and "New School" Presbyterians but strong agreement on abolition and temperance. James Hall and William McGuffey represented the "Old School," while Lyman Beecher was "Old School" orthodox Presbyterian (at times reactionary). The College of Teachers, with its Presbyterian roots, would help spread abolitionism throughout Ohio and Transylvania. Presbyterian Oberlin College in Oberlin, Ohio, and the Western Reserve of Ohio became the first to admit blacks in 1835.

Still, the College of Teachers' public educational approach forged a Christian yet nondenominational path in public schools. Religious differences seemed to strengthen this group that loved intellectual debate. Eventually, the Catholic bishop of Cincinnati became a member of the college. McGuffey avoided taking sides in religious debates between denominations. In 1905, a writer noted the contribution of the College of Teachers: "It accomplished much for a cause of supreme importance, and workers in educational fields in Ohio owe it a debt which can be paid only in life-long gratitude, shown by handing on down the torch which these men lighted."[10]

The College of Teachers also was a testing ground for the first national textbooks, *McGuffey's Readers*, which William McGuffey had started working on in the early 1830s. The College of Teachers was pushing for common public schools with *Readers* prepared for the West. Daniel Drake, who belonged to no church, fought hard to ensure that the group's charter forbade teaching any sectarian theology or dogma. McGuffey, while a conservative Presbyterian minister, agreed that public education should be nonsectarian, although Christian. This belief, of course, did not restrict McGuffey from freely using Christian and biblical references, which would be totally acceptable and even expected at the time. The highly Christian but nondenominational approach would be the model for all *McGuffey's Readers*. McGuffey used this Christian foundation to promote temperance and abolition. While *McGuffey Readers* became the standard national textbook, the editor produced southern editions that took out antislavery references (until after the Civil War).

The College of Teachers played a pioneering role in the advance of education in America. The organization fought hard from 1834 to 1837 for state regulations for public schools. William McGuffey would often be the one from the group to make presentations to the state legislature. In 1837, Ohio Whigs passed a law providing for state and local school superintendents, and Samuel Lewis became the first Ohio school superintendent in 1838. At the time, the state contained 8,000 schools with 490,000 students. Lewis started a complete survey of Ohio educational institutions. In addition, a state school fund was set up, and conditions such as a minimum of three-month terms were defined. The state allotted $0.14 per student, or about $25.00 per student in today's money, for a total of $65,000 ($1.2 million today). Lewis's survey showed an additional $200,000 ($3.7 million) was needed, as well as 5,000 additional teachers. He suggested a tax on alcohol to raise the additional funds, but the legislature failed to act. However, districts were given the authority to raise money for schools. Lewis resigned in 1839 but continued his role in the temperance movement, the abolition movement, and the College of Teachers. Public education would become a core value in Ohio republicanism and part of the legacy of Ohio's presidents.

The College of Teachers was, by most standards, an activist group as well. Its members realized that torchlight parades and riots would not change the balance of political power in moral issues. Educating the youth and adopting common textbooks could, however, change the balance and become the value system for Ohio republicanism. The problem, of course, was that educational revolution was 30 to 50 years out. Still, education could make dynamic shifts in public opinion, and Ohio President Rutherford Hayes reinforced his home state's educational views at a national level. Ohio republicanism was a movement with an 80-year longevity, enough to change several generations of thought.

In the long run, it was not the abolitionist movement of the 1830s that ended slavery, but rather the moral education of decades that changed attitudes toward slavery. In many ways, the College of Teachers and the *McGuffey Readers* offered a model for long-term change. For the College of Teachers, the idea was simple; if you wanted moral behavior in society, then you needed moral education. McGuffeyism and Ohio republicanism made the link between democracy and ethics. Over 150 years later, Pope John Paul II made the same argument: "As history demonstrates, a democracy without values easily turns into open or thinly disguised totalitarianism."[11] The impact of moral values education was not immediate, but the result was decisive.

The Ohio educational movement built the groundwork for Whigs and eventually the Republican Party. *McGuffey Readers* changed generations of Americans from the 1820s to the 1860s. McGuffeyism is tied to Whig economics and moral values with Ohio republicanism. *McGuffey Readers* in the North adeptly addressed instilling antislavery views in students. Editions of the textbooks for Deep South schools had to edit out material relating directly to antislavery, but their impact in Border States was powerful.

McGuffey Readers had become the childhood textbooks of all future midwestern political leaders and U.S. presidents, spreading Ohio republicanism throughout the nation. Almost every president from William Harrison to Harry Truman was educated using these texts. Not surprisingly, Ohio's first native president, U. S. Grant, came from a Whig background and was educated with *McGuffey Readers* in a one-room Ohio schoolhouse. He had become a pro-abolition Whig though his early learning experiences using the books. Grant noted his political evolution in his memoirs: "I was a Whig by education and a great admirer of Mr. Clay. But the Whig Party has ceased to exist before I had the privilege of casting a ballot; the Know-Nothing had taken its place, but was on the wane; and the Republican Party was in chaotic state and had not received its name yet." Grant would vote in 1856 for the Democrat James Buchanan for president to avoid war; but four years later he supported Abe Lincoln, who better fit his own Whig economic principles. Rutherford Hayes, in the 1850s, became a believer in the use of *McGuffey Readers*, and while practicing law in Cincinnati, he joined a branch of the College of Teachers known as the Cincinnati Literary Society. President Hayes would be the first to propose public schools for blacks in the South to help heal the nation after the Civil War. He also promoted the use of *McGuffey Readers* to spread moral values, exceptionalism, temperance, and antislavery views.

The value system and Christian principles in the *McGuffey Readers* set the foundation for Ohio republicanism for future generations. The combination of economics and abolition would eventually fracture the Whigs and morph them into the Republican Party, but Whig economics would be the glue of this new Republican Party in the 1850s. Ohio Whig economics united East Coast Republicans with Midwest Republicans. It was the masterstroke of Abraham Lincoln, a former high-tariff Whig, that brought Republican protectionism to the forefront. Lincoln focused on tariffs to safeguard workers and infant industries. The idea of protecting infant American industry had been initially designed by Alexander Hamilton in 1794 based on the need for a self-sufficient military.[12] Lincoln would hold to American-made protectionism even during the initial shortages of the Civil War.

Chapter Three

Birth of the Republican Party

The Ohio and Transylvania and Western Reserve Whigs would form the nucleus of the Republican Party. The Whig Party of the early 1850s was divided much like the nation itself. New England Whigs and the southern Whigs opposed the nationalistic tariff policy of the party. In New England, it was the shipping industry that wanted open trade; and in the South, it was the cotton and tobacco planters. Southern Whigs were also slaveholders. The Transylvanian core of the Whig Party had taken on many social issues such as abolition and temperance. Southern Ohio, the home of the Harrison family, led the movement for a slow approach to abolition by Whigs. The Compromise of 1850, which addressed slavery in new states, had fractured the Whigs along pro- and antislavery lines. The party's division into factions would lead to a breakup like that in the nation itself. Midwestern Whigs and antislavery Democrats would form the Republican Party. The real demise of the Whig Party had started in the 1840s. In 1848, the Democrats had control of the White House, and the Whigs were looking for a popular leader to bridge the national divides of slavery and tariffs.

In the election of 1848, Zachary Taylor (1784–1850) became the last elected Whig president.[1] The election of 1848 underscored the important role of slavery in national politics. Democratic president James K. Polk did not seek reelection in 1848. Democrats nominated Senator Lewis Cass of Michigan, who created the concept of popular sovereignty (the settlers of a new territory would decide whether to permit slavery). Antislavery groups formed the Free Soil Party, whose platform promised to prohibit the spread of slavery, and chose former Democratic president Martin Van Buren of New York for president.

The Whigs' nomination of Zachary Taylor for the presidential election would split the party between the North and the South. Taylor was a famous general of the Mexican War. He was a southerner and slaveholder, but he had popularity as a national hero. In addition, Taylor displayed little political allegiance to the Whig Party; instead, his loyalty was rooted in the wants of the South. The southern wing of the party was known as the "Cotton Whigs." As a slaveholder, Taylor was unable to carry the Whig strongholds of Ohio, Indiana, and western Pennsylvania. In Ohio, the strength of the antislavery Whigs divided the party badly.[2] The slavery issue created additional parties in the Whig bastions of southern Ohio and Ohio's Western Reserve. The Liberty Party and Free Soil Party had antislavery platforms and took over 10 percent of the vote in Ohio in the national election, as well as almost the same percent of the national vote. The Free Soil Party tried to offer a bit of a compromise in trying to stop slavery's expanding to the western territories. In Ohio, many Whigs left the party to join the Free Soil Party; and in Ohio's Western Reserve, many Free Soilers won local elections. At the state level, it was said that "the emergence of the Free Soil Party was a turning point in state political alignments."[3] Ohio's fractured electorate over slavery issues would augur the end of the Whigs on a national level.

The revolt of the Ohio Whigs in the 1850 national election was deeper than the slavery issue alone. One historian noted the heresy of President Taylor's approach: "Taylor was equally indifferent to programs Whigs had long considered vital. Publicly, he was artfully ambiguous, refusing to answer questions about his views on banking, the tariff, and internal improvements. Privately, he was more forthright. The idea of a national bank is dead, and will not be revived in my time. In the future the tariff will be increased only for revenue."[4] In the Western Reserve and the Youngtown area, where industry was surging, the idea of removing the high protective tariff in favor of the low rates of a revenue-only tariff was unacceptable. In effect, Taylor had left the Whig Party leaderless and trashed its core platform of decades.[5] National elections in 1848 showed the Whigs were in decline, and the local 1850 election sealed the deal. The Western Reserve of Ohio was searching for a new national party to take on the evil of slavery while maintaining an aggressive economic policy of protective tariffs and internal improvements.

The Western Reserve of Ohio covered the northeast part of Ohio. Originally the area was a western colony of Connecticut and was settled by Puritan descendants wanting further freedom from the Protestant congregations of New England. The Western Reserve was a deeply religious area as well as a region of Whig economic support. Like its southern Whig counterpart of Transylvania, the Western Reserve would play a key role in Ohio republicanism and the Republican Party. Presidents James Garfield and William McKinley both had Western Reserve roots, and so did Ohio senator and kingmaker Mark Hanna. The reserve was one of the leading antislavery regions. Its leaders often worked with those in southern Ohio to bring Ohio firmly into the national antislavery movement. In addition, the Western Reserve was a key part of the Underground Railroad taking fugitive slaves to Canada. The antislavery plank of the newly formed Republican Party can be traced to Western Reserve congressman and activist Joshua Giddings (1795–1864).

Joshua Giddings shifted from the Whig Party to the Free Soil Party with the presidential nomination of Zachary Taylor in 1848. In the 1840s, Giddings helped support the Underground Railroad in Ohio to help fugitive slaves reach freedom. He led a true revolution in the state. In the presidential election of 1848, Zachary Taylor won by supporting slavery and with backing from southern Whigs and some New England Whigs. However, the Western Reserve went strongly for the Free Soil Party's candidate, Martin Van Buren, and pulled the state's support to the Democrat. For many historians, this event augured the death of the Whig Party, and Cleveland newspapers of the time also noted as much.[6] In 1854 and 1855, Giddings became one of the leading founders of the Republican Party. His vision for the party was to combine the social issues of the Free Soilers with the economics of the Whigs, creating a reflection of his Ohio district in the Western Reserve. Giddings campaigned for Abraham Lincoln, although the two men disagreed over the uses of extremism in the antislavery movement. Gidding had been an antislavery radical as a congressman from 1843 to 1859. He was censured in 1842 for violating the gag rule against discussing slavery in the House of Representatives when he proposed a number of resolutions arguing against federal support for the slave trade. Giddings led the congressional opposition by free-state politicians to slavery's westward expansion. He condemned the annexation of Texas, the Mexican War, the Compromise of 1850, and the Kansas-Nebraska Act, all of which contributed to the growth of slavery in the West.[7]

Giddings would be the founder of the congressional caucus known as "Radical Republicans," which evolved out of an Ohio fracture in the Whig Party. The movement had deep roots with the College of Teachers in southern Ohio and activists in Ohio's Western Reserve. Radical Republicans had their origins in the Whig Party and became the wedge that helped form the Republican Party. The radicals strongly opposed slavery during the war. After the war, they distrusted ex–Confederates, demanding harsh punishments for the former rebels and emphasizing equality, civil rights, and voting rights for the ex-slaves. This Ohio-born movement went far beyond the moderate wing of the Republican Party led by Abraham Lincoln. Radical Republicans found national support with old Whigs, such as William Seward, a leading presidential contender in 1860 and Lincoln's secretary of state; Thaddeus Stevens of Pennsylvania; and Horace Greeley, editor of the *New York Tribune*, the leading radical newspaper. Ohio presidents Grant, Hayes, Garfield, Benjamin Harrison, and McKinley were supporters of the radical movement.[8] Giddings had started the congressional movement as a Whig.

The Whig Party fatally divided north and south with the successful introduction of the Kansas-Nebraska Act of 1854, which dissolved the terms of the Missouri Compromise and allowed slave or free status to be decided in the territories by popular sovereignty. Joshua Giddings and a number of congressmen issued a national appeal to resist the act. The party revolution in the Western Reserve in the early 1850s spread rapidly in the North. In 1854, antislavery Whigs began meeting in the upper midwestern states to discuss the formation of a new party. One gathering of 10,000 in Wisconsin on March 20, 1854, is generally considered the founding meeting of the Republican Party. The Republican Party began as a coalition of antislavery conscience Whigs and Free Soil Democrats opposed to the Kansas-Nebraska Act, which spread slavery. The New England Yankees and their Ohio cousins were the strongest supporters of the new party. This was especially true for the Congregationalists and Presbyterians, along with the Methodists and Scandinavian Lutherans. The Ohio Quakers were a small, tight-knit group that was also heavily Republican. Old Transylvania, centered around Cincinnati, Ohio, was another anchor of the new party. In Cincinnati, Alphonso Taft, father of future president William Taft, was a Republican Party founder.

The Republicans rapidly gained supporters in the North's former Whig districts; and in 1856 their first presidential candidate, John C. Fremont (1813–1890), won 11 of the 16 northern states. Fremont of California was extremely popular in Ohio with his national effort to restrict the spread of slavery west. He was from the Free Soil branch of the Democrats. In 1849 the residents changed the name of Lower Sandusky to Fremont, in honor of John C. Fremont.[9] In 1873, future president Rutherford B. Hayes moved into a family home in Fremont called Spiegel Grove.

Giddings played the major role of rallying midwestern Whigs amid western concerns over the spread of slavery. Ohio supplied its huge 23 electoral votes to the new Republican Party, overwhelmingly supporting the Western Reserve and Joshua Giddings in 1856. The strong nationalist economic platform of the Republicans resulted in the majority of former northern Whigs backing the new party. John C. Fremont would be the link between the antislavery voters and the Republican Party on a national level.

Giddings wasn't the only Ohio congressman who was influential in the formation of the Republican Party in 1854. John Sherman (1823–1900), a former antislavery Whig, became a candidate for Ohio's 13th District (Cleveland and parts of the Western Reserve) in the federal House of Representatives. The 13th District was the heart of the Ohio canal system, which had created a booming regional economy. It also was home to the Underground Railroad and antislavery activists. A local convention nominated Sherman over two other candidates in 1854 to represent what was then called the Opposition Party (later to become part of the Republican Party.) The new party was a fusion of Free Soilers, Whigs, and antislavery Democrats in the Cleveland area.

John Sherman (brother of General William Tecumseh Sherman) would be a dominant force behind Ohio republicanism and its philosophy. He served as an Ohio Republican in the U.S. House of Representatives from 1855 to 1861. From 1861 to 1877, he served as a U.S. senator. From 1877 to 1881, Sherman served Ohio President Rutherford Hayes' as secretary of the Treasury. Subsequently, he returned to the Senate, where he became famous for the Sherman Antitrust Act. In 1898, Ohio president William McKinley appointed Sherman secretary of state. Sherman was the perennial potential candidate for president and a power broker in the new Republican Party.

Sherman helped develop the strong stand of Ohio republicanism toward civil rights and Radical Reconstruction. He also counseled fellow Republicans to play the middle road on temperance by personally avoiding alcohol but keeping alcohol out of politics. In addition, he defended the gold standard, convincing Grant, Hayes, and Garfield to maintain it. Sherman asserted, throughout his career, the importance of business and capitalism, but he also felt strongly about regulating against corporate corruption with his Antitrust Act. This belief in promoting but monitoring business growth would become a unique part of Ohio republicanism. John Sherman would be the defender of Ohio republicanism's trade views to protect industry but scrutinize it for abuses. This regulatory/growth formula would eventually be challenged by the progressive Republicans and divide the party in the 1900s. Sherman, of course, was one of many Ohio Republicans who came to leadership with the Civil War.

During the critical reelection of Lincoln in 1864, the rise of the peace movement in old Transylvania brought concern among the Republicans (known at the time as Unionists) that Lincoln could not win. The problem was internal to the Republicans, who split on being more radical than Lincoln, and such a split would give Ohio to the Democrats. In Ohio, favorite son Salmon Chase arose as a possible challenger to Lincoln, who was considered a weakling by more radical Republicans.[10] It would be Senator John Sherman and Representative James Garfield (future president) that turned the Ohio delegation back to Lincoln, probably saving his reelection.[11]

Chapter Four

The Civil War in Ohio and the Republican Party

The Civil War would be the training ground for Ohio presidents—Ulysses S. Grant, Rutherford Hayes, James Garfield, Benjamin Harrison, and William McKinley—and a testing ground for Ohio republicanism. Ohio abolitionists had formed the backbone of the Republican Party that brought on the Civil War. Ohio's industrial might would a big reason for the Union's success in the Civil War. Ohio future presidents would learn leadership, logistics, and humility in the Civil War. The experience would bring a strong vein of nationalism into Ohio republicanism that would be reflected in the philosophy's economic policies. Nationalism would become the glue to bring industrialists and laborers into the Republican Party. President Lincoln would hold to Whig scientific protectionism of manufacturers even with the demands of the Civil War. American manufacturing rose to meet these needs, and the incoming tariffs helped to finance the war. By 1900, the blend of nationalism and economics under Republican presidents would give America leadership in steel, glass, manufacturing, and electrical industries. In addition, civil rights for all would become one of the legs of social policy for Ohio presidents. The economic platform of the Whig Party prior to the Civil War stood for a Federalist approach to government, a strong banking system, and the growth of American industry. But party members' rise to power was on their support of protective tariffs, a national bank to supply investment capital, and a strong network of roads and canals to support commerce.

The Civil War was not totally about slavery; there was an underlying economic issue involved. Southern cotton growers opposed any tariffs on British goods, believing Britain would retaliate with tariffs on cotton and tobacco. The major portion of the South's cotton and tobacco went to Great Britain for processing. Furthermore, even the northeast representatives were torn between the New England textile manufacturers and the merchants who favored free trade. Ohio and midwestern farmers also tended to oppose tariffs, believing they increased prices on basic needs. The tariff debate was changing as America moved from an agricultural nation to a manufacturing nation. It would be a debate that Ohio Republicans learned to balance.

The debate on tariffs goes back to the earliest day of our republic but heightened in the 1820s with the rise of Henry Clay and formation of the Whig Party. In 1824, Congress moved to debate even more extensive tariffs. Clay, the orator, would emerge as leader of this industrial movement. He thundered in Congress with an eloquence reminiscent of Patrick Henry a generation earlier: "Is there no remedy within the reach of the government? Are we doomed to behold our industry languish and decay yet more and more? But there is a remedy, and the remedy consists in modifying our foreign policy, and adopting a genuine American System."[1] "We must naturalize the arts in our country, and we must naturalize them by the only means, which the wisdom of nations has yet discovered to be effectual by adequate protection against the otherwise overwhelming influence of foreigners. This can only be accomplished by the establishment of a tariff."[2] In Ohio, where the glass, railroad, and iron industries were keys to the economy, tariffs were believed necessary for these businesses' prosperity.

South Carolina was particularly upset with the Tariff of 1828 backed by the Whigs. Andrew Jackson's vice president, Whig John Calhoun, was from South Carolina and the author of the tariff. Behind the scenes, Calhoun opposed the measure. Jackson did sign a reduced tariff in 1832, but it was not enough to appease states like South Carolina. Calhoun resigned in December of that year, and the party and its heads were divided on the importance of action by Jackson to reduce the tariffs. A radical movement started in South Carolina, culminating in 1832 with a state convention. The conference called for South Carolina to demand nullification of the tariff on the grounds it was unconstitutional and unenforceable. The convention further advocated preventing the federal government from imposing protection tariffs. This action led to the Nullification Crisis, with Andrew Jackson sending naval ships to enforce the tariff. The nation went to the edge of war when Henry Clay and John Calhoun came together in Congress to propose the Compromise Tariff of 1833. This bill gradually reduced tariffs over a ten-year period to the 1816 levels of 20 percent. This rate was considered revenue producing versus protective. The compromise averted the Nullification Crisis, but it would be a precursor to the states' rights argument of the Civil War. The high tariff levels were again reinstated in 1842 and extended for specific industries under Whig administrations of the 1850s.

The Pig Iron Aristocrats of eastern Ohio and western Pennsylvania pushed for more protection of their iron industry.[3] This would be the region that supplied the votes for Lincoln's presidency in 1860. Lincoln's victory owed to his success in the old Iron Whig districts of Ohio and the other Pig Iron Aristocracy districts in Pennsylvania, Maryland, Connecticut, and western Virginia. These areas were rewarded for their votes with the 1862 Tariff Act, which was the highest ever on pig iron at 32 percent. As the Pig Iron Aristocrats responded with massive investments in industry, Congress moved the rate to 47 percent by 1864. The pig iron industry grew an amazing 65 percent during the Civil War. By the end of the war, the Pig Iron Aristocrats were a real national political force with wealth and the ability to employ tens of thousands. In fact, the American pig iron industry was the world's greatest. Lincoln and the Republican Party held firm on tariffs during the Civil War.

The Civil War defined the rise of Ohio republicanism through the rise of national leaders on the battlefields. It was the Civil War that honed the leadership skills of future Ohio presidents—Ulysses S. Grant, Rutherford Hayes, Benjamin Harrison, James Garfield, and William McKinley. Ulysses S. Grant, of course, became the popular winning general of the war. Harrison was a colonel in the Indiana 70th, Garfield was a colonel in the Ohio 42nd, Hayes was a general, and McKinley was a major in the Ohio 23rd. Many other Ohio politicians, such as Republican kingmaker Mark Hanna and Ohio senator John Sherman, came to public notice during the Civil War. The key relationship, however, would be the comradeship of Rutherford Hayes and William McKinley during the war. The Ohio presidential legacy really had its heart in the 23rd Ohio Regiment.

Ohio's most popular president started his career in the Civil War. William McKinley began as a private, unlike the other Ohio presidents. He and his cousin Osborn joined the Poland (Ohio) Guards in Columbus, Ohio. Pay for a recruit was $13 a month with a signing bonus of $400. Later, in 1863, men could avoid the draft by paying $300 to substitutes, but McKinley was an ambitious and willing recruit. The Poland Guards joined nine other volunteer units forming the 23rd Ohio Volunteer Infantry, becoming Company E. William S. Rosecrans was named first colonel, and future president Rutherford B. Hayes was named first major. The regiment was mustered at Camp Jackson, a few miles west of Columbus on the National Road.

Future Ohio presidents Rutherford Hayes and William McKinley learned an early lesson on the need for American manufacturing as a national defense priority. The manufactured goods shortage during the Civil War would emphasize the need for American industry, but it was an old theme in American politics. The Federalists of the 1790s believed firmly in the function of government to regulate commerce. Federalists were supporters of tariffs to protect American agriculture, but they foresaw a day when a different movement would be necessary to promote manufacturing.[4] James Madison also argued that the regulation of foreign commerce was a function of the federal government.⁵ Alexander Hamilton saw America's freedom as rooted in its ability to achieve economic freedom through manufacturing and banking. Hamilton the soldier was well aware of the role of technology and industry in the ability of a nation to win wars, and he believed that manufacturing was fundamental to America's freedom. As a young officer, Hamilton found the colonial army constrained by lack of iron cannon and rifles because of the lack of American manufacture.

Years later, McKinley would read about a similar experience of the nation's first secretary of the Treasury, Alexander Hamilton. McKinley's economic roots can be traced to the Federalist Hamilton, whom he often quoted. Like McKinley, Hamilton learned his economics as an army supply officer. On Washington's staff, Hamilton struggled to get the soldiers clothing because of America's dependence on British goods. He also learned the hard lesson of inflated dollars, as merchants rejected government notes. These experiences would be the foundation for Hamilton's classic 1791 *Report on Manufactures*, which prophesied much of post–Civil War America. The work would augur McKinley's governmental approach to national industrial planning. Hamilton was the first to suggest a scientific plan for tariffs versus across-the-board revenue tariffs. First, defense and national industries were to be protected, followed by targeted infant industries. Hamilton argued for lower tariffs on raw materials to help industry. America moved to cheap dumped British iron after the Revolutionary War, only to be caught short of manufactured arms again for the War of 1812. It would be a lesson repeated in the Civil War.

Uniform shortages during the Civil War were an inconvenience, but the lack of muskets presented another problem. When the muskets did arrive, they were smoothbores of 1812 design that had been manufactured in the 1820s. These young soldiers felt they deserved the very best American arms, but in general the Union armories had mostly 1840-vintage armaments. Still, five of the regiment's ten companies, including McKinley's, refused them. Emotions ran high as a small rebellion and standoff ensued. McKinley recalled years later: "none of us knew how to use any kind of a musket at the time, but we thought we knew our rights and we were all conscious of the importance."⁶ This musket rebellion was not unique to the 23rd Ohio, but was being repeated across the nation.

The rifled Springfield musket had been well advertised in the 1850s as a triumph of American manufacturing. The Springfield rifle had even been adopted by the U.S. military for general use, but in 1861, the available rifles could arm only 10 percent of the regiments. Still, Lincoln gave priority to American firearms, using imported ones only after domestic sources had been exhausted. The president had been a Whig committed to American manufacturing over foreign imports before the Whigs morphed into the

Republican Party. His heart was in the right place, but the country had become dependent on overseas industries. Lincoln personally took an active role in the encouragement of American inventors to bring on new manufacturing technology.

Lincoln's policies were directly involved in the shortage of arms, but the problem existed throughout the supply chain. Even the special iron needed for barrels was scarce and would have to be imported from Europe. America, at best, produced only 15,000 rifles from 1861 to 1862. Lincoln was forced to purchase foreign rifles, which supplied more than half of the Union regiments. The president also made a political decision to deliver the new American weapons to Border State regiments such as the Ohio 23rd to keep them in line. Orders for over a million rifles went out to Europe, but half of them were never delivered, and the balance were of poor quality. In later years, international banker J. P. Morgan was implicated in arms sales fraud, and this may have been part of the cooling between him and McKinley in his presidential years. Still, the supply shortages would be the philosophical root of future Ohio presidents such as Hayes, McKinley, Garfield, and Taft, as well as the dominant trade policy until the 1920s.

For the 23rd Ohio, Rutherford Hayes settled the rifle controversy with the help of Lincoln and just in time for the regiment's departure for western Virginia. The troops were being shipped to Virginia to prevent Confederate raids and protect the Baltimore and Ohio rail tracks. McKinley and Company E were stationed at the small town of Weston. The 23rd was involved in some guerrilla actions and a few minor battles until settling at Fayetteville in November for winter encampment. McKinley adapted—but slowly. It also appears Mother McKinley visited him in western Virginia to lift his spirits. As a private, McKinley performed the basic duties of camp life with care and attended to every detail. He reminisced as governor: "I always look back with pleasure upon those fourteen months in which I served in the ranks. They taught me a great deal. I was but a school-boy when I went into the army, and that first year was a formative period in my life, during which I learned much of men and of affairs."[7]

In the spring, McKinley was promoted to commissary sergeant. In this position, he learned the need for logistics and manufactured goods to make an army function well. McKinley took to the clerical as well as the planning requirements of the work, excelling at the tasks most wanted no part of and proving to be a logistics genius. In the Battle of Antietam, McKinley would earn a battlefield promotion to lieutenant. This engagement, which occurred on September 17, 1862, would be remembered as the war's bloodiest day. With part of the regiment beaten down and fatigued and lacking food, McKinley packed wagons of supplies and moved to the front lines to relieve his comrades. The Union army suffered through the night, with the bodies of the dead stacking up at Burnside's Bridge. McKinley continued to get provisions to the front throughout the battle. He earned not only a promotion but also, two years after his assassination, a memorial erected in his honor at Antietam. McKinley was promoted to second lieutenant of Company E, and he served on General Hayes's staff.

In 1863, General Rutherford B. Hayes took a real interest in McKinley's career. Hayes moved him to brigade quartermaster and also to his staff as an adjutant officer. McKinley was now in a position that was normally reserved for those of wealth or importance. He would meet many of America's future leaders and best families. The year would be a defining one for young McKinley, who reenlisted in 1863.

General Hayes wrote the following on the request for McKinley's promotion: "That battle began at daylight ... without breakfast, without coffee, they went to fight, and it continued until after the sun had set. Early in the afternoon, naturally enough, with the exertion required of the men, they were famished and thirsty, and to some extent broken in spirit. The commissary department of the brigade was under Sergeant McKinley's administration and personal supervision. From his hands every man in the regiment was served hot coffee and warm meats—a thing that had never occurred under similar circumstances in any other army in the world."[8]

McKinley viewed his promotion to the officer ranks as the turning point in his life. He reminisced in an 1888 letter to Hayes: "let me tell you General, that the proudest and happiest moment of my life was in 1862. I was sent from the regiment on recruiting service with other sergeants, and upon arriving at Columbus, found that you had my commission to 2nd Lieutenant, and that it had been issued upon your personal recommendation, for what as a boy, I had done at Antietam."[9]

McKinley also admired Hayes, who was a major influence on McKinley's political formation. Hayes was a lawyer from Cincinnati with a wealthy family background. He had graduated from Kenyon College in 1842 and Harvard Law School in 1845. Hayes was a Whig, Republican, and abolitionist. As a lawyer in Cincinnati, he had defended runaway slaves. Ultimately, Hayes would become president in the election of 1877. While he opposed most formal religion, his wife, Lucy, was a strict Methodist who, as first lady, banned alcohol from all state functions. Hayes carried an extensive library in camp, and McKinley was well schooled by reading books in his free time. Lucy helped train McKinley in social graces that would prepare him for his future. The first Ohio-born president would, however, be a country boy and a soldier lacking those charms.

The Civil War was not only the resource of Ohio's Republican presidents, but it formed the core of their philosophies of protectionism. President Lincoln, a former Whig, had actually run on a strong economic policy of American protectionism and the advance of technology. Lincoln had been the first national candidate since Henry Clay to have the united support of labor and manufacturers. That alliance would include the manufacturing districts of Illinois, Pennsylvania, Ohio, Kentucky, southern Michigan, and Virginia that carried Lincoln to the presidency. It was no surprise that the Republican Party had been born at an 1856 convention in Pittsburgh at the heart of Whig country. Lincoln carried industrial Pittsburgh's Allegheny County by a record 10,000 votes. He called the concentration of support in this manufacturing area "the State of Allegheny." Lincoln's winning margins were similar in the iron districts of Ohio, where Iron Whigs and protectionist Democrats had found a new home in the emerging Republican Party. This "state of Allegheny" and Ohio would become the voting foundation of the Republican Party.[10] In western Virginia, the Pig Iron Aristocrats' support of the protectionist Lincoln split the state and created West Virginia. These Pig Iron Aristocrats had forged an alliance with iron labor as well. The Ohio Republicans became the party of the iron industry.

The German and Irish immigrants of the 1840s came to Transylvania for economic opportunity, and they united with wealthy Scotch-Irish to form a new Republican machine in the iron-making districts of the middle states. Industry growth took priority over unionism and profits. These districts knew the recessions caused by free trade policies, believing the still-lingering Panic of 1857 was a result of the Democrats passing lower tariffs. As a result of war and protectionism, the pig iron industry would see great advances in technology and employment. The Pig Iron Aristocrats were rewarded for their votes with Lincoln's 1862 Tariff Act, which was the highest ever on pig iron at 32 percent. As the Pig Iron Aristocrats responded with massive investments in industry, Congress moved the rate to 47 percent in 1864. The pig iron industry grew an amazing 65 percent during the Civil War. By the end of the war, the pig iron industry was a real national political force with wealth and the ability to employ tens of thousands. The American pig iron industry was the world's greatest after the Civil War, overtaking that of England.

There is no demand such as that of war. Sixty percent of the iron used in the war was made in Ohio. As much as 25 percent of the Union's artillery (15 percent at Fort Pitt Foundry alone) was made in Pittsburgh. At least 80 percent of the Union's naval iron plate for ships was made in Ohio and rolled in Pittsburgh. All of the artillery carriage axles and most railroad axles were forged in Pittsburgh. But most of the raw pig iron, however, came from Ohio. In 1860, Cleveland, Ohio, had no iron foundries; but after the war, Cleveland had over 50 foundries. The Pig Iron Aristocrats (iron manufacturers, as they were known) were not only the ones who won the war, but also the ones who profited the most. The Republican tariffs assured a boom in national production for years to come. The great iron triangle of Ohio, West Virginia, and

Pennsylvania saw growth as never before. The war would also stimulate huge leaps in pig iron technology, railroads, and manufacturing. The huge profit margins in the pig iron–related businesses assured the money was poured back into the businesses because it offered the highest return on the dollar. Just as important, the pig iron end users, such as the railroads, experienced similar growth. The expansion of American industry during the war would be the infrastructure in place to make the United States the premier industrial nation. Lincoln took chances by promoting infant industries during the war rather than buying off European sources. While this course proved to be smart business, by war's end, the Union controlled its own destiny and was immune to foreign boycotts or pricing. In the end, Union manufacturing overwhelmed the South.[11]

Lincoln's protectionism was born out of the early work of Ohio Republicans prior to the war. When the 36th Congress met in 1859, action remained blocked over who would be the Speaker of the House until 1860, when Republican William Pennington of New Jersey was elected. A pro-tariff Republican majority was appointed to the Ways and Means Committee, and John Sherman of Ohio became chairman. Sherman had included protectionism in the founding principles of the Republican Party. The national Republican victories of 1860 resulted in the famous Morrill Tariff Act. The Morrill Tariff of 1861 was an increased import tariff in the United States adopted on March 2, 1861, during the lame duck administration of President James Buchanan, a Democrat. It was the 12th of 17 planks in the platform of the incoming Republican Party, which had not yet been inaugurated, and it appealed to a new voting alliance of industrialists and factory workers as a way to foster rapid industrial growth. The Morrill Tariff inaugurated a period of continuous trade protection in the United States, a policy that remained until the adoption of the Underwood Tariff Act of 1913.

Lincoln used tariffs to raise money for the war as well, which was a basic use of tariffs as proposed by the Federalists earlier. Lincoln's economic advisor, Henry C. Carey, was a huge supporter of Clay's American System, as was Speaker of the House John Sherman. Carey became a key political ally of Clay's, forming the Pennsylvania Society for the Encouragement of Manufacture, as well as the American Industry League. In addition, Carey was a prolific writer in support of tariffs throughout his career. He requires some note because he was the most influential economist of the 1850s, 1860s, and 1870s and the philosophical root of Ohio republicanism. Carey was for easy money and strong tariffs, ideas supported by Henry Clay, President Grant, President Hayes, President Garfield, and, later in the 1890s, by President McKinley. Moreover, Carey understood the nature of the money supply as a stimulus and supported the printing of greenback dollars. Today, of course, he would be considered an inflationist; but he argued that while inflation hurt the bankers, it helped the manufacturers. Carey correctly identified the "enemy" as the eastern banking concerns and banking monopolists who favored importing and trade. He argued that these financiers were actually hostile to American industrial enterprise. Carey also predicted the bankers' take-over of the railroad industry to control trade. His writings foreshadowed the rise and dominance of J. P. Morgan in the McKinley era. Carey was the major influence on Ohio Republican tariff policy that would become the policy of the Republican Party for many decades. Carey's disciples in the Congress, such as Pig Iron Kelley, James Garfield, William McKinley, and Thaddeus Stevens, carried the protectionist banner in the time period between Henry Clay and Herbert Hoover. These men also demanded congressional oversight to ensure profits gained from tariff protection were invested back into the industry to create employment.

The Lincoln presidential victory of 1860 was attained through his success in Ohio's Western Reserve, the old Iron Whig districts of Ohio, and the other manufacturing districts in Pennsylvania, Maryland, Connecticut, and western Virginia. Lincoln's protectionist policies ensured that these districts would remain Republican for many decades. The vote in these districts set new majority records, as Lincoln's protectionism played as well as his antislavery stand. Lincoln's victory would bring war to the nation but prosperity to the iron districts of the North and the manufacturing regions of the Midwest. It would build a long-term Republican majority and an industrial base for America's future. Congress passed the highest iron tariffs ever, along with an increase in tariffs across the board during the Republican supremacy. At the time, the government's main source of income was tariffs (not income taxes). Almost all industries benefited, but iron, glass, textile, forgings, tinplate, and mining boomed. The protectionist representatives wrote the tariff bill, ensuring iron received the highest level of protection. This political alliance of labor and capitalists would guarantee Republican protectionist policies for the next 70 years. It would also lead to the voting success of President Grant. Of course, it would be the popularity of General Ulysses Grant that assured the national platform of the new Republican Party.

The Civil War made civil rights a key part of the Ohio republicanism movement. It made Ohio presidents committed to personal liberties and a bit antagonistic toward the old South. Benjamin Harrison, like the other Ohio presidents, served with honors and passion. In 1889, his Inaugural Address was still celebrating the individual rights Civil War soldiers fought to protect: "Mill fires lighted at the funeral pile of slavery. The emancipation proclamation was heard in the depths of the earth as well as in the sky; men were made free, and material things became our better servants."[12]

Chapter Five

President Grant and the Foundation of Ohio Republicanism

Ulysses S. Grant is not associated with any form of lasting legacy as an Ohio president. For many biographers, Grant was defined by his faults even in the face of his success. He was Lincoln's favorite general because of his achievements, and he would become the nation's favorite general. Yet Grant is often remembered for his legendary drinking and his scandal-ridden presidency. When Lincoln was asked about his general's drinking, he said he wanted to find the brand of his favorite spirits and send a barrel to his other generals.[1] Grant is known as a problematic character for biographers. A recent scholar noted: "He has been an enigma not only to Grant biographers but also to generations of historical generalists and scholars, their difficulty in assessment betrayed by their inability to write about him with anything approaching the objectivity."[2] Fortunately, this work is not a biography; its task is to look only at his role in forming the philosophy of Ohio republicanism. In this regard, Grant's role is as clear as his straightforward approach to giving military orders.

Grant's legacy was to ensure the growth of the embryotic new political party. The Republican Party had its roots in antislavery, but it also had roots with the old Whig Party. It was pro-business, supporting banks, the gold standard, railroads, and high tariffs to protect factory workers and grow industry faster. Grant would become the standard-bearer for Ohio republicanism and Lincoln's legacy. Like Lincoln's, his philosophy was centered on bringing slaves to full citizenship, and Ohio was the center of support for this plan. Grant supported Radical Reconstruction and the Radical Republicans' programs in the South, the 14th Amendment, and equal civil and voting rights

President Ulysses S. Grant delivering his first Inaugural Address on the east portico of the U.S. Capitol, March 20, 1869. Photograph by Mathew Brady retrieved from the Library of Congress, https://www.loc.gov/item/00650932/. (Accessed June 23, 2017.)

for the freedmen. On the economic front, he supported government backing of the country's growing railroad system. As an Ohioan, Grant had seen firsthand the prosperity brought by railroad and canal systems. He would also initiate the survey and study that would, decades later, lead to the building of the Panama Canal. Somewhat lost in the records of the Grant legacy was his formation of a scientific approach to tariffs, which would become the hallmark of Ohio republicanism.

Grant's rise to the presidency was grounded not in his political views or experience, but in his popularity as a Civil War general. With the assassination of Lincoln, his vice president, Andrew Johnson assumed the presidency. Johnson had been a former slaveholding Democrat and a compromise pick by Lincoln and the Republicans. In 1864, Lincoln had run as a unity candidate under the National Union Party. The National Union Party was the general name used by the Republicans to bring in southern-leaning supporters. Andrew Johnson was the perfect choice to attract Democrats and southern Whigs. Johnson actually opposed civil rights for African Americans, which would be his demise as a Republican candidate in 1869. He favored letting the South return to many old ways of discrimination, putting himself at odds with the Republicans in Congress and his army commander, Ulysses S. Grant. The majority of Republicans were "Radicals," wanting civil rights for former slaves and punishment of old Confederate leaders, and the Radical Republicans would support Grant's nomination.[3] Grant's presidency would be, for many, Lincoln's second and third term.

President Johnson lacked the support of his own party, since he sided with the Democrats of the South on restricting the rights of ex-slaves. General Grant supported the Reconstruction plans of the Radical Republicans in Congress, which favored the 14th Amendment and full citizenship and civil rights for African Americans. The Democratic platform condemned Negro supremacy and demanded a restoration of states' rights, including the right of southern states to determine for themselves whether to allow suffrage for adult freedmen. The Republican platform supported black suffrage in the South as part of the passage to full citizenship for former slaves. Party policy agreed to let northern states decide individually whether to enfranchise blacks. Johnson's support of the Democratic platform was clearly a step backward. By 1868, Johnson had alienated many of his constituents and had been impeached by Congress. The Radical Republicans led the effort to impeach him and drive him out of the party. Although Johnson kept his office by one vote in the Senate, his presidency was crippled and his future candidacy lost. Johnson would not be the Republican candidate in 1868; General Grant would emerge as the party's contender.

Grant was a son of the frontier and of Ohio. His family went back to Plymouth in 1630, but his father, Jesse, had moved to a number of points west in search of business success. President Grant was born in the heart of Transylvania in Point Pleasant, Ohio, on the Kentucky border. He was educated in nearby Georgetown, Ohio, starting school at a one-room schoolhouse using the *McGuffey Readers*. He was clearly impacted by frontier politics, being geographically in the center of the Transylvania abolition movement. The western frontier of the time had little toleration for slavery. It would be the antislavery platform of the Republican Party that would change him from Democrat to Republican.

Besides his one-room schoolhouse experiences, Grant's attendance at West Point would hone his patriotism, leadership skills, and love of technology. The West Point of the time was really an engineering school to educate officers in the technologies of the telegraph, cannon, and artillery. Politically, most military officers tended to be southern Whigs, but the slavery issue prevented Grant from joining their ranks. He preferred to steer away from any political party. Grant made his mark for bravery as an officer in the Mexican War, but he would return to civilian life in peacetime. He briefly sided with the Ohio Democrats because he hated war, feeling that the strong stand of the Republicans on slavery would provoke hostilities. Still, Grant saw slavery as a great evil. By birth, he was a Methodist, but not a practicing one. He came to strongly believe that the Civil War was God's punishment for slavery.[4] This was a common belief throughout religious communities in Ohio.

Grant would merge his frontier spirit with his war experiences to cement the philosophy of Ohio republicanism. He embraced the ideology on both the social and economic fronts. Grant believed wholly in Lincoln's protection of American industry. As a general, he was well aware that a successful standing army required a domestic supply chain to support it. It had been Grant's strong advocacy against slavery that attached him to the Republican Party, and this viewpoint would be the moral backbone of his later presidency. Grant was not a natural politician; he had always been a military commander. In his youth, he had been a Democrat, and he was often asked if he was truly a Republican. In an 1880 speech Grant delineated his reasons for being a Republican: "The Republican party is a party of progress, and of liberty toward its opponents. It encourages the poor to strive to better their children, to enable them to compete successfully with their more fortunate associates, and, in fine, it secures an entire equality before the law of every citizen, no matter what his race, nationality, or previous condition. It tolerates no privileged class.... I am a Republican, as between the existing parties, because it fosters the production of the field and farm, and of manufactories, and it encourages the general education of the poor as well as the rich."[5] Grant was always clear that it was Abraham Lincoln who was the cornerstone of the emerging Republican Party, and he would adhere to Lincoln's polices throughout his career.

While Grant was not a politician, his military rise was as much political as founded on his military record. Republican congressman from Galena, Illinois, Elihu B. Washburne would be a sponsor of Grant early on. Washburne became active in politics as a Whig and served as a delegate to the Whig National Conventions of 1844 and 1852. In 1852, Washburne was elected to the United States House of Representatives. He was reelected eight times and represented northwestern Illinois from 1853 to 1869. In 1854, Washburne supported Abraham Lincoln's unsuccessful candidacy for the United States Senate. In the mid–1850s the Whig Party dissolved, and the Republican Party was founded as the major antislavery party. Washburne joined the Republican Party and became an early force in its development. While from Illinois, he had a frontier philosophy consistent with Ohio republicanism.

Though Grant had no rank or commission at the start of the war, he took the initiative to recruit a company of volunteers in Galena, Illinois. Grant discussed with the district's congressman, Elihu Washburne, his views on war and civil rights, and Washburne was impressed at first meeting him. Grant's hope was that his West Point education and previous military experience would lead to a field command. Washburne promised to discuss the matter with Governor Richard Yates. Yates quickly offered Grant a militia commission to serve as mustering officer and to continue training the volunteer units which were being raised to rapidly expand the army. Grant accepted but continued his efforts to obtain a field command. With Washburne's sponsorship, Grant was commissioned a colonel of volunteers on June 14, 1861, and appointed to command the 21st Illinois Volunteer Infantry Regiment. In September 1861, the congressman sponsored Grant's promotion to brigadier general and leadership of a brigade, and his subsequent promotion to major general. Washburne was also an advocate for Grant's advancement to lieutenant general and commander of the entire Union army.

Washburne would also be the key link to Grant's rise to the presidency. As a leader of the Radical Republicans, Washburne opposed the Reconstruction policies of President Andrew Johnson and supported African American suffrage and full civil rights. During the war, Grant aligned himself with the Radical Republican goals of ending slavery and incorporating African Americans into the military. The leader of the Radical Republicans in Congress at the end of the war was Washburne. At first, Grant's former backing of the Democratic Party made Republicans leery of him. Grant's support for the Democrats had been rooted in his opposition to war, which many found hard to believe. Still, Grant's actions left little doubt with the Radical Republicans that he was one of them. He changed political affiliation, and success on the battlefield made him a likely contender for president as a Republican. Washburne supported Grant's successful campaign in 1868.

The Union victory had allowed Republicans to emerge again. By 1868, the Republicans felt strong enough to drop the Union Party label, but they needed to nominate a popular hero for their candidate. Presidential contender Grant was popular but lacked any political record. The Democratic Party still controlled some of the big northern states and Border States that had been split by the Civil War. After numerous ballots, the Democrats nominated former New York governor Horatio Seymour to take on the Republican candidate. Grant was one of the most popular men in the North due to his efforts in concluding the Civil War successfully for the Union. Still, while Grant had an Electoral College landslide, the popular vote was close. Civil rights of the ex-slaves had replaced slavery as a national issue. What had gone unnoticed in the post–Civil War electorate was the transformation of America into a manufacturing nation.

Grant's second election in 1872 was more decisive despite a split in the party and much corruption tied to his first administration. Republican division was again over civil rights and the treatment of the southern states. The core economic issues of Ohio republicanism were widely accepted in the northern states and the party. Grant's decisive reelection was achieved in the face of disruption that resulted in a third party of Liberal Republicans nominating Horace Greeley to oppose Grant. The Liberal Republicans demanded civil service reform and an end to the Reconstruction process, including withdrawal of federal troops from the South. This action caused the Democratic Party to cancel its convention, support Greeley as well, and not nominate a candidate of its own. Grant won an easy reelection over Greeley by a margin of 56 percent to 44 percent. Grant had 286 electoral votes to what would have been 66 electoral votes for Greeley. The general's popularity was a cornerstone of his presidency in the face of a split in his own party and strong opposition from the Democratic Party. Grant would stand for full civil rights of ex-slaves and the old Whig economic policy of fostering and protecting American industry. His legacy of securing the role of Ohio republicanism both in the party and nation is overlooked by most biographers.

As president, Grant would hold to Lincoln's protectionism against rising political opposition from the southern and northern farmers, as well as international pressure. Grant was squarely focused on the development of industry that had brought the Union success in the war. He stated the following to Congress in 1873: "For centuries England has relied on protection, has carried it to extremes and has obtained satisfactory results from it. There is no doubt that it is to this system that it owes its present strength. After two centuries, England has found it convenient to adopt free trade because it thinks that protection can no longer offer it anything. Very well then, Gentlemen, my knowledge of our country leads me to believe that within 200 years, when America has gotten out of protection all that it can offer, it too will adopt free trade."[6] Grant did add the necessity of government oversight on military purchasing orders. As General Grant, he had attacked many American manufacturers for their substandard quality. This concept of oversight and limited regulation of industry given federal trade protection would be a foundation for Ohio republicanism.

Grant's protectionism is often overlooked by historians, but he was aggressive and believed that American labor had a right to be protected from foreign manufacturers.[7] Grant would establish a new plank to Ohio republicanism that would be strongly supported by all Ohio Republican presidents to follow. He maintained that American laborers had been asked to give their blood and treasures to defend the nation, and he required the government to put these workers' jobs ahead of any other factors in trade decisions. Furthermore, veterans were the core of Republican voters, and protection for jobs of returning veterans was a plank of the Republican platform. The alliance of veterans, laborers, urban voters, and manufacturers made protective tariffs extremely popular. Grant's success was to make this new voter amalgamation into a political force that became Ohio republicanism. It would, however, be a decade-long struggle to fuse Ohio republicanism with the new Republican Party.

Grant faced a huge war debt, and the Republicans wanted the war income tax eliminated. Grant realized that tariffs not only protected the American worker and manufacturer but also were a huge source of revenue. In this respect, Grant extended Lincoln's tariff policy into a supply of funds to run the government and finance war debt. Grant was not without political opposition. He faced it from America's largest industry, the railroads, which imported all their rails from Europe at the time. Grant held firm, and in doing so, he created the American steel industry. In 1875, Andrew Carnegie opened the world's largest steel mill and factory to produce steel rails for the tracks. Edgar Thomson Works at Braddock, Pennsylvania (near Pittsburgh), was named after Edgar Thomson of the Pennsylvania Railroad. Within 20 years, American steel went from a specialty manufacture to the world's largest industry, employing millions of Americans. The Grant tariff policy would be studied for the next 50 years as an economic foundation of industrial America. Capitalists such as Andrew Carnegie would be forever linked to the Republican Party, but political success depended on bringing Carnegie's workers into the fold.

One of Grant's pieces of genius would be his welding of two premises of Ohio republicanism into a strong policy. Protectionism and patriotism had been core values of Ohio republicanism. After the war, the Grand Army of the Republic (GAR) was a fraternal organization composed of veterans of the Union army, Union navy, marines, and U.S. Revenue Cutter Service who served in the American Civil War. The group had natural links to the Republican Party, which favored Civil War officers for political offices. Democrats, on the other hand, had natural ties to the old South and the antiwar movement. Grant and the Republicans used the large surpluses generated by tariffs to develop a generous pension program for Union soldiers. One historian viewed the merger as follows: "The revenue generated from protection, in turn, supported a vast pension system for Union veterans who, through the Grand Army of the Republic, subsequently enlisted in the tariff coalition, further underpinning republican dominance within the manufacturing belt."[8] This voting alliance would be one of the most powerful in American history, and it would form a key part of victories for Ohio presidents Rutherford Hayes, James Garfield, Benjamin Harrison, and William McKinley.

Another basis for the tariff policy was to eliminate the income and inheritance tax that had been imposed for the first time to finance the Civil War.[9] In 1862, Abraham Lincoln had signed a bill that imposed a 3 percent tax on incomes between $600 and $10,000 and a 5 percent tax on higher incomes to fund the war. The bill had been amended in 1864 to levy a tax of 5 percent on incomes between $600 and $5,000, a 7.5 percent tax on incomes in the

$5,000–$10,000 range and a 10 percent tax on everything higher. The flow of tariff revenue allowed Grant and the Republican Congress to repeal the income tax in 1872. America would be free of income taxes until the late 1890s. Furthermore, the country's major political problem became how to spend the surplus created by revenue-producing tariffs.

Grant helped formulate the scientific approach to tariffs that would be refined by later Ohio presidents. This approach required a detailed look at products, rates, and markets instead of across-the-board or unfocused tariffs. Grant stated in his 1874 report to Congress:

> I would suggest to Congress the propriety of readjusting the tariff so as to increase the revenue, and at the same time decrease the number of articles upon which duties are levied. Those articles which enter into our manufactures and are not produced at home, it seems to me, should be entered free. Those articles of manufacture which we produce a constituent part of, but do not produce the whole, that part which we do not produce should enter free also. I will instance fine wool, dyes, etc. These articles must be imported to form a part of the manufacture of the higher grades of woolen goods. Chemicals used as dyes, compounded in medicines, and used in various ways in manufactures come under this class. The introduction free of duty of such wools as we do not produce would stimulate the manufacture of goods requiring the use of those we do produce, and therefore would be a benefit to home production. There are many articles entering into "home manufactures" which we do not produce ourselves the tariff upon which increases the cost of producing the manufactured article. All corrections in this regard are in the direction of bringing labor and capital in harmony with each other and of supplying one of the elements of prosperity so much needed.[10]

Grant's tariff model would become part of Ohio republicanism, which would be championed by Presidents Hayes, Garfield, and McKinley.

Grant's interest in manufacturing and economic growth went far beyond scientific tariffs. He was a supporter of federal assistance to railroads to extend to the West. Grant's Ohio background made him a big supporter of canals as well, and his 1869 inauguration as the 18th U.S. president brought new impetus to American canal policy. His personal interest in the subject went back to July 1852, when, as an army captain, he had led the American Fourth Infantry across the Isthmus of Panama to garrison duty in California. In his first address to Congress as president in 1869, Grant called for the construction of a canal connecting the Pacific and Caribbean through the Isthmus of Panama.[11] He believed that such a canal would be a great boon to American commerce, and he sent seven expeditions to survey the practicability of canal construction between 1870 and 1875.

President Grant was an active supporter of the world's fair in Philadelphia, known as the Centennial Exposition, to highlight American technology. This first world's fair held in the United States celebrated the 100th anniversary of the Declaration of Independence. Grant officially opened the 1876 Centennial Exposition on May 10 of that year. The event celebrated the emergence of the United States as a world industrial power. While nearly every nation exhibited at the fair, the exposition showcased the developing industrial power and abundant natural resources of the United States. President Grant himself had suggested the Smithsonian Institution get involved in the Centennial Exposition, and with his lobbying, Congress provided a new home for the exhibits. Today, many of these displays remain in the Smithsonian's Arts and Industries Building.

Even the scandals of the Grant administration would be formational in the evolution of Ohio republicanism, and they would augur future problems. These disgraces had highlighted the dangers inherent in a pro-business platform. It would become a tenant of Ohio republicanism that government oversight would be necessary, and Rutherford Hayes and, later, William McKinley would successfully address the political balance needed. Government supervision would also mark a major failure in a future Warren Harding administration in 1921. This oversight would result in overregulation and the birth of the progressive wing in the Republican Party that was often at odds with Ohio republicanism. Teddy Roosevelt would be the face of the progressive Republicans with his aggressive trust-busting policies. Grant's railroad scandals did point to corruption.

The public, however, did not fully hold President Grant accountable in the 1872 election. However, there was a conservative-liberal split in the Republican Party over Radical Reconstruction in the South. Grant's decisive reelection was achieved in the face of this rift, which resulted in a third party of Liberal Republicans nominating Horace Greeley to oppose Grant. The Democratic Party canceled its convention and supported Greeley. This early split of the Republicans almost ended the new party, but Grant's popularity and the firm stand of Ohio Radical Republicans held the center. Grant was reelected in the largest popular-majority victory for a Republican in the 19th century. He won 55.6 percent of the popular vote and 286 electoral votes to Greeley's 66. However, the election had challenged the very heart of Ohio republicanism at its geographic core of old Transylvania.

On the social planks of Ohio republicanism, Grant not only held to temperance and abolition but advanced on both issues. The temperance movement had a strong political backing in Ohio. Grant had been known for his drinking, but most historians see this reputation as overstated.[12] Still, he at many times during his life was a heavy drinker, and he probably would be considered an alcoholic today. Believing he had a drinking problem, Grant became a member of the Sons of Temperance. In his first term as president, he allowed the Republican temperance plank to remain. Grant was ambivalent about the temperance movement, but it had the forceful support of the Republican governor of Ohio, Rutherford Hayes (1868–1872). The severity of Grant's drinking problem was magnified by rumor, but he was largely able to control his impulses thanks to the help of people close to him and his own willpower and sense of duty.[13] At the political level, he supported the temperance movement; however, the party did drift away from a strong public stance on the issue in its 1872 platform.

On slavery, Grant remained a strong supporter of civil rights and Radical Reconstruction during his presidency. In 1868, the 14th Amendment was passed by Congress and ratified by the states, guaranteeing former slaves citizenship and equal rights, but not the vote. Grant also had the overwhelming support of the Radical Republicans in Congress. With the leadership of Representative James Garfield of Ohio, the House Speaker and a future president, congressmen marshaled the vote for the amendment's passage. Grant then pushed and lobbied the 15th Amendment through Congress, and when it was ratified in 1870, the amendment gave blacks the vote. Section 1 of the 15th Amendment reads: "The right of citizens of the United States to vote shall not be denied or abridged by the United States or by any state on account of race, color, or previous condition of servitude." Grant and Ohio republicanism had a deep hatred of racism in all forms. The Civil War general and Radical Republicans fought hard for full integration of ex-slaves into society. Grant continued to fight as he had during the war for blacks in the military and government. To bolster the 15th Amendment, Grant relied on the army; and in 1870, he signed legislation creating the Justice Department to enforce federal laws in the South. Grant also pressured Congress to draw up legislation that would seat black state legislators in Georgia who had been ousted by southern Democrats. Congress responded through special legislation; the members were reseated in the state legislature, and Georgia was required to adopt the 15th Amendment to gain representation in Congress.[14]

Surprisingly, the real fight for ratification of the 14th and 15th Amendments was centered in the old Transylvania region of Ohio, Indiana, and Kentucky. This was the very area that had spearheaded the abolition movement. The battle would be led by President Grant and two future presidents from Ohio–Rutherford B. Hayes and James Garfield. The split in the Republican Party over radicalism helped to fuel this Democratic spring in Ohio. Resistance to the 14th and 15th Amendments centered on the surge in the Democratic Party at the end of the war and a stirring of "new liberalism."[15] Another view was that the Republican Party had lost its "crusading fervor" and relied on past glories.[16] The grassroots peace movement of Copperheads[17] in the last years of the Civil War morphed into organized fear of pushing Radical Reconstruction as a root for more violence and war. These desires for peace were the main issues for German farmers, whom Democrats won over with a liberal view of civil rights. The state elections showed the success of the Democrats in taking the state legislature and voting down the 15th Amendment. However, Rutherford B. Hayes did win the governorship, even with his support for the amendment. Hayes refused to give up and fought disappointment with a renewed effort.

The peak of the Democratic resurgence in the presidential election saw the Democrats join the Liberal Republicans. This resurgence and coalition would particularly divide the Republican Party in Ohio and old Transylvania. In the presidential election of 1872, Grant had a landslide win nationally, but in Ohio, the Democrats swept the state congressional seats. Still, Grant's victories nationwide and in Ohio were attributed to the hard work of Ohio's Republican governor Rutherford Hayes and Republican representative James Garfield.[18] However, even Hayes lost his Senate bid.

A closer look at the Democratic surge of the late 1860s and earlier saw a breakdown in Ohio republicanism. Ohio republicanism was always tied to a coalition of civil rights and economics. The Republicans had also lost the initiative on economic issues important to the voters. In 1870, Governor Hayes would package the 14th and 15th Amendments with a weak economic platform. Hayes went throughout the state in 1870 promoting the 15th Amendment. In January 1870, the Ohio State Assembly passed the amendment with a 57–55 vote, and the Ohio State Senate passed it with a 19–18 vote.[19] Rutherford Hayes would emerge as a leader of the Republican Party and help solidify the core philosophy of Ohio republicanism. The Democrats' advocacy of the old slavery and civil rights would peak in 1872 as Grant and Republicans proceeded to address poor treatment of the blacks.

Grant went much further in his quest for the full civil rights of ex-slaves. In 1871 with the help of President Ulysses Grant, Congress passed the Ku Klux Klan Act. Also known as the Third Enforcement Act, the bill was a controversial expansion of authority designed to give the federal government additional power to protect voters. It established penalties in the form of fines and jail time for attempts to deprive citizens of equal protection under the laws, and it gave the president the authority to use federal troops. In addition, Grant signed the Civil Rights Act of 1875, guaranteeing blacks equal rights in public places and prohibiting their exclusion from jury duty. The act was declared unconstitutional by the Supreme Court in 1883. Nevertheless, it created an important precedent. Radical Reconstruction and black civil rights would be a big part of the legacy of Ohio presidents from Grant on.

The biggest challenge to Grant's presidency and Ohio republicanism was not civil rights or scandals but the Panic of 1873. Like most financial crises, the Panic of 1873 had started in New York with investment house problems. The panic started as a bank crisis, but within a few days the stock market closed for the first time in its history. The event soon became known as the Great Depression and held that title until 1930. The result of railroad speculation after the Civil War, the Panic of 1873 hit the nation and Ohio hard. Over a five-year period, 30 percent of Americans were unemployed and another 40 percent were working for less than seven months a year. Nationwide, three million would lose their jobs, and daily wages would fall 25 percent. In Ohio, railroad workers suffered a 35 percent decrease in pay. Miners' wages for coal dug had been reduced throughout the years of panic from $1.00 a ton to $0.65 a ton. The canals started to dry up for lack of farm traffic.

The year 1874 was probably the worst year of the panic for Ohio, with 11,442 of the state's 22,650 employees working less than 50 weeks.[20] America and Ohio noticed an increase of "tramps" on city streets. In fact, the papers suggested getting a dog with good teeth as protection. The price of oil had dropped from $3.00 a barrel to $0.50 cents a barrel. Agricultural products' value had dropped a similar percentage, causing farms to fail and railroad profits to decrease dramatically. Financial and political scandals of the period further rocked investor confidence. Nationally, a quarter of the nation's 360 railroads failed, as well as 20,000 other businesses. The Panic of 1873 was the first international depression that America had experienced, and that would leave its mark on Ohio republicanism. It would also bear witness to Americans voting with their pocketbooks.

Initially, the Panic of 1873 had little direct political impact on the movement of Ohio republicanism. In fact, it created a uniform call by farmers and industrialists for higher tariffs. The political makeup of the electorate did change the support of the Republican Party as more focused political parties evolved. The Panic of 1873 had a heavy impact on the lives of Ohioans and Americans and resulted in some groundswell political movements that split Ohio republicanism at the grassroots level. These interest groups were consistent with Ohio republicanism but took votes from the Republican Party. In Ohio, the People's Party was formed of Liberal Republicans and mainline Democrats from the 1872 coalition of the two. The People's Party held that the corruption of the Grant administration had caused the 1873 depression, but its adherents never became a political force. In the East, silver and paper money advocates formed the independent Greenback Party. The Greenback Party aggressively supported monetary policies favorable to manufacturing and farming, policies many believed the Republicans had left behind. A greenback was paper money not backed by either silver or gold, which was believed responsible for monetary expansion and growth. The party's 1876 candidate, Peter Cooper, was a nationally known iron manufacturer. As a special focus party, like the People's Party, the Greenback Party had a minor influence. The political impact of the Panic of 1873 would show up in the contentious presidential election of Rutherford Hayes.

Chapter Six

Ohio Republicanism and the American Empire— Rutherford Hayes

President Hayes's nomination at the Republican Convention in Cincinnati, Ohio, and subsequent election would begin what many historians call the "Ohio Dynasty."[1] The so-called dynasty came from not only Ohio's 23 electoral votes (behind Pennsylvania at 30 and New York at 36), but also the dominance of Ohio in the Republican Party's infrastructure. President Hayes was at heart a populist and a nationalist, but his campaign had been funded by the eastern big-money Republicans. Still, Hayes had the support of Ohio's strongest senator and national statesman, John Sherman. Hayes's populism would be challenged throughout his presidency, but Ohio republicanism was always bottom driven by the voters.

Rutherford B. Hayes (1822–1893) was born in 1822 in Delaware, Ohio, to Rutherford Hayes and his wife, Sophie Birchard Hayes. Descended from a long line of Presbyterians, he could trace his lineage to New England in 1625 and Scottish colonists. While Hayes had adhered to various faith institutions over the years, his beliefs were probably best described as Unitarian.[2] As a boy, he had attended one-room schoolhouses, then had become a student at Methodist Norwalk Seminary in 1833. He went on to Kenyon College and then Harvard to study law. Hayes had also learned German, which would serve him well with the growing German population of Ohio and the Midwest. He opened his first law practice in 1850 in Cincinnati, Ohio. Since his college days Hayes had been a committed Whig, but he also developed a support for antislavery parties of the time. He took on a number of fugitive slave cases in his law practice. He soon adopted the emerging Union Party (Republican Party) in 1853, and in 1856 he was a delegate to their first convention. That convention nominated General John Charles Fremont (1813–1890), who had been a Free Soil Democrat, for president in 1856.[3] Hayes strongly supported the antislavery platform and played a major role in the early Republican Party's founding. One issue with the German population was that it often included abolitionists and opponents of war, which required some compromise, but Hayes never questioned that slavery had to end. The English stock of Ohio's Western Reserve took an ambivalent stand on slavery as well.

Hayes became an avid supporter of Abraham Lincoln in 1860 and worked for his election. With the war, Hayes joined the Union army and rose to the rank of general. He led the Ohio 23rd with another officer, William McKinley, who would become president. While still in the army, Hayes was elected as a representative to Congress in 1864. He served two years but felt more comfortable returning to his law practice. It was a short sabbatical, however, as friends forced him into running for governor of Ohio in 1867. Hayes would run and win three times, beating some of the best hopes of the Democratic Party.

As governor, Hayes championed civil rights in an era of a split Republican Party and rising Democrats. He battled hard for the 14th and 15th Amendments in Ohio. His efforts would cost him a Senate seat in 1872, but he incorporated civil rights into Ohio republicanism for the future and built a foundation for an Ohio Republican Party stronghold. Hayes would also mold the frontier diversity of old Transylvania into a political philosophy. This process was a difficult balancing act. The German farm base opposed tariffs, while the emerging Ohio industrial centers wanted protectionism. The temperance movement also split the state in the 1870s. In addition, the newly formed Republican Party was often split on social and economic issues, requiring adept leaders to solidify the vote. Ohio republicanism was populistic, nationalistic, and moralistic. While the political environment would often divide the Republican vote, Democrats of the period remained unified in opposing civil rights and tariffs. In these factors, Ohio reflected the diversity of the nation. Success in Ohio would also mean success in national elections. Even more so than Grant, Hayes was the first to realize this state of affairs.

Hayes's nomination in 1876 highlighted the old split between Liberal Republicans and Radical Republicans, who supported Ohio-style republicanism. While the Radical Republicans were on the way out of the party, new factions arose. The Stalwart Republicans were East Coast Republicans aligned more closely with the Democrats in their support for lower tariffs. Stalwarts also were in favor of political machines and spoils system–style patronage. Ohio republicanism represented a groundswell movement that demanded civil service reform, while the Stalwarts supported the old patronage system in government. The Ohio republicanism movement was similar to the "Drain the swamp" sentiment of today and the "Throw the bums out" movement of the 1980s. The Stalwarts opposed many core moral values of conservative Ohio republicanism. In particular, they had little interest in the social issues of midwestern Republicans, such as temperance, radical civil rights, and education. The Stalwarts formed a faction of the U.S. Republican Party that existed briefly during the 1870s, in the Gilded Age after Reconstruction. But their impact lasted for decades; the Stalwarts would deeply divide the party. Some of this fault line is still visible today, as eastern Republicans have less interest in social issues such as abortion and religious liberty.

The Stalwarts tended to be eastern Republicans with big bankers' support. Led by U.S. senator Roscoe Conkling of New York—also known as "Lord Roscoe"—Stalwarts were sometimes called Conklingites.[4] Other notable Stalwarts included Chester A. Arthur (future vice president and president) and Thomas C. Platt, both of whom were in favor of 18th U.S. president Ulysses S. Grant's running for a third term. Not that Grant was the Stalwarts' ideal, but they feared the rise of Ohio candidates John Sherman and Rutherford Hayes. Another group of eastern Republicans known as the Half-Breeds also arose. Stalwarts invented the derisive epithet "Half-Breed" to denote those whom they perceived as being only half–Republican. Led by Maine senator James G. Blaine, the Half-Breeds supported civil service reform and a merit system. Many Ohio Republicans were with the Half-Breeds because of their stance on higher tariffs, and Ohio republicanism was still a core principle for most in the party.

Hayes's success in Ohio immediately elevated him to the top ranks of Republican politicians under consideration for the presidency in 1876. The Ohio delegation to the 1876 Republican National Convention was united behind Hayes, and Senator John Sherman did all in his power to bring Hayes the nomination. When the Stalwart Republicans failed to get Grant to run again, they turned to Maine's James G. Blaine. The convention assembled with Blaine as the favorite, but while he started with a significant lead in the delegate count, he could not muster a majority. As Blaine failed to gain votes, the delegates looked elsewhere for a nominee and settled on Hayes on the seventh ballot.

Hayes was a popular Ohio congressman, Ohio governor, and former army officer. He was considered by Ohio Republicans to be an excellent standard-bearer for the 1876 election campaign. As a result, the state delegation mounted a major floor campaign for him. Hayes's political views were more moderate than the Republican Party's platform, although he agreed with the proposed amendment to the Ohio state constitution that would guarantee suffrage to black males. Hayes could count on the Half-Breeds if their candidate failed to get the vote. On economic issues, Hayes believed in Ohio republicanism and protective tariffs. His slight moderate view on some issues allowed him to gain enough Stalwarts to win the nomination. Hayes was, in this respect, a bridge and compromise candidate for a struggling Republican Party that had lost the energy of abolition in its formation. The difficult nomination process augured a difficult national campaign. However, this election would be the first where the Republican and Democratic Parties would become the main representatives of the United States.

Hayes would win the presidency under questionable circumstances. The election of a Republican to follow President Grant was extremely problematic in many ways, and the 1876 presidential election was one of the most contentious and controversial in American history, at least until the 2000s. The results remain among the most disputed ever, although it is not disputed that Democrat Samuel J. Tilden of New York outpolled Ohio's Rutherford B. Hayes in the popular vote. After a first count of ballots, Tilden won 184 electoral votes to Hayes's 165, with 20 votes unresolved. These 20 electoral votes were in dispute in four states. In the case of Florida, Louisiana, and South Carolina, each party reported that its candidate had won the state. In Oregon one elector was replaced after being declared illegal. The question of who should have been awarded these electoral votes is the source of the continued controversy concerning the 1876 presidential election. An informal deal known as the Compromise of 1877 was struck to resolve the dispute; this measure awarded all 20 electoral votes to Hayes.[5] The compromise also resulted in the national government pulling the last federal troops out of the South, which ended the Reconstruction era. Through the compromise, Republican Rutherford B. Hayes was awarded the White House over Democrat Samuel J. Tilden on the understanding that Hayes would remove the federal troops from the South, whose support was essential for the survival of Republican state governments in South Carolina, Florida, and Louisiana.

The election did identify a new geographic strength for the Republican Party. This was the industrial Midwest, which included Ohio, Michigan, Illinois, Wisconsin, Iowa, and Pennsylvania. This area would become a key voting bloc for future Republican victories as the South turned Democratic. The end of Reconstruction cost the Republicans the southern states. After the Compromise of 1877, the Democrats controlled all the southern states, and disenfranchised blacks, who were Republicans, had their voting rights challenged. The Democrats would restrict black voting to maintain control. The southern black vote had helped Grant and Hayes win their elections. Furthermore, the Democrats would control the South until the 1980s. Future Republican presidents would find tough resistance to their plan of expanded civil rights for blacks. In Ohio, the call for civil rights for ex-slaves would continue.

The hardest policy for Hayes was the withdrawal of troops from the South. Military occupation had assured the control of the Radical Republicans at the state level. Moreover, the black vote was solidly Republican. But even

Grant had called for an end of the occupation. The Compromise of 1877 would effectively end the role of the Radical Republicans and allow Democrat-controlled state legislatures to suppress the black vote. The Republicans still had a split between the Liberal Republicans and the old Radicals. The compromise and the party divisions weakened the Republican Party.

While President Grant had a high favorability rating, his administration had been one of the nation's most corrupt ones. Grant had personally avoided the scandals of his government, but the blame was put on many of the Radical Republicans in Congress, which further expedited their fall. All of these circumstances allowed Hayes to put some of the wounds of the Civil War behind him while still fighting for civil rights embodied in Ohio republicanism. Even so, the southern states under Democratic control did take a step back in civil rights.

President Hayes brought with him strong ties in Ohio's south and its Western Reserve, and with those ties came a strong view of Ohio republicanism. Having served three terms as Ohio governor, Hayes understood the meaning of Ohio republicanism and was in a position to establish it on a national level. He would maintain the Republican Party's protective tariffs while expanding black education, civil rights, and economic growth. Hayes was a staunch believer in temperance, but he failed to take it to a national implementation.

Temperance had always been an issue with Hayes. He did not serve alcohol in his house or at political rallies, and his wife, Lucy, took this policy to the White House. The ban on serving liquor and wine at White House entertainments was attributed to Mrs. Hayes, and critics derisively nicknamed her "Lemonade Lucy."[6] Hayes, in turn, had few social visitors to the White House except Congressman William McKinley, a fellow Ohioan. Hayes realized early in his career that the Ohio German farmers and Irish canal workers would not stand for a temperance law. In the 1850s, he had made several public speeches on temperance and had been silenced by the strong backlash.[7] However, he realized that temperance could create another fault line in an already divided party. After leaving the White House, Hayes would continue to cajole Ohio presidents to maintain some level of support for temperance to prevent further division over social issues.[8] He did give priority to matters such as education and prison reform.

Hayes was successful at bringing the Ohio and midwestern McGuffey common-school approach to education. With his time in the Cincinnati area, Hayes had become deeply involved in the branches of the earlier College of Teachers, McGuffeyism, and common schools. he firmly believed that education had taken a small (but persistent) abolition movement in the 1820s and 1830s to a national movement. One biographer sees the importance of schooling for Hayes, stating: "Hayes thought education as the solution to most of the nation's problems. With education at all levels Hayes thought that the South would become more like the North, adapting the commercial society of the late nineteenth century. Unfortunately, it took another century for that to happen. With education ex-slaves could be productive and free, advancing economically as earlier immigrants had done."[9] Even after his presidency, Hayes continued his work with the education of ex-slaves through the Slater Fund for Freemen.

Hayes had been one of the founding members of the Cincinnati Literary Society, which discussed the future and important role of education. The society was rooted in the earlier College of Teachers and the McGuffey movement. Among the organization's famous guests were Charles Dickens, Oscar Wilde, Samuel L. Clemens, Ralph Waldo Emerson, Booker T. Washington, and Robert Frost. Among the Cincinnati Literary Society's distinguished members were U.S. presidents Rutherford B. Hayes and William Howard Taft. Cincinnati's Literary Club remains the oldest such group in the United States. For Hayes, the society and public education would be lifelong loves. After h presidency, he would attend and serve on many college boards, including those of Case Western Reserve University and Ohio State University.

President Rutherford B. Hayes and his wife, Lucy. Library of Congress.

Ohio republicanism brought to education not only common schools and textbooks, a Christian and patriotic basis, and schooling for blacks and prisoners, but a practical addition of manual arts needed for industry. More than prior presidents, Hayes saw education as the heart of industrial success. His Cincinnati connections put him in the early network of philosophical debates on American public education. These discussions would become a plank in future Republican platforms.

On a national level, the Hayes administration faced some tough times with labor, including problems with workplace safety. The railroads were also unpopular with farmers because of overpricing. Scandals had plagued the railways since the Grant administration, and the public had a negative view of them as a result. America's railroads were becoming known for their monopolistic practices and had found resistance from organizations such as the Grange. The rate schedules had drawn criticism from many segments of the population, including businesses. Furthermore, the Pennsylvania Railroad was in a direct battle with Standard Oil in Cleveland. The Pennsylvania Railroad was trying to force Rockefeller to refine more oil in Pittsburgh because it was to the railroad's advantage. Congressman William McKinley had spoken against these practices, but the real problem would be the growing employee problems. In mid-July 1877, the Pennsylvania Railroad and the Baltimore and Ohio, still struggling from the Panic of 1873, decided to cut wages of the brakemen and firemen by 10 percent. In addition, the companies announced their intention to run "doubleheaders." A doubleheader meant two locomotives and 34 freight cars versus one locomotive and 17 cars. It effectively cut the workforce in half while doubling the labor of the remaining employees. President Hayes and the Republican Party were now facing a political problem.

The struggle reached the crisis point on July 17, 1877, at Martinsburg, West Virginia. There, a protest strike started at the Baltimore and Ohio railroad hub. State militia was called in, and one of the strikers was shot. At Baltimore's Camden Yards, the strike closed down what was then the nation's hub. Troops again confronted the strikers, and ten strikers were killed. On July 21, a full riot broke out in Pittsburgh as citizens joined the picketers, destroying 1,383 freight cars, 104 locomotives, and 66 passenger cars. Freight was looted, and Union Depot burned down. Pittsburgh militia refused to shoot at the locals, so Philadelphia troops were sent in. The mobs surrounded the troops, and over 25 were killed and hundreds wounded. In Ohio, miners took up arms against the railroad, and Hayes had to augment the National Guard with federal soldiers. The nation's sympathy was with the strikers, and the Republican Party was hurt by the use of troops.

Chicago, at the time, was suffering from a major heat wave. The weather combined with the city's large number of socialists to make conditions ripe for riots. Uprisings did break out as crowds took to the streets shouting, "Pittsburgh, Pittsburgh, Pittsburgh!" The socialists, realizing the nation's sympathy was with the strikers, took advantage of the unrest to make a statement against capitalism. Striking lumbermen and butchers joined in. Hayes was forced to send in troops as the headlines called the riots a "reign of terror."

In the end, 30 men and boys died, most of them Irish. The railroad strike hurt the Republicans nationally with labor, immigrants, and the Irish. Democrats used the strike to help stop the growth of a labor coalition in the Republican Party that protective tariffs had fostered.

In the same year, Irish gangs in California were attacking Chinese immigrants. These immigrants had flooded the West Coast to supply cheap labor to the railroads, and they had displaced mostly Irish laborers. In San Francisco, the Irish were killing Chinese on the streets. Congress then passed a law to ban Chinese immigration. American businessmen not only wanted cheap Chinese labor but also saw China as a great opportunity for market expansion. Hayes vetoed the ban, which helped turn what few Irish Republicans existed to the Democratic Party. However, Ohio republicanism would evolve and later would support restricted Chinese immigration during the Garfield and McKinley administrations. The Republican Party was now becoming the party of industry and the eastern bankers. The alliance, however, was one of convenience. These easterners had little support for frontier congressmen from Ohio such as Hayes, Sherman, McKinley, and Garfield. Still, the East was home to the Republican donor class. What the eastern bloc lacked was the popular vote. Republicans would have to live with eastern money and western votes by finding a compromise.

The devastation of railroad equipment, cars, and locomotives during railroad riots in Pittsburgh, July 22, 1877. Library of Congress.

Eastern Republicans and Stalwarts were former Whigs, but they represented the shipping industry that wanted international trade and low tariffs. The eastern bankers wanted international trade as well, since they profited from the volume of trade regardless of whether it favored American industry. The eastern Republicans also backed the railroad management versus labor.

Railroad scandals had always been a stone around the neck of Republicans in Ohio. Ohio politicians in particular tended to be more labor oriented, and this circumstance was behind the rise of Congressman William McKinley. While the eastern wing of the party lacked the votes, it had the financing. The divide would always require compromise, and east-west tension would be a notable characteristic of the Republican Party to this very day.

This east-west divide became clear in the 1880 Republican Convention. Hayes's secretary of the Treasury, former Ohio senator John Sherman, started as the favorite from the Ohio delegation and the committed votes. Sherman was a bulldog on protectionism even through the great economic downturn of the 1870s. The convention was held in Cincinnati, reflecting the importance of Ohio in national politics. Overall there was a strong movement for Grant to be nominated again. James Gillespie Blaine (1830–1893) had the strong support of the eastern banking wing of the party. An American statesman and Republican politician who had represented Maine in the U.S. House of Representatives from 1863 to 1876, Blaine had served as Speaker of the U.S. House of Representatives from 1869 to 1875, and then in the United States Senate from 1876 to 1881. He had been a moderate on strict protectionism but a pioneer in the idea of trade reciprocity (which later Ohio presidents would embrace). After a number of ballots, it was clear that Ohio's Sherman could not win.

John Sherman at the time was the heart and soul of the Republican approach to trade protectionism, and he would never yield on his trade policy. He clearly opposed James Blaine because of his free trade tendencies and eastern banking connections. The philosophical struggle over trade and protectionism was a national issue and an issue within the Ohio Republican Party. James Garfield, John Sherman's manager, was himself struggling with this argument, but he had came over to the forceful view of Sherman in Congress. The views of the two men could be summarized in this manner: "For some years Garfield tried to reconcile the logic of free trade with the indisputable benefits of protection. Sherman never troubled to doubt whether they agreed or not or even could be reconciled."[10]

Sherman's delegates could swing the nomination to either Grant or Blaine, but Sherman refused to release them through 28 ballots in the hope that the anti–Grant forces would desert Blaine and flock to him. Eventually, the delegates did abandon Blaine. But they shifted their votes to Ohio congressman James A. Garfield instead of Sherman; and by the 36th ballot, Garfield had 399 votes, enough for victory. Garfield offered somewhat a of compromise, as he had led the Ways and Means Committee in Congress and believed in strong protectionism. However, he was willing to embrace reciprocity suggested by Blaine to expand trade, which eastern bankers wanted, while protecting American industry. As manager of Sherman's campaign,

James Garfield adhered to the emerging philosophy of Ohio republicanism.

It would be the nomination of James Garfield that would set in motion the unique policy of scientific protectionism associated with Ohio republicanism. The idea of strong protection had been settled with John Sherman's unswayable commitment to it with key Republicans. Eastern bankers, who supported Blaine, wanted a liberal trade policy. These bankers had deep international ties and made money on the volume of trade regardless of the nations involved or the direction of product flow. Garfield's compromise to include Blaine's idea of reciprocity would allow for business to expand exports while protecting against cheap dumping of products. Reciprocity required a balanced approach on trade amounts and pricing with trading parties. These concepts addressed the fears of potential trade wars by proponents of free trade and gave hope to eastern bankers for increased trade volume. Garfield added his own important twist to Republican trade policy, requiring congressional review of tariffs and companies. The idea was to ensure that companies that benefited from tariffs would reinvest in American plants and jobs. Otherwise, Congress would reduce the tariff. This Ohio-born policy of reciprocity and oversight would govern American trade until the 1920s and lead to the international ascendency of American manufacturing. It would unify, at least for the upcoming presidential election, east and west Republicans, as well as protectionists and free traders in the party. James Garfield offered the perfect compromise for the times and future Republican platforms.

Chapter Seven

The Rise of National Capitalism versus Internationalism

James Abram Garfield (1831–1881) was the 20th president of the United States (1881–1882), serving from March 4, 1881, until his assassination later that year. He had served nine terms in the House of Representatives, which is where he left his mark on Ohio republicanism. Garfield represented the transition of Ohio republicanism from an artifact of the Civil War to a national policy. Garfield entered the U.S. Congress in 1865 and would remain there until his presidency in 1881. He would bridge the gap between Grant and McKinley as to policy. Furthermore, Garfield would chair the House Banking Committee and Appropriations Committee, and he also served on the House Ways and Means Committee.

Garfield would become a financial expert for the Republicans. He took a moderate approach on tariffs compared to Presidents Lincoln, Grant, and Hayes, who had generated cash through tariffs to finance the war, pay veterans, and generate large surpluses. Garfield believed tariffs should be used to protect American industry but not be so high as to generate extra revenue for the government. Early in his career, this idea put him in opposition to most Republican leaders. Garfield's beliefs played well, however, in his Western Reserve district, which included farmers who generally opposed tariffs. This varying reception was also representative of a new, evolving divide between rural and urban centers in Ohio and other midwestern states over the impact of tariffs in the late 1870s. The growing political bloc of farmers was being cultivated by the Democrats. Garfield would, however, maintain support that tariffs should be used to protect American industries and laborers. He managed this balance with a scientific approach that looked at specific needs of an industry, product, and consumers. Garfield's protégé, Congressman William McKinley, would spend hours developing tariff tables that addressed specific products and countries.

While short, a recent article in the *Washington Post* gives a powerful endorsement of Garfield's record: "James A. Garfield, who may have been the best president we never had, or hardly had. Garfield was fatally wounded only months into his presidency by a deranged office seeker with a handgun, and the memorials to him—statuary, parks, streets, schools here in Washington and elsewhere—reflect not just the nation's grief over his martyrdom but also a genuine admiration felt across a great part of the country and especially among its most downtrodden."[1] One characteristic of Garfield that separates him from the purer ideals of other Ohio presidents was his independent thinking. He hated to focus on extremes or simple solutions. He struggled with many big issues; today he would have a hard time with his evolution on political issues and appear to be inconsistent. Garfield often moderated the concepts of earlier Ohio republicanism, and he was also flexible and capable, yielding to his voters and fellow Republicans. However, Garfield reflected the state of Ohio and its evolution on matters of the day. At the time, voters were more accepting of a politician's changing views to better reflect the changing environments. Yet many of Garfield's political peers were just as rigid on this topic as they are today.

Some of Garfield's independent thinking might have come from his diverse background and experiences. His family, like President Grant's, could trace its roots to Plymouth in the 1630s. Garfield's father came to Ohio in the 1820s to build a section of the Ohio Canal in the Western Reserve.[2] Garfield was born on November 19, 1831, in the small village of Orange in Cuyahoga County. This was the northern part of Ohio's Western Reserve. The Garfields were not, however, political sons of the Western Reserve. James Garfield and his family belonged to a fundamental Christian sect known as the Disciples of Christ. The Western Reserve was known for Christian diversity, such as in locations where Mormons and Shakers intermixed with traditional Protestant sects. Most inhabitants, however, were abolitionists. While not supporting slavery, the Disciples were more accepting of slavery. The Disciples of Christ represented a backlash against the rigid denominationalism of the early 1800s. Disciples maintained an openness and a fear of rigid beliefs and philosophies. It seems that Garfield's mother adopted this movement, which evolved out of Kentucky and central Transylvania. Garfield would remain with the Disciples of Christ and their views, and he seemed to have moderated the furor of the area's strong antislavery movement ideas early in his life. He would also remain a lifelong Disciple and serve as an active minister as a young man.[3] Garfield would marry Lucretia Rudolph, who was also a Disciple of Christ, in 1858.

Garfield's family had been active in canal building. Much has been made of Garfield's six-week career as a canal mule boy, but it really only proved to himself his love of academic pursuits. Garfield had enjoyed the classics and mathematics in his early boyhood studies, using the *McGuffey Readers* in the one-room schoolhouses of the Western Reserve. He had to work as a janitor to further his schooling, and he went to New England for a college education.

At Williams College in Williamstown, Massachusetts, Garfield became strongly influenced by abolitionists, who brought him more in line with his Ohio roots in the Western Reserve. He graduated in 1856. A year later, Garfield entered politics as a Republican and served as a member of the Ohio State Senate from 1859 to 1861. He received a commission as a colonel in the 42nd Ohio Infantry Regiment as the Civil War started. The 42nd Ohio existed only on paper, so Garfield was tasked with the mission to fill its ranks. He did so within a few weeks, recruiting many of his neighbors and former students. Garfield was promoted to major general in the Union army during the Civil War, and he fought and won distinction in the Battles of Middle Creek, Shiloh, and Chickamauga. He was revered as a war hero, which made him a popular choice for political office. Garfield was first elected to Congress in 1862 to represent Ohio's 19th District of the Western Reserve.

His Civil War experience further moved Garfield toward the importance of civil rights, for which he would become an activist. "Initially, Garfield thought the Bible supported the presence of slavery, but his views began to change in the 1850s. During his service in the Civil War, he experienced things that put him in greater sympathy with the abolitionists."[4] While in the military, Garfield related the following experience about a runaway slave: "Not long ago my commanding general sent me an order to have my camp searched for a fugitive slave, I sent word that if generals wish to disobey an express law of Congress, which is an order from the War Department, they must do it themselves."[5]

Garfield's congressional experiences further evolved his views on civil rights to a more radical stand on Reconstruction. As a congressman, Garfield not only favored abolition but also became a member of the Radical Republicans. He and the Radicals believed that the leaders of the Confederate rebellion had forfeited their constitutional rights. Garfield and his allies also supported the confiscation of Southern plantations and the punishment of rebellion leaders. Yet he slowly moved away from many of the Radicals' policies, as did the nation. Garfield was a difficult man to put labels on. One historian notes: "Yet, for all his desire to see slavery ended, he did not want to see African-Americans given 'special treatment.' Garfield could not agree with Pennsylvania Radical Congressman Thaddeus Stevens, who wanted to equalize the pay of white and black soldiers.... Though he praised black troops for their devotion and service to the Union, Garfield would not 'pat the black man on the back merely because he is black,' and he would not attempt to make 'political capital by showing an excessive zeal for the black man.'"[6] Yet Garfield became more aggressive over the years on civil rights.

At his Inaugural Address, Garfield stated: "The elevation of the negro race from slavery to the full rights of citizenship is the most important political change we have known since the adoption of the Constitution of 1787, no thoughtful man can fail to appreciate its beneficent effect upon our institutions and people. It has freed us from the perpetual danger of war and dissolution.... No doubt this great change has caused serious disturbance to our Southern communities. This is to be deplored, though it was perhaps unavoidable. But those who resisted the change should remember that under our institutions there was no middle ground for the Negro race between slavery and equal citizenship."[7] This was a powerful summation of Ohio republicanism over the years on civil rights.

James Garfield had made his mark on Ohio republicanism and the nation as a congressman, but Ohio republicanism also impacted his views. Garfield was, more than previous Ohio presidents, influenced by the state's opinions on abolition, tariffs, the gold standard and economic development. In today's world, he would be called a flip-flopper, but he was the eternal student studying and evaluating issues and remaining open to new views. He certainly was amenable to deferring to the will of his Ohio district on many issues. Garfield's thinking on civil rights clearly evolved to become consistent with the activism of Ohio's Western Reserve. On economic issues he helped moderate core Republican approaches with his own study and beliefs. There always seemed to be a struggle versus unwavering belief in any position.

Garfield struggled personally as a Republican with the radicalism of Reconstruction as well as the protective-versus-revenue-tariff question. Tariffs were a core issue of Ohio republicanism, but they divided the eastern Stalwart Republicans. The matter seemed particularly perplexing to Garfield. Some of the problem was the mixed politics of the Western Reserve, which included anti-tariff farmers and tariff supporters in industrial cities such as Cleveland, Akron, Niles, Youngstown, and Canton. One biographer puts it best: "Garfield should have been an adamant free-trader, for the theory was as orthodox and respectable a part of laissez-faire doctrine as sound money. Yet on the tariff his stand was ambiguous. In part, this was because the tariff issue lacked a clear-cut moral certainty of the money question, but, to a greater degree, his wobbling was due to the pressure of political realities."[8] For example, Garfield's congressional district around Youngstown was headquarters of the Ohio Wool Growers Association, which lobbied for low tariffs. Yet Youngstown was also the center of the old Iron Whig industrialists, who had built a huge iron industry in the district and demanded high tariffs. In fact,

Garfield's district had 19 iron furnaces and was one of the biggest iron making districts in the United States. Early on, his middle-road approach cost him the chairmanship of the Ways and Means Committee, which had been dominated for years by protectionists such as Pig Iron Kelly of Pennsylvania, the chairman. Garfield would also be pushed by a young (future Ohio president) William McKinley of the same Ohio area to support high tariffs. Garfield walked a tightrope; but he clearly leaned more protectionist as he approached the presidency.

In 1878 in his journal, Garfield noted the following on the tariff issue: "I am distressed by the curious state of conflict in my own mind upon the phases of it. To be an extreme man is doubtless comfortable. It is painful to see too many sides of a subject."[9] This struggle was also being played out in his state of Ohio as it was in the nation. Ohio was representative of the discord between the industrial America of Hamilton and the agrarian one of Jefferson. In the last half of the 19th century in Ohio, you could see iconic iron furnace stacks with farm animals feeding nearby. Often the small farmer was also an employee of the iron company. In addition, the very success of the American farmer was based on the industrial might exemplified by the railroads and canal systems. In the 1870s, Ohio grain shipments to Europe were booming thanks to the railways and canals. Ohio was at the crossroads of industry and agriculture, and thus of the tariff issue. Ohio republicanism would need to become some type of compromise to adapt to its citizens.

Ohio, in particular, was developing in a very different way from the past. The European model of industrialization had been the growth of centralized manufacturing cities. This was somewhat true in America, but Ohio was seeing the rise of the rural industrial town. The town would evolve around an industrial entity such as an iron furnace, glass furnace, or rubber company. Farmers found both customers and employment in these small company towns, and this mix confused the political logic on economic issues such as tariffs. Ohio in the last quarter of the 19th century saw the explosion of these industrial burghs, with glass towns such as Bowling Green, Tiffin, Fostoria, North Baltimore, and Findlay; rubber towns such as Barberton and Akron; and iron towns such as Niles, Canton, and Warren. In the state and the electorate opinions became intermixed on tariffs, so the politicians could no longer live at the political extremes of farming versus industry. Furthermore, Ohio was leading the movement in the American West toward industrial small towns. Indiana and southern Michigan were also seeing the emergence of the industrial town. These developments hurt the voting base of the Democrats in the North, but they also complicated things for Republicans. Garfield understood this shift in the electorate better than most.

In his biographical notes, Garfield described the struggle clearly: "I was denounced by extreme protectionists as a free trader; and denounced by free traders as a sort of protectionist ... the only position in my life that has been a middle between two extremes. I have been at one pole or the other; there I stood on the equator ... and I esteem it as one of the greatest of my achievements in statesmanship to have held that equipoise."[10] It was a necessity for a politician of the Western Reserve to maintain that middle ground; however, Garfield proved to be a protectionist in most congressional votes. Still, he would cut a new scientific approach to eliminate revenue-producing high tariffs on common goods while protecting job-creating industries.

It was on the tariff issue that Garfield's views impacted Ohio republicanism the most. He tried to moderate Ohio republicanism by defining the tariff issue as one of protectionism versus revenue. During the Grant and Hayes administrations, duties not only protected industry but were placed higher to generate federal revenue. Garfield would argue for protection only, but the distinction was difficult to apply perfectly to tariff rates. Still, protection-based tariffs had more popularity in the agricultural and industrial mix of Ohio. It took years for Garfield's more moderate view to win over the national Republican Party, with the Stalwart wing in the East opposing it. Garfield's study and hesitation helped form the cornerstone of America's scientific approach to duties. With the aid of a young congressman, William McKinley of Ohio, he formed a review subcommittee on tariffs. At the same time, Ohio republicanism was more aligned with the Stalwarts on tariffs and civil service. Instead of across-the-board tariff rate changes, rates were adjusted based on the needs of industry and consumers. For example, the steel industry wanted taxes on incoming foreign steel, but it needed duty-free iron ore from other countries. Oversight was also required to adjust any windfall profits due to protection invested in factories and jobs. Young William McKinley would become the congressional expert on scientific tariff rates.

Garfield would be one of the first presidents to deal with the impact of cheap immigrant labor taking American jobs. He favored limiting Chinese immigration, though he preferred to do so by negotiating a treaty with China. The issue may have been one of the first October surprises in a major presidential election. Before the election in October 1880, Democrats published a letter, attributed to Garfield, that supported unrestricted mass entry of cheap Chinese laborers to be used by the railroads on the West Coast. Though the letter damaged Garfield in the western states, he protested that it was a forgery (which it was). Even so, the damage had been done.[11]

Another practical moderate position of Garfield's Ohio republicanism was temperance, a dividing issue in the 1870s and early 1880s. Ohio had strong, well-organized local temperance organizations, but the German and Irish populations offered voting-bloc resistance. Somewhere in between was where most of the population's opinion lay. Garfield and his wife, Lucretia, were themselves light drinkers. He was bothered not by drinking itself, but its results in communities. As a congressman, Garfield had supported bills to restrict the sale of alcohol without eliminating it. He refused to bow to the pressure of temperance groups to maintain the Hayes ban on spirits in the White House. Garfield continued to publicly support limitations on alcohol without expending political capital on the matter. He would often take this wait-and-see attitude on issues before taking a strong stand. Finding middle ground was often the best option. In general, Ohio republicanism wanted to limit alcohol, not ban it. But like abolition, temperance had deep roots in Ohio republicanism that required some concessions.

Eventually, politicians in Ohio passed a number of laws placing taxes on alcohol sales and licensing and eliminating Sunday sales.[12] These events occurred after the Garfield presidency, and courts overturned many of these laws. The Ohio Republicans put two amendments to voters—one to prohibit sales and the other to allow sales. Amazingly, both amendments failed! Still, Democrats took state seats, and these victories would hurt at the national level in the presidential race of 1884. Ohio had a divide that was reflected in the nation as a whole. The urban eastern European population, German farmers, and the Irish opposed temperance, while the traditional Protestants, Calvinist congregational sects originally from New England, and many women's groups strongly supported it. These opinions were typical of the movement, in which the majority of Ohio voters were reflected in the direction of state politics even when there were crosscurrents. Garfield found himself in a similar situation with the gold standard.

Most of the Republican Party stood with the eastern bankers for the gold standard. Since gold tended to be of a finite, slow-growing amount, it limited the money supply. The gold standard tightened money, and this particularly hurt farmers. Farmers needed mortgages, and they were sensitive to interest rates and the money supply. Using silver could help increase the money supply and bring down interest rates. The Grange, a national organization of farmers, supported the most liberal money standard, which was known as "free silver," that is, silver exchange not based on gold. Generally, the Democratic Party had supported the farmers and the silver issue. It was a very polarized subject, with eastern bankers believing in the necessity of gold. This conviction came from the need to deal with other countries that mostly supported the gold standards. Western farmers, right or wrong, believed silver was the answer for eliminating debt and reducing interest rates. Ohio voters' opinions were mixed and confused on the gold issue, as were the politicians' views.

Ohio republicanism had already been suspicious of the gold standard, but the state's early Republican representatives generally went along with the eastern bankers. Eastern bankers saw gold as necessary for international trade and banking, and, of course, they were the financiers of the early Republican Party. Garfield had been a gold standard backer, but he started to question that wisdom as the electorate in Ohio also became more suspicious. These misgivings were part of the old Whig east-west fault line. Republican presidential candidate James Garfield urged government debt payments in gold. Although he opposed free silver, Garfield expressed interest in a bimetallic standard before his assassination. At the same time, some Ohio manufacturers started to agree with farmers that the gold standard limited economic growth. Garfield had realized a shift in the view on the gold standard, and his fellow Ohio Republican William McKinley would eventually change the Republican view on the subject. The gold standard would become a very hot issue after the Garfield assassination.

The incumbent in 1880, President Rutherford Hayes, had no interest in seeking a second term. After 36 ballots, the Republicans nominated a dark horse Ohio representative named James Garfield. The nominee had gone to the convention as manager of the campaign of Secretary of the Treasury John Sherman, Ohio's most venerable statesman. Garfield had emerged as a candidate after delegates were impressed by his nomination speech for Sherman. In his address, Garfield offered a transition from the Radical Republicans, who were declining in popularity, to a more moderate approach. He would better position the Republicans nationally as the southern states were reunited with the nation. The newly reunified southern states strongly opposed the radical civil rights that Republicans had imposed on them. When Garfield won the Republican nomination for president in 1880, Arthur, an eastern Stalwart Republican, was nominated for vice president to balance the ticket.

The presidential race of 1880 was a tough one for Republicans. Ohio congressman William McKinley and John Sherman stumped the state for Garfield, who was running against General Winfield Scott Hancock, a Democrat and the hero of Gettysburg. Hancock opposed any tariff, and McKinley became worried that should Hancock win, Ohio republicanism would be challenged. Prosperity had returned to the nation, and tariffs were losing support; civil rights was no longer a passionate movement, and temperance was in decline. Nationally, the election was another close fight, with Garfield winning by only 7,018 votes. The Greenback-Labor Party gave 308,578 votes for James Weaver. Garfield carried the big states, however, and won in the Electoral College by a vote of 214 to 155. Congressman McKinley fared better, beating his Democratic opponent 20,221 votes to 16,660 votes. McKinley was instrumental in Garfield's selection of eastern Republican James Blaine as secretary of state. The Democratic Party's national strength was building with their alliances with Catholics and labor. Republican platforms were pro-gold and anti-immigration, and, with the exception of a few like McKinley, Thomas Kelly of Pennsylvania, and James Blaine, most Republicans were neutral on

James A. Garfield, Republican candidate for president, and Chester A. Arthur, Republican candidate for vice president, 1880. Library of Congress.

tariffs. Seeing his own party split over protective revenue tariffs, McKinley started to work on his concept of reciprocity in tariff applications. This idea would evolve with McKinley and would be featured in his second administration in the late 1890s.

Garfield's campaign gave rise to Ohio's presidential kingmaker. The Western Reserve industrialist Mark Hanna (1837–1904) helped found a businessman's fundraising club to cover Garfield's personal expenses in the campaign. Hanna had become a millionaire by age 40 in 1877—he had built an industrial empire on the shipping and mining of iron ore. He had started by fundraising on a limited basis for Rutherford Hayes, but he stepped up with his support of John Sherman and James Garfield. Hanna would play a unique role in the success of Ohio republicanism. He was able to bring in big business supporters for Ohio politicians, offsetting the money advantage of the big eastern bankers in picking Republican candidates. Hanna represented the heart and complexity of Ohio republicanism. Though his historical legacy was tarnished by the hatred of influential publisher William Randolph Hearst, in reality, Hanna was neither a true kingmaker nor a villain, but a reflection of Ohio republicanism.[13] Hanna needs to be understood to fully comprehend Ohio republicanism. He represented a fusion of labor and management at an elementary level.

Hanna was from New Lisbon, Ohio (southern Western Reserve, north of Youngtown), and he came from a strong Whig, abolitionist, and prohibitionist background. When he was a teenager, his family moved to the city of Cleveland, where he attended high school with John D. Rockefeller. The Hanna family had been unsuccessful investors in attempts to expand the Ohio Canal. Hanna moved into his father-in-law's firm of Rhodes and Company (later M. A. Hanna and Company), which dealt principally in coal and steel, but under Hanna, the business expanded into many fields. The firm had close dealings with the railroads—especially the Pennsylvania Railroad, which carried much of its freight. Hanna later became director of two railroads, including the Pennsylvania Railroad. During Grant's first four-year term, Hanna began to involve himself in politics. At first, he took a purely local interest, supporting Republican candidates for municipal Cleveland and Cuyahoga County offices. In 1873, disgusted by city scandals, Hanna and other Republicans briefly abandoned the party to elect a reform and pro-business Democrat, Charles Otis, running for mayor of Cleveland. Hanna, who had made a fortune, turned into an activist and community organizer. From then on, however, he would be an *Ohio* Republican first and foremost.

Hanna presented an unusual figure in politics, maybe the archetype for what would become commonplace in presidential politics. In this respect, Hanna is often compared to Carl Rove, the "architect" of the George Bush administration.[14] An early biographer, Thomas Beer, saw Hanna as a political engineer: "It was not until 1880 that Mr. Hanna shrugged and consented, and perhaps the experience of hearing himself called a rich busybody.... He knew by that time, that machinery ruled in politics.... Behind this apparatus was the point of reality; one might quietly rule in politics without being a politician. One might be an engineer."[15] Hanna was a visionary believing that Ohio politics were good for America. He wanted to make Ohio republicanism a national vision that vision included a McGuffey-style education like he had received in Ohio. Hanna had won an election to the Cleveland School Board, but business kept him from flourishing in that role. His vision was also one of industrial growth bringing prosperity to business, labor, and community.

Like most Republicans of the time, Hanna was a reformer of government. He and others viewed corruption as embedded in political infrastructure. Hiring political friends to government offices and paying for vote operations were the major evils. In Republicans' view, the Boss Tweed–type operations were the source of the real corruption. These political bosses ruled urban districts by supplying favors for votes. Big business was not yet seen as part of the corruption in government. The Grant railroad scandals were the beginning of a new type of business and government corruption, but the public still focused more on political bosses as the problem. In the late 1870s, the banner of a pro-business party was up for grabs for Republicans and Democrats.

Even Hanna's in-laws were strong pro-business Democrats. Hanna saw a pro-business strategy as pro–American by tying it to jobs. It would not be until the 1890s that big business and the robber barons would become public enemy number one. Hanna believed in 1880 that the Republican Party had to become the party of big business. He believed that business and labor could forge an alliance of common goals and become a uniform voting bloc. He also understood that banks funded politicians of the East, and that these ties promoted open trade at the expense of American manufacturing businesses and workers. Hanna realized that big banking and big business were not a single entity. He saw an alternative means of financing Ohio politicians through the emerging midwestern industries of iron, steel, railroads, glass, oil, and electrical products. The old Whig party had been controlled by eastern banks, but Hanna saw the new Republican Party as capable of breaking the eastern financial bonds.

Hanna's epiphany was that he would have to make that vision a reality, not as a politician but as a political engineer. His first major effort was the Businessman's Republican Campaign Club to collect donations from business for James Garfield's presidential run. Another part of Hanna's approach was newspaper support. In 1880, he added the *Cleveland Herald* to his business empire. While Hanna focused on the Midwest, his biographer in 1912 said: "Mr. Hanna had as much to do with the election of Mr. Garfield as any single individual in the country."[16] Garfield's assassination and death within his first six months in office was a major setback for Hanna and Ohio republicanism.

Chapter Eight

Ohio Republicanism in the Wilderness

James A. Garfield, the 20th president of the United States, was assassinated at 9:30 a.m. on July 2, 1881, less than four months into his term as president. He was shot by Charles J. Guiteau at the Baltimore and Potomac Railroad Station in Washington, D.C., and he died in Elberon, New Jersey, on September 19, 1881. Guiteau was a disgruntled government employee, a man fed up with the reduction of the patronage system by James Garfield and the Half-Breeds. With the shot, Guiteau cried out, "'I am a Stalwart of the Stalwarts! I did it and I want to be arrested! Arthur is President now!'"[1] Other reports say he shouted, "I did it. I will go to jail for it. I am a Stalwart and Arthur will be President."[2] Mortally wounded, Garfield was taken back to the White House, but the severe summer heat was considered life threatening. In an effort to relieve the president from the heat of a Washington summer, navy engineers rigged up an early version of the modern air conditioner. Fans blew air over a large box of ice and into the president's sickroom; the device worked well enough to lower the temperature 20 degrees.[3] Garfield was taken to the once-famous resort town of Elberton, New Jersey, as the summer heat became overwhelming, but he came back to Washington in September. Thomas Edison offered the use of a prototype X-ray machine and sent it Washington. While the X-ray machine was never used, Alexander Bell did try to find the bullet with a prototype of the metal detector (induction coil). Garfield never recovered but struggled until his death on September 20. His body was taken to Washington, where it lay in state for two days in the Capitol Rotunda before being taken to Cleveland, Ohio. The funeral was held on September 26, and arrangements were handled by Mark Hanna.

Guiteau's trial was one of the first high-profile cases in the United States where the insanity defense was considered. Guiteau vehemently insisted that

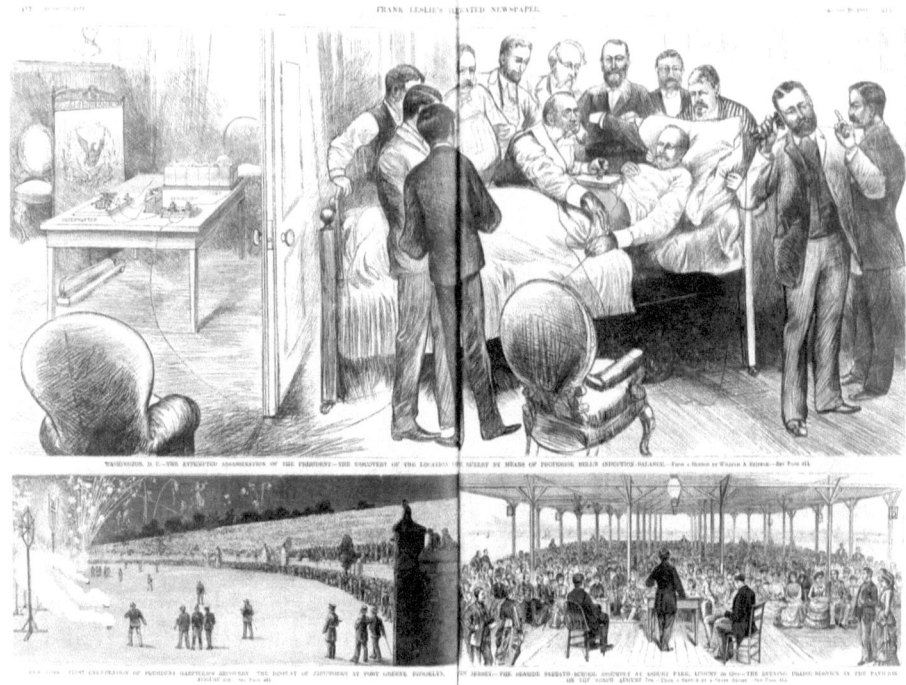

Events related to the assassination of President James Garfield, 1881. Prints show Alexander Graham Bell using his induction-balance device to locate the bullet in Garfield's body; funeral fireworks at Fort Greene in Brooklyn, New York; and an evening service at Asbury Park, New Jersey. Retrieved from the Library of Congress, https://www.loc.gov/item/2004671448/. (Accessed June 23, 2017.)

he had been legally insane at the time of the shooting. The court found him guilty, and he was hanged on June 30, 1882. The highly publicized insanity defense led to part of Charles Guiteau's brain being preserved and put on display at the Mütter Museum at the College of Physicians of Philadelphia.

Driven by political pressure, Chester Arthur, a strict Stalwart Republican, became flexible and implemented reforms to the patronage and spoils system for filling government jobs. Garfield's assassination caused Ohio republicanism's spirit of civil service to become a national issue. Even Ohio Democrats took up the cause. The result was the Pendleton Act of 1883, proposed by Ohio Democrat George Pendleton, which established the principle that government jobs should be awarded on the basis of merit, not patronage. In addition, the act created the Civil Service Commission to implement merit exams for civil servants. Pendleton's measure also made it illegal to fire, demote, or harass civil servants for political reasons. After Democratic congressional victories in the 1882 elections, Arthur had no choice but to make reforms.

Garfield Memorial in Cleveland, Ohio, 1895. Library of Congress.

Waiting two years had given the credit to the Democrats for cleaning up Washington. Arthur also implemented Garfield's moderate tariffs, eliminating revenue but maintaining protection. The president surprised many by keeping the flame (albeit a small one) of Ohio republicanism burning with the exception of tariffs.

Congressional victories in 1882 gave the Democrats the House of Representatives. With President Arthur hitting lows in popularity, the Democrats hoped to challenge Ohio republicanism on its economic planks. Congressman William McKinley was given the torch of maintaining Ohio republicanism for America, and his national reputation on tariffs brought in extra money. However, 1882 brought a major challenge to McKinley's Ohio seat, and the Democrats nationally targeted him for his defense of high tariffs. Initially, things looked bright. State Republicans, through redistricting, returned Stark County (Canton, Ohio) to its old district with Mahoning and Columbiana (Youngstown area). But the real threat came from within McKinley's own party. Tradition at the time was that a congressman should step down after two terms; in addition, Ohio congressional districts rotated candidates between the counties in the districts. The Republican chairman of Columbiana County challenged McKinley to step down and let a candidate from Columbiana take the nomination. The battle against tradition dragged into the fall elections of 1882. Arthur was very unpopular at the time, and the election trend favored Democrats. As a result, McKinley won the election by only eight votes. A large part of his narrow victory owed to his anti-liquor stand based on his moral beliefs. McKinley's beliefs cost him heavily with the Germans and Irish that dominated his district. He had nothing to gain politically from his opinion on alcohol, but he held to it as a tenet of Ohio republicanism. Nationally, the Democrats still resisted the election results. The Republican-controlled state legislature certified McKinley, but his opponent Jonathan Wallace took the contest to Washington, where the Democrats held power. The real issue was that McKinley led the tariff caucus. A committee was formed to look at the election results as McKinley took his seat in Congress and on the Ways and Means Committee.

President Chester Arthur also seemed willing to modify Ohio Republicans' orthodoxy decreeing support for a high tariff. His second annual message called for reductions in duties on such important items as cotton, iron, steel, sugar, molasses, silk, wool, and woolen goods. Arthur's conversion was, in part, a product of his discomfort with a Treasury surplus, which tariff collections had helped to generate; he believed it was better to have the money out in circulation. The president's change was also a follow-up to the report of a special Tariff Commission created by law in 1882. Although heavily weighted with protectionists, the commission believed many duties could and should be lowered. Thus it proved to be more liberal than McKinley had hoped. Congress, while recognizing a growing pressure for tariff modification, proved customarily susceptible to strong lobbying from industry and Ohio politicians, and the result was a weak tariff compromise known as the Mongrel Tariff.

McKinley stood as the main defense on tariffs as President Arthur and Ohio senator John Sherman wavered. The liberal Tariff Commission also folded under the political wave election of Democrats in 1882. With the conference report of the Tariff Commission accepted, the Democrats moved for a bill with a 20 percent across-the-board reduction. Known as the Morrison Bill, the measure probably overplayed the Democratic hand by extending the reduction across the full list of protected products. The blanket approach allowed McKinley to build support with Democrats in manufacturing districts. In the end, he prevailed with a 156–151 vote in the House, and he succeeded in bringing over 41 Democrats. It was a huge victory for Ohio republicanism.

McKinley's leadership and speaking ability had become a significant problem for the Democrats, and his success in defeating the Morrison Tariff Bill was short-lived. A few weeks later, the House Elections Board recommended McKinley be unseated. The strongly Democratic House delivered a 158–108 decision to that effect. McKinley accepted the conclusion, and Jonathan Wallace took the seat on May 27, 1884. McKinley returned to a hero's welcome in Canton, Ohio, but the event was a low point in many ways. Local crowds hailed him as the "Napoleon of Protection." The name would stick, as cartoonists often drew McKinley as Napoleon throughout his career.[4]

In 1884, McKinley was a delegate to the Republican National Convention in St. Louis. James Blaine was once more considered the favorite for the nomination, but President Arthur was contemplating a run for election in his own right. Eventually, Arthur backed out for health reasons, and Blaine got the nomination. The Ohio delegation was behind Ohioan John Sherman. McKinley became the key player in keeping the party together.

Ohioan William McKinley was made chairman of the Ohio Republican Convention. As a delegate to the Republican National Convention, he was promptly made chairman of the Resolutions Committee responsible for the national platform. McKinley worked hard on the platform, which stood for high tariffs with a scientific look at reform, railroad reform, bimetallism, curbs on Chinese immigration, and the eight-hour day. National party policy was a reflection of the state of Ohio republicanism, but it lacked a true champion. In addition, the eastern donor class of the Republican Party headed by J. P. Morgan opposed the platform. The convention was a wild one—fistfights were common. William McKinley opposed his own Ohio delegation, which supported John Sherman, by voting for James Blaine. As always McKinley's support depended on the tariff issue, and John Sherman, though an Ohioan, was weak on tariffs in McKinley's view. Blaine won the nomination, but McKinley's platform gave the Republican Party a labor plank to stand on. This amazing platform addressed most of the problems of the emerging middle class, business leaders, laborers, and farmers.

The addition of a call for the eight-hour day was particularly friendly to labor. McKinley, however, had always maintained management was part of the labor problem, and he often spoke for better managers. This platform was, however, representative of McKinley's middle-class following. James Blaine and Republican policy appeared to be a winning combination except for two weaknesses. Blaine was not as strong on tariffs as the platform, and that would cost the Republicans labor votes. The eight-hour-day plank was visionary, but it seemed doubtful that the Republican Party donors could fully endorse it. In most manufacturing businesses, the twelve-hour day was standard. J. P. Morgan became the major opposition, turning the donor class toward the Democrats and candidate Grover Cleveland.

The presidential election of 1884 was a tough because scandals haunted the Republicans. James Blaine had a suspect record, having been named in some scandals. That weakness, coupled with his support of railroads and the gold standard, caused many Republican industrialists such as George Westinghouse to vote Democratic. These reform-minded Republicans were known as Mugwumps, and they denounced Blaine as corrupt. However, even as the Democrats gained support from the Mugwumps, they lost some blue-collar workers to the Greenback Party, led by Benjamin F. Butler. Blaine's weakness on tariffs hurt him with blue-collar workers. McKinley could certainly relate to most of the Mugwump Republicans, wanting a stronger stand on tariffs.

The Democrats nominated Grover Cleveland, a conservative with strong eastern banking ties. Cleveland was a middle-road Democrat with business support from the likes of Charles Goodyear, J. P. Morgan, Andrew Carnegie, and George Westinghouse. Cleveland actually counted the "Prince of Capitalism," J. P. Morgan, as a friend. They frequently lunched together in downtown New York. The Democratic Party avoided the gold issue, while Cleveland supported the gold standard privately. Grover Cleveland, in many ways, looked more like a Republican than Blaine. Cleveland ran on a reform platform pointing to the endless scandals and abuses in the business community. He also had the strong support of the Grange and farmers, who were particularly upset with railroad abuses and high tariffs.

Cleveland was the perfect candidate for the Democrats in the midst of a major movement of Ohio republicanism. He was really a conservative in concert with the core principles of Ohio republicanism. In a recent book on Cleveland's conservatism, Lawrence Reed, president of the Foundation for Economic Education, notes: "Cleveland believed that government has nothing to give anybody, except that which it has taken first from somebody else and that a government big enough to give us everything we want is big enough to take away everything we got."[5]

Cleveland was the leader of the pro-business Bourbon Democrats who opposed big government, bimetal or silver currency, inflation, imperialism, and subsidies to businesses, farmers, or veterans.[6] Bourbon Democrats were promoters of a form of laissez-faire capitalism that included opposition to protectionism.[7] Bourbons led the fight against the famous New York Tweed Ring, and Cleveland had been a reform governor of New York. The anti-corruption theme thus earned the votes of many Republican Mugwumps. While many historians refer to Cleveland as pro-business, he was really pro-banking. This stand gave him the support of big Republican East Coast bankers such as J. P. Morgan and August Belmont, as well as the railroad bosses. The bankers loved Cleveland's gold standard approach, while Ohio republicanism had pushed the Republican Party to the use of silver to increase the money supply and grow industry. Public support for high tariffs was wavering because of the huge government surpluses, and this helped mollify Republican voters about Cleveland's tariff views. While his conservative views identified him as pro-business, his tariff stand put him in opposition to Ohio republicanism.

In the end, the election was not a rejection of Ohio republicanism but of corruption. The issue of personal character was paramount in the 1884 campaign and determined the outcome. James Blaine had been prevented from getting the Republican presidential nomination during the previous two elections because of the stigma of the Mulligan letters. These letters were sent to a Boston bookkeeper named James Mulligan, who had located correspondence showing that Blaine had sold his influence in Congress to various businesses. Grover Cleveland, in many ways, looked more like a Republican than Blaine. Cleveland ran on a reform platform pointing to the endless scandals and abuses in the business community. In particular, he had the strong support of farmers. The Republican platform addressed the issue, but Republicans lacked the record of support. Cleveland also stood against the anti–Catholic and anti-immigrant stand of many Republicans. Still, it was believed that Blaine could win Irish Catholic support since his mother was an Irish Catholic and his sister a mother superior at a convent. In the end, James Blaine carried Ohio by 30,000 votes but lost the national vote. The separation nationally was fewer than 100,000 votes, but it was enough to elect the first Democratic president in 28 years.

William McKinley reentered politics again, running for Congress. His congressional District was gerrymandered in 1884 and included Stark, Summit, Wayne, and Medina Counties, which tended to vote Democratic. McKinley's loss of the seat suggested his effort to take it back would be easily defeated, especially as the national trend was once again Democratic. Yet he reversed the trend and carried the district by 2,000 votes. His return to Washington was a great personal victory and established him nationally as a leader. In many ways, it was McKinley's greatest victory since Cleveland carried Ohio and his district. McKinley's stand and victory against the Morrison Tariff Bill had strengthened his industrial base. Still, he and his wife, Ida, returned to their somewhat monastic routine in Washington. In the House, he once again faced a substantial Democratic majority, and he could expect Cleveland to push for tariff reforms (lower tariffs).

In 1885, McKinley made one of his famous protection speeches in Petersburg, Virginia. He responded to the rural Jeffersonian writers who talked of factories bringing cholera: "I tell you, manufactories do not bring cholera—they bring coin, coin: coin for the poor man, coin for the rich, coin for everybody that will work; comfort and contentment for all deserving people. And if you vote for increasing manufactories, my fellow citizens, you will vote for the best interests of your own State, and you will be making iron, and steel, and pottery, and all leading products."[8] McKinley was not just a great orator; he was a student of economics. He often studied journals and statistics into the early morning. He built a small library on trade and economics, and few were as well versed in these subjects as he was, even at our best universities. McKinley was always well prepared for even minor debates. Democrats feared him because he had the ability to persuade opponents; and it was a necessary skill, since he mostly faced a Democratic majority during his career.

In 1886, Congress prepared for new battles on tariffs, as Grover Cleveland was determined to reduce them. McKinley prepared by lining up his support from unions and manufacturers in Ohio, Illinois, and Pennsylvania. He had strong backing from union leaders, which gave the Democrats pause at the local level and widened the tariff issue within their party. In early 1886, William Morrison of Illinois, chair of the Ways and Means Committee, drafted a bill for tariff reduction. McKinley once again built a floor alliance with the protectionist Democrats and defeated the measure. The Democratic Party remained split while the Republicans remained united, thanks to McKinley. Grover Cleveland, however, continued to push for tariff reductions against the McKinley House alliance.

With the corruption issue settled for Cleveland, the 1887 annual presidential address to Congress focused on one topic—tariff reduction. Congress was again Democratic, and Cleveland was confident in victory. The government had a surplus, so the Democrats argued tariff revenue was unnecessary. A battle was building, and McKinley was gathering statistics and rallying industry and labor leaders again. This time his opposition was Roger Mills of Texas, who was now chairman of the Ways and Means Committee. Mills was representative of the southern Democrats that opposed tariffs because of their negative impact on the cotton industry. There was still a protectionist

Cartoon showing monster, "tariff question," in large bag, "surplus," saying, "Here I am Again! What are you going to do with me?" in House chambers, 1888. Library of Congress.

wing of the Democratic Party, but Cleveland was applying pressure for a party vote. McKinley's effort to kill a bill for tariff reduction in committee failed as the Democrats moved it to the floor.

This time, McKinley and the supporters of Ohio republicanism met the full force of the Democratic administration. Cleveland lobbied the protectionist Democrats using special favors. In exchange, the Democrats would load the bill with pork barrel amendments. Mills lined up America's best academic minds to testify for free trade. McKinley looked for middle ground, but Cleveland wasn't interested. Eastern protectionist Democrats weakened in their opposition. The floor debate started on April 17, 1888, but McKinley sized up the turning tide and didn't rise to speak until May 18. The Republican added amendments and moderated the reduction level. McKinley had a very effective grassroots operation even beyond Ohio. In Pittsburgh and eastern industrial cities, he was becoming a national figure. He had the necessary popular support, but Cleveland and Democrats were in control. When McKinley did speak, he spoke to the people more than to Congress: "I would rather have my political economy founded upon the everyday experience of the puddler [union steelmaker] or a potter than the learning of the professor, or the farmer and factory hand than the college faculty."[9] McKinley realized the fight was lost on the floor but extended the debate. In early summer the Mills bill passed the House, but the Senate tied it up until the fall elections with the help of future president Benjamin Harrison, an Ohio Republican.

McKinley had lost his first big floor battle on tariffs, but he gained the people's support nationally. The floor fight was well covered throughout America, making tariffs the key issue in the 1888 presidential elections. Indiana U.S. senator Benjamin Harrison (Ohio born) had also gained national attention in this losing tariff fight. Grover Cleveland's popularity was hurt with his push to end protective tariffs as labor pulled its support. The protective tariffs of Ohio republicanism were continuing to gain labor and business backing in old Transylvania, as well as in the new industrial centers of Pittsburgh, Buffalo, New York, Chicago, St. Louis, and growing East Coast manufacturing towns.

Congress was also split on the need to regulate the railroads, which were increasingly coming under public pressure for reform. The issue really cut party lines and slowed legislative reform. The root of the problem was an obvious and glaring inconsistency between higher short-haul rates and low long-term rates. Eastern merchants, small farmers, and manufacturers were the losers, while western farmer-businessmen had a huge advantage. The low rail rates from the West to the East had, in large part, made American wheat dominant in the world market. The matter was complicated even more by rebates to big rail users such as Rockefeller's Standard Oil and Carnegie Steel. Big-money interests such as J. P. Morgan headed the railroad trusts. Railroad practices hurt the smaller manufacturers of William McKinley's district. McKinley thus supported the passage of the Interstate Commerce Act, which regulated such actions. It was yet another example of McKinley's breaking from the big-money Republican wing.

The Interstate Commerce Act of 1887 was extremely popular with the public and had been part of the presidential election. This United States federal law was designed to regulate the railroad industry, particularly its monopolistic practices. The act required that railroad rates be "reasonable and just," but it did not empower the government to fix specific charges. Additionally, railroads could no longer provide secret beneficial rates to certain shippers. In fact, the Interstate Commerce Act required rates to be published so everyone could see them. The effectiveness of the act depended on its implementation by the executive branch, which allowed President Cleveland to sign it but limited its use.[10] Of course, the measure was opposed by the eastern banking wing of the Republican Party that owned the railroads, but it remained a core issue of Ohio republicanism.

Another more disturbing event was the 1886 Haymarket Riot, which would change the political landscape for decades. Happening during President Cleveland's presidency, this event hurt the Democrats with labor interests.[11] The union movement had been building in the United States since the mid–1870s. The Great Railroad Strike of 1877 had demonstrated the power of the movement and some of the public concerns. Working conditions at the time were abysmal. Workers often worked twelve-hour days seven days a week, and safety and benefits were nonexistent. While pay was much higher than in Europe, American salaries were perceived as being too low. Furthermore, the length of the working day in the United States was considered particularly oppressive. A national labor organization—the Knights of Labor—was gaining popularity with its campaign for an eight-hour day. Prior to the Haymarket Riot, the eight-hour day had broad popular support in the United States. Under the leadership of Terence Powderly, the Knights had won a major strike against Jay Gould's Wabash Railroad in 1882. The membership of the Knights boomed to 700,000 nationally.

The early spring of 1886 pitted union workers at the McCormick Harvesting Machine Company against management with regard to the twelve-hour-plus working day. At the same time, the Federation of Organized Trades and Labor Unions had called for a May 1 parade and march in American cities for union support. The Knights of Labor joined the national day. The march in Chicago had the strong support of German immigrant radicals as well; the city was the heart of German immigrants and socialists. Attendance estimates for the crowds in Chicago on May 1 were over 80,000. Nationwide, the approximate attendance at the May Day march was over a half million. Albert Parsons, an anarchist and founder of the International Working People's Association (a Marxist/socialist group), led the Chicago rally. It was an opportune time for the locked-out workers of McCormick to form an alliance with this massive popular movement. On May 3, a protest outside of the McCormick plant resulted in a death. The McCormick factory was under the protection of outside Pinkerton guards and privately hired police because strikebreakers had been hired to run the plant.

The death ignited an outcry among the young German radicals present for the May 1 protests. Even though the strikers were Irish American, the German population rallied with them at the prodding of the socialist German radicals. These anarchists took over the McCormick strike to use for the broader purpose of the eight-hour day and the socialist movement. On May 4, a crowd of 1,500 to 2,000 gathered in Chicago's Haymarket Square, where farmers sold their products. The protesters had expected a crowd of 20,000, but a rainy day kept turnout down. Rioting turned into a bloodbath as Cleveland sent federal troops to the scene. Police had gathered to break up the peaceful demonstration, and during some of the small scuffles, someone threw a pipe bomb, wounding police officers. The scene then erupted in police fire. Eventually the cross fire resulted in the death of eight police and four civilians. In addition, over 100 were wounded. Panic followed, and the violence turned the general public against the organizers of the eight-hour-day movement. The Democrats and Cleveland took the blame, opening up an opportunity for Republicans to make more inroads into labor. While union leadership supported the Democrats, working union members looked toward the Republicans. The Democrats' support of lower tariffs through the 1880s also appeared to be anti-labor. Grover Cleveland faced a difficult election in 1888 if the Republicans could find a candidate.

Chapter Nine

Benjamin Harrison

Ohio Republican Benjamin Harrison (1833–1901) would return the nation to Ohio republicanism. President Benjamin Harrison and then Congressman William McKinley would push the famous McKinley Tariff Act of 1890. Prior to that, Harrison supported another Ohio-backed bill known as the Sherman Silver Act. The Silver Act caused a major split in the party's weak alliance with New York Republican bankers demanding a gold standard. J. P. Morgan would claim the Silver Act resulted in an economic downturn, and he would once again look to Democrat and former president Grover Cleveland to run for office. The final problem with Harrison's presidency would be the need to maintain the rule of law with difficult labor riots. Harrison arrived at the point of great labor and economic turbulence. In addition, the business cycle had reached an end of expansion. The economic downturn would open all Republican programs as suspected causes, which the Democrats effectively pinned on the Republicans. The Democrats effectively identified all Republican programs as suspected causes of the economic downturn. The McKinley Tariff Act, the Silver Act, major labor strife, and an oncoming depression would, at first, seem to end the popularity of Ohio republicanism and ensure the party's loss of the presidency in 1892. The massive defeat of Republicans and President Harrison in 1892 would actually be the future of the Ohio Dynasty. In 1896, McKinley reestablished the dynasty after the setback. Unfortunately, Benjamin Harrison would be the major casualty of 1892. Still, he would have an important role in the building of the legacy of Ohio republicanism.

Benjamin Harrison was also a grandson of U.S. president William Henry Harrison. The younger Harrison was born on August 20, 1833, in North Bend, Ohio (on the border of Ohio and Indiana), to a family that was Whig, pro-temperance, and strongly abolitionist. Harrison's early education was in a one-room schoolhouse using *McGuffey Readers*. In 1850, he went to Miami

University in Oxford, Ohio, and he graduated in 1852. After becoming a lawyer, Harrison moved to Indianapolis, where he practiced law and campaigned for the newly formed Republican Party. He helped put together a volunteer unit for the Civil War. Subsequently, he commanded an Indiana brigade at the Battles of Resaca, Cassville, New Hope Church, Lost Mountain, Kennesaw Mountain, Marietta, Peachtree Creek, and Atlanta. When Sherman's main force began its March to the Sea, Harrison's brigade was transferred to the District of Etowah, and it participated in the Battle of Nashville. Harrison returned home a war hero. In 1865, President Lincoln made him a brevet brigadier general of volunteers.

The revolt of reform Republicans and Republican donors against the candidacy of Senator James G. Blaine of Maine in 1884 had forced the party to return to the roots of Ohio republicanism. Benjamin Harrison carefully walked the middle ground to help unite the Republicans. In February 1887, he lost reelection to the United States Senate in the new Democrat-controlled state legislature of Indiana. United States senators were selected by the state legislatures rather than by popular vote until 1913. One year later, Harrison announced his candidacy for the Republican presidential nomination, running on a return to Ohio republicanism. The words "Rejuvenated Republicanism" became the slogan of his campaign.

Harrison had strong support in Ohio, having headed up the Indiana caucus that had given James Garfield the nomination years earlier. Harrison represented Ohio republicanism, wanting a return to high tariffs, a move to silver currency to help farmers and manufacturers, and a strong civil rights stance. He proposed a scientific approach to tariff rates to protect manufacturing while allowing basic necessities, such as sugar, rice, coal, ores, iron, fruits, cotton cloths, and other products, to enter the United States free. Ohio farmers had often changed the results of elections when things like sugar were highly taxed. Years later, after success, Harrison noted: "The placing of sugar upon the free list has saved to the consumer in duties in fifteen months, after paying the bounties provided for, $87,000,000. This relief has been substantially felt in every household upon every Saturday's purchase of the workingman."[1] He further embraced the idea of reciprocity, which had evolved through Ohio republicanism. In addition, he would support the expansion of exports with the upgrading of our merchant marine and the building of a South American canal. These ideas were a winning formula for the Republicans. The party had to bring in enough Democratic voters and bring home the Cleveland Republicans of the last election to win.

One area where Harrison would leave his mark on Ohio republicanism was the currency. Garfield had maintained the gold standard to placate eastern bankers, but he had personal doubts about it. In old Transylvania and Ohio, popular opinion had moved to silver or a bimetal currency base. Ohio congressman William McKinley and Ohio's John Sherman had embraced the bimetal or silver approach because it stimulated manufacturing growth and jobs. As the party nominee, Harrison embedded this policy in the platform. After his election, he would team up with Sherman and McKinley to pass the Silver Act. Bimetallism would become a foundational part of Ohio republicanism moving toward the 20th century. Harrison's embrace of bimetallism would strengthen his popularity in old Transylvania and the Midwest. The policy was key for strengthening Ohio republicanism as a program for American growth.

In the bitterly contested nomination fight that followed, Harrison became everyone's second choice in a field of seven candidates. When Senator John Sherman of Ohio, the first choice of most, faltered in the balloting, Harrison's support surged ahead, winning him the nomination on the eighth ballot. The convention picked banker Levi P. Morton of New York as Harrison's running mate to recapture the eastern donor base. Democrats, at their national convention in St. Louis, rallied behind incumbent Grover Cleveland of New York and his running mate, Allen G. Thurman (1813–1895), the conservative senator from Ohio. Nominating Thurman was a weak effort to gain Ohio votes—his proslavery and anti–civil rights views were far from Ohio republicanism. Born in Virginia, Thurman played better in the South than as a son of Ohio.

Benjamin Harrison did, however, have some key advantages. When Sherman dropped out, Ohio financier Marcus Hanna jumped onboard, but not with the enthusiasm he had had for the Garfield campaign. As noted by an early Hanna biographer, Harrison said: "Well, Harrison was born in Ohio, anyhow."[2] Matthew Stanley "Matt" Quay (1833–1904) was a Pennsylvania political boss whom Harrison called a "kingmaker." Quay was, at the time, a United States Senator; and from 1888 to 1891, he was chairman of the Republican National Committee. Moreover, he served as Benjamin Harrison's campaign manager in the 1888 presidential election. Quay hailed from nearby southwestern Pennsylvania, and his Radical Republican family was heavily focused on civil rights and protection for the American worker. On a national level, Matthew Quay brought in the great leaders of the Pittsburgh steelmakers, such as Henry Clay Frick and Andrew Carnegie. The steel industry was a natural ally of Ohio republicanism and was located geographically in the old Whig Party heartland. Harrison would be the first Ohio president to fully recover the Whig vote for the Republicans. With his election, Ohio republicanism would become a national movement. People started to look at Ohio as the barometer of prosperity for the nation.

For the Republicans, the congressional election of 1888 was as important as the presidential election. McKinley needed help in the House on tariffs, and the Democrats had to be unseated. The Republicans targeted three free traders—William Ralls Morrison of East St. Louis, Speaker of the House John Carlisle of Kentucky, and Frank Hurd of Toledo. Morrison had been a target of Republican gerrymandering for years, but all such efforts had been unsuccessful. The year 1888 was different in that Republicans had strong national labor support, in particular from members of the Knights of Labor. Strangely, the Knights might publicly support a candidate, but its members would secretly campaign for another. Local Knights chapters often went against national endorsements to support high-tariff Republicans. Labor leadership was now becoming openly Republican. The Master Workman of the Knights of Labor Union, Terrence Powderly, is believed to have issued a directive to defeat Morrison.[3] The new Republican labor coalition would show its national popularity and strength in 1888.

Another Knight and shady Republican operative was John Jarrett. Jarrett had been a leader of the Labor Knights and a Pittsburgh lodge member, and he had also served as president of the Amalgamated Association of Iron and Steel Workers. He had become invested in the iron and steel industry over the years, although the sources of his investments and money were not clear. Jarrett was sent to East St. Louis to oppose Morrison with a bag of money. Officially, he represented the Workingman's Tariff Club, which some believed to be a front for the owners' American Iron and Steel Association. Additionally, Jarrett was active in Carlisle's Kentucky district. In Toledo, the Knights and the various glassworker unions united to target Hurd. Republican money poured in to labor unions such as the Window Glass Workers. The glass industry of northwest Ohio had been a huge benefactor of the Republican tariffs. In the end, the Republicans and the Knights took down Morrison, Carlisle, and Hurd in stunning upsets. In particular, the defeat of the anti-robber baron, anti-capitalist Speaker of the House showed a shift in the electorate. Labor sent a strong message of its support for high tariffs.

The 1888 election was known as the "election of education" targeted at labor. "John Bull baiting"[4] could be tied into the tariff issue and help gain Irish laborers' support. McKinley skillfully reminded the Irish that free trade had been used by the British to destroy Ireland. To ensure success, Republican candidates spoke of "independence" for Ireland. The deflection of the Irish and the Knights even helped shake the Tammany Hall Democratic machine in New York. With the exception of William McKinley and Ohio Republicans, few Republican politicians realized that the Irish vote could become a Republican strength.

The presidential election of 1888 for the fourth time in a row was close. While tariffs were the main issues, a number of political tricks may have given the Republicans the victory. A solicited letter from the British minister supporting Cleveland hurt Cleveland with the eastern Irish vote. Cleveland's anti-capitalist platform was not popular for workers now facing a major recession. The Union Labor Party (a third party) had attempted a combination of farmers and laborers that probably took up to 150,000 votes from the Democrats. Cleveland actually won the popular vote by 90,000 votes, but he would lose the Electoral College by losing the big states such as New York. Benjamin Harrison received 233 electoral votes to Cleveland's 168. It was the second time in twelve years that the Democrats won the popular vote but lost the presidency. The Democrats, in particular, had shown strength in farming districts and states. McKinley won in 1888 by his largest majority of 4,100 votes, which also reflected his new national reputation. He had won the votes of the Knights, defeating their own Democratic candidate.

President Benjamin Harrison, circa 1893. Library of Congress.

But really the issues for labor were tariffs and jobs, not robber barons or oppressive capitalists. Labor pulled their votes from third parties such as the Labor Party and Greenback Party to give Republicans the victory. The Republicans nationally had a slight advantage in the House and Senate. Harrison had an aggressive plan of legislation.

President Harrison, House Ways and Means Committee chairman William McKinley, and Ohio senator John Sherman pushed through the famous Tariff Act of 1890 and the Sherman Silver Act (these will be dealt with in the next chapter). Both of these major pieces of legislation would be used against the Republicans in the congressional elections of 1890. While neither act had time to impact the economy, the Democrats successfully blamed the measures for the economic downturn known as the Depression of 1892. In the interim elections, the House Republicans lost 93 seats, and Democrats swung comfortably into a commanding majority. Harrison would be blocked in his efforts to further legislate Ohio republicanism.

Harrison's presidency would also be impacted by events outside his control. The year 1892 would be a Waterloo for Harrison and many Republicans, as labor and economic problems plagued the nation. 1892 would also bring major labor problems in the steel and mining industries, as well as an economic recession. The very alliance of big industry that had brought Harrison success would now play against him and the Republicans. The labor vote that had helped him in the 1888 election would turn against him after the Homestead Steel Strike of 1892.

The Homestead Strike would leave an indelible mark on American business and the Republican Party. Andrew Carnegie's largest steel mill was located on the river floodplain of Homestead, across from Pittsburgh. This mill was a huge melting pot of immigrants, skilled nativist labor, and politics. The relationship between socialism and American trade unionism would be forged in the blood of the workers and managers of Homestead in 1892. American unionism would become distinct from that of Europe after Homestead. U.S. labor organizations had been focused on the skilled craftworker, leaving out the day laborer. Homestead was also the icon of growing American industrialism, and it had been a Republican stronghold. Moreover, it represented a toxic mix of opposing ideas and forces: nativists versus immigrants, skilled workers versus unskilled laborers, free trade versus protectionism, Democrats versus Republicans, and socialism versus capitalism. More importantly, for the Democrats the Homestead Strike offered an opportunity to break the Republican and labor alliance that had been growing under Ohio republicanism.

Homestead's steel mill was a craft union and Republican town, but across the railroad tracks was a shantytown of low-paid, nonunion immigrant laborers. It would be here that America's strongest union would face America's largest company of Carnegie Steel. It would the beginning of the end of the Amalgamated Association of the Iron and Steel Workers; but like the Alamo, the Homestead Strike would be the rallying cry of American unionization for decades. The strike changed management, the union, and the public's view of concepts like property rights and European-style union socialism.

Both the Carnegie steel empire and the Amalgamated union (Amalgamated Association of Iron and Steel Workers) approached July 1892 at the peak of their power. Carnegie was the richest man in the world, and his company was the biggest and most profitable. Homestead was one of America's great melting pots, as Slavs and Hungarians poured in to fill the thousands of unskilled jobs created in America's largest factory. The local natives, skilled Western European Americans, were angered by this new influx of untrained workers. Amalgamated union was a skilled crafts union that excluded the majority of the unskilled labors in the workforce. The ethnic mix of its members would become a major complication in the struggle. This strike was far from America's bloodiest or biggest, but it is one of the most remembered.

As the possible strike approached in July 1892, hundreds from the national press filled Pittsburgh hotels as both sides fought for public support. National politicians came and framed the conflict as part of the tariff / free trade debate of the time. The Democrats cited Carnegie's profits and poor wages as evidence that the years of protective steel tariffs had failed to help the workers. Homestead was to be the location of Armageddon for the showdown of labor and steel management.

Homestead represented a stand for management as well as reinforcement of property rights and control of the means of production. It also signified the massive change of steelmaking from skilled workers to automation. Carnegie and his general manager, Henry Clay Frick, had eliminated hundreds of skilled workers as they adeptly timed the confrontation. The economy of 1892 was now in a downturn, which gave Carnegie the upper hand that he had played so well in the past strikes.

For most, the facts of Homestead are surprising. The skilled union workers at Homestead numbered 800 out of about 3,800 total employees. The Amalgamated Association of Iron and Steel Workers represented an even smaller group of 325 highly paid and skilled workers. The wage argument was initially with those 325 laborers. Even more surprising might be the fact that the average American worker at the time made $8.50 a week, while a union steelworker at Homestead averaged $35.00 a week. In terms of a percentage cut proposed by Carnegie, it meant a cut from 40 percent to 20 percent for the skilled workers only.[5] Some 3,000-plus nonunion unskilled laborers joined the strike, having no place to go or anything to gain. They were being paid a mere $0.50 a day.

Henry Clay Frick set up an 18-foot wooden fence with barbed wire and allegedly with rifle slots. Sewers from the mill were provided with gratings and bars. Arc light searchlights were also installed on twelve-foot towers. It was rumored (falsely) that the barbed wire was electrified, using Westinghouse's new alternating current. In early June, Frick had contracted with Pinkerton for an army of 300 guards. The hiring of Pinkerton guards, while unpopular, was not uncommon. However, the number needed for America's largest industrial plant was unusual. Pinkerton was short on trained guards because of prolonged strikes in the mines of Utah and Colorado. The company had been advertising in western U.S. cities for armed guards at a salary of five dollars a day plus food and lodging. These raw recruits, a mix of college students, drifters, and laid-off workers, mustered in Chicago. The union similarly prepared their forces, which included the unskilled workers. They patrolled the river, railroad tracks, and the bridges. Assuming scabs would be sent in, scouts on horses were sent up and down the river to warn the town of any approaching company men.

The union used socialist agitators to work up the army of unskilled laborers, even though they were not represented by the union and had nothing to gain. The Pinkertons moved to the Homestead via two barges on the Ohio River. These vessels were equipped with dining halls and kitchens and staffed with a hired steward and 20 waiters. As the barges moved toward the plant, fog and early morning darkness helped cover their approach. A horseman spotted the barges and was sent to awake Homestead, and the Homestead Electric Works sounded a whistle alarm. Residents and workers, like the minutemen of old, got out of bed and picked up old family guns. There was some pushing at the mill, and then shots rang out. Three steelworkers were killed on the spot and dozens wounded. An old 20-pounder Revolutionary War cannon was fired, missing the barges and hitting and killing a steelworker.[6] Inaccurate cannon fire and shots continued as the Pinkertons huddled in their floating forts. The huddled Pinkertons had some protection, but the barges lacked air conditioning and were becoming sweaty iron furnaces. In Pittsburgh, Frick tried to use the courts to put pressure on the governor to send troops. Homesteaders added to the barrage by tossing dynamite. Telegraph wire reports to Washington and Congress brought calls to repeal the tariffs that had helped Carnegie Steel. Meanwhile, the Homesteaders poured oil on the Monongahela River and started a few surface fires. At this point, the Pinkertons had had it and so raised a white flag. The count was 13 dead and 36 wounded. Captured Pinkertons were then forced through a crowd of angry workers who freely beat them with clubs.

The sheriff struggled to find deputies, and the union leadership in Homestead struggled to regain control of the town. Union men in Chicago talked about sending men and guns. The United States Congress debated daily. The governor finally sent troops after Pittsburgh political bosses pulled every string possible. With the town under military control, Congress sent a special committee to hold hearings, and the Democrats seized on the political advantage. The union appealed by letter on July 16 asking Republican president Harrison to allow the organization to save some face by reopening the negotiations. President Harrison's appeal to Frick, however, failed; the strong-willed Frick sensed a victory. On July 17, union members went to a national meeting in New York to try to win over Republicans who were counting on the labor vote for high tariffs in the fall presidential election.

The socialist and anarchist movements in the United States had been following the action at Homestead and hoped to use it to their political gain. Socialists had always looked for opportunities to get involved in labor strife. On July 23, a clean-cut socialist and activist in a suit, Alexander Berkman, entered Frick's office at the *Chronicle-Telegraph* Building on Pittsburgh's Fifth Avenue. Berkman was carrying a gun, and he rushed in and fired, hitting Frick in the shoulder. Frick fell, and Berkman fired again, hitting Frick in the neck. Berkman's entrance into the crisis changed things—the union wanted no part of his act. While the press continued to villainize Frick, they also hailed his courage. Frick survived and remained in control from his bedroom, and the public turned against the union. Still, the public had little stomach for the use of Pinkertons and troops in labor disputes. Democrats were winning the messaging on the national level.

Pennsylvania governor Robert Patterson was a Democrat, and the Homestead uprising played into the politics to break the workers' support for Republican tariffs. The White House was watching the problems at Homestead closely. President Benjamin Harrison was struggling and needed the labor vote, while the Democrats were linking Homestead to the Republicans. Harrison privately was opposed to the use of armed Pinkertons, but Henry Frick ignored his personal requests. The president sent in troops to end the strike, and Frick replaced the picketing workers with scabs and started steel operations. Democrats felt they could carry western Pennsylvania for the first time since the formation of the Republican Party in the 1850s and make inroads in the old Whig roots in Republican territory. Torchlight parades in Homestead had floats portraying protectionism as black sheep, as politicians injected their own brand of racism into the crisis. Senate Democrats came to Homestead to hold hearings. Homestead cost Harrison and the Republicans the election, and the Democrats would effectively repeal the great protective Tariff of 1890.

The 1892 presidential election was fought between former president Cleveland and Harrison. Thanks to the hard work of Republican Ohio governor William McKinley, the Republicans held the labor vote in Pennsylvania and Ohio but lost the election. Cleveland won both the popular and electoral vote, thus becoming the first and, to date, only person in American history to be elected to a second nonconsecutive presidential term. The Democrats won the presidency and both houses of Congress for the first time since 1856. The election was lost in the midwestern states, where the farm vote opposed the tariffs.

Chapter Ten

Congressman McKinley and the Rise of Ohio Republicanism as a National Movement

Ohio republicanism would split the East Coast money Republicans, but it would gain the party a new voting coalition of blue-collar workers from the Democrats. Never comfortable and still holding a disparaging view of frontier Ohio Republicans, the East Coast money interests would compromise. Eventually, by the 1920s, they would take back the party; but until then, Ohio republicanism was the voting bloc that gave them victories. Behind the victories of Rutherford Hayes, James Garfield, and Benjamin Harrison was the work of Ohio congressman William McKinley. McKinley was the center of Ohio republicanism. He built his career by building expertise on tariffs. McKinley's political career deserves consideration in a bit more detail, for he built Ohio republicanism into an engine of prosperity for the nation.

William McKinley came to Congress in 1877. He was given a piece of advice by his old commanding officer, current president Rutherford B. Hayes: "To achieve success and fame, you must pursue a special line. You must not make a speech on every motion offered or bill introduced. Confine yourself to one particular thing. Become a specialist. Take up some branch of legislation and master that. Why not take up the subject of the tariff? That being a subject that will not be settled for years to come, it offers a great field of study for years to come."[1] Of course, Hayes was well aware that it was almost preordained that this would be McKinley's field of study. Hayes's advice may well have been a bit of Republican revisionist history, since he was never a strong supporter of protectionist tariffs. However, future Ohio president James Garfield had a seat on the powerful Ways and Means Committee, which controlled trade. Another mentor, William "Pig Iron" Kelly of Pennsylvania, then chair of Ways and Means, would point McKinley in the same direction. Pig Iron Kelly had taken up the mantle of protectionism from the late Whig leader Henry Clay. Within a year, McKinley and Garfield would be known as "Kelly's Lieutenants."[2] McKinley would settle the decades-old debate on tariffs by applying product-specific rates and inserting reciprocity in trade deals between other countries.

McKinley did make tariffs his specialty, and in doing so, he fought both Democrats and Republicans. Often, like Henry Clay, his farming constituents deserted him. Three Republican presidents opposed him as well. His closest friends often opposed him as well. Because of his tariff views, Democrats forcibly tried to remove McKinley through gerrymandering. National Democratic money poured in to support his local opponents. Critics, including college professors, saw McKinley as simpleminded in his economics. He could compromise on most anything except tariffs. He generally faced a Democratic majority in the House of Representatives, making his tariff bills difficult to pass. In his own party, the old Whig branch of wealthy eastern Republican bankers such as J. P. Morgan opposed him. In the end, McKinley's views would even cost him his congressional seat.

McKinley lived far below middle-class standards, having only a small apartment in Washington for himself and his wife. While he had financial campaign support from business interests, he barely managed to stay at breakeven personally. Republican donor Henry Clay Frick had to purchase McKinley a tuxedo for the inauguration. Capitalism was not a real benefit to McKinley individually. His investments turned out no better than the average investor's, if not worse. He had no aptitude for business, and his law firm income barely put him in ranks of the lower middle class. McKinley entered Congress with $10,000 in assets, and he was bankrupt when he left for his first term in the White House. He was as far as you could get from the robber barons that many called his "cronies."

As a freshman, McKinley was in the 45th Congress. The Democrats controlled the House with 153 members to the Republicans' 140 members, but the Speaker was a protectionist Democrat, Samuel Randall of Pennsylvania. The Republicans held power in the Senate with 39 members to the Democrats' 36. One senator was independent. A weakened President Hayes controlled the White House due to the Supreme Court decision over his election vote count. The national debate concerned the silver-versus-gold issue, and McKinley was immediately on the hot seat. President Hayes, the Republican Party, and major New York bankers supported gold. McKinley favored silver, believing it better for manufacturing in his Canton, Ohio, district. With the silver question, he could offer a new path and coalition for the Republicans. The first bill that McKinley faced was the "Bland Bill" of Richard "Silver Dick" Bland of Missouri. Congressional Republicans and their floor leader and friend,

James Garfield of Ohio (a future president), opposed the pro-silver bill. The freshman McKinley stood alone in his party to vote for silver because he believed it was good for American workers.

President Hayes used the veto, but the House overrode it, with McKinley voting to override. Many overlook McKinley's early courage to go against even his party for the benefit of American workers. Too often he has been characterized as a puppet of his party when his conviction was rooted in the good of U.S. manufacturing. How many of today's freshman congressmen would go against their party on a major bill in their first vote? McKinley's actions were not only a mark of courage but also a measure of his commitment to the country's laborers. He helped initiate a coalition between workers and capitalist owners that would define the Republican Party and Ohio republicanism for decades. The *Canton Repository* noted in 1877: "Major McKinley voted for the re-monetization of silver the other day, like a man who has the courage of his convictions."[3] On the day McKinley was shot, he was carrying a well-worn silver nugget in his trousers as a remembrance of his stand on silver money.

Another important event of McKinley's term was a tariff bill. In 1877, the eastern and southern Democrats wanted to reduce tariffs from protectionist levels to revenue-only levels. Southern Democrats opposed duties because they depended on shipping cotton to Britain for processing. Farmers opposed tariffs because they believed they increased prices for basic goods and made it necessary to ship grain to Europe. Recall that duties were the main revenue of the United States prior to income taxes (established 1913). The Democrats had run on a revenue-only approach, and President Hayes even mildly supported at least a reduction in the rates. House Republicans lacked leadership on protectionism, and their opinions on the matter were mixed. New York congressman Fernando Wood brought a bill to the floor to reduce the tariff. Word got out, and the steelworkers of Ohio brought a petition to William McKinley to stop the bill. There was some popular support for the lower prices that tariff freedom would supposedly bring, and free trade also had the support of academics and theorists. The Republicans had a champion in Pig Iron Kelly of Pennsylvania, but he was considered self-serving since such backing was a necessity in his district. Democrats controlled the House, and without Republican leadership, the bill was expected to pass.

When freshman congressman McKinley took the floor in his first speech, he represented a split district (farming and manufacturing) more representative of Congress. He rose with the petition of Ohio laborers in hand and roared: "Reduce the tariff and labor will be the first to suffer.... Home competition will always bring prices to a fair and reasonable level and prevent extortion and robbery. Success, or even apparent success, in any business or enterprise, will incite others to engage in like enterprises, and then follows healthful strife, the life of business, which inevitably results in cheapening the article produced."[4] McKinley argued forcibly that lower prices meant nothing to the unemployed. He espoused a national type of capitalism reminiscent of the ideas of Henry Clay, whom he had studied endlessly in preparing this first speech. Moreover, McKinley argued that free trade between the states (not countries) was all that was needed, and that it afforded our national security. He asserted, as a veteran, that American products had a blood component cost from workers who had fought for the government in wartime. The freshman congressman sparked the leadership needed to defeat the Wood free trade bill in the Democratic House.

Academics of the time turned against the shameless nationalism and populism of McKinley. However, McKinley argued that protection might not be "favored in colleges, but it is taught in the school of experience, in the workshop, where honest day's labor, and where the capital seeks the development of national wealth."[5] He completely rejected the fashionable theories of Adam Smith in favor of the simplistic nationalism of Henry Clay. With the defeat of the Wood bill, McKinley took a leadership role and united his party around protectionism, bringing in President Hayes. McKinley was the congressman best versed in the whole subject, and he routinely studied long into the night. His national coalition of steelworkers, miners, glassworkers, and laborers and started to make inroads in Democratic voting strongholds. His success made him a major national target for the Democrats.

Back in Ohio in 1878, the Democrats controlled the legislature and had the ability to redistrict. By gerrymandering, they put Stark County in the 16th District with rural Ashland, Portage, and Wayne Counties. By doing so, they took away from McKinley his strength and the heavily industrial Columbiana and Mahoning Counties. Columbiana, in particular, was considered a Republican stronghold with roots going back to Henry Clay. On paper, these counties had a Democratic majority of 1,300 votes. The Democrats were gaining with labor and the Irish during the late 1870s. The party seemed sure of McKinley's defeat in 1878, but to make defeat a reality, it nominated Aquila Wiley. Wiley had an outstanding military record that would help mute McKinley's advantage with veterans. Now factory workers and manufacturers in Stark County rallied behind McKinley. It was an uphill fight, but McKinley won 15,489–14,255. His silver vote had helped him with the farmers (who opposed him on tariffs) enough to diffuse large Democratic majorities in Ashland and Wayne Counties. Furthermore, McKinley had survived a rising national Democratic movement in the election. The victory only strengthened the resolve to defeat McKinley, whose popularity was rising on a national level with his tariff stand.

McKinley's second term was less dramatic, but he was appointed to the powerful Ways and Means Committee. He introduced some anti-liquor legislation, which was an old plank of Ohio republicanism. Additionally, he started building a closer relationship with the Grange, and he supported bills on railroad regulations. McKinley also took an interest in railroad safety, which was becoming a problem in Ohio. More importantly, McKinley's view on Henry Clay's American System was gaining support within his own party. For his part, McKinley, like Clay before him, loved to tour factories and mills throughout the nation. He was building a national following as well. Manufacturers were starting to help support his political career beyond his district base. McKinley loved to speak to anybody who would listen about the role of protectionism and American prosperity. He had won over two more Republicans, James Garfield of Ohio and James Blaine of Maine. His passion was now becoming part of the national Republican strategy.

The year 1880 brought McKinley another challenge to his seat and additional duties in supporting his friend James Garfield's run for the presidency. This time the Republicans gained the state legislature and returned Stark County to its affiliation with Mahoning and Columbiana as a voting district. It was the first time McKinley's district would be a solid Republican one. With some security for holding his seat in Congress, he was elected chairman of the Republican state convention. On a national level, McKinley supported the strong protectionist James Blaine as the Republican candidate. James Garfield submitted fellow Ohioan John Sherman's name for the Republican nomination. Sherman had been Hayes's Secretary of Treasury. When Hayes chose not to run for a second term, he lent his support to Sherman, who had the backing of eastern money. Sherman also had the strong support of Cleveland industrialist Mark Hanna. Sherman had been a senator since 1861, and he remained a dominant force in Ohio politics into the 1890s. McKinley saw him as weak on protectionism for American industries and supportive of a strict gold standard, a judgment that proved wrong in the long run. Senator John Sherman had risen through the ranks, but he was incompatible with McKinley on the protection of American industry—he didn't go far enough for McKinley. Backed by Mark Hanna, Sherman tended to favor business over the more balanced approach of McKinley for labor. In 1878, Sherman told a struggling coal dealer in the Mahoning Valley to go west to find a better future. McKinley, on the other hand, had been close to the coal miners while he was a lawyer representing them against unfair owners.

The gold standard would be another fault line for Ohio and the nation. This issue would always be a problem for McKinley within his own party, as most Republicans stood with the eastern bankers supporting the gold standard. The gold standard tightened money, and this particularly hurt farmers. Farmers needed mortgages, and that made them sensitive to interest rates and the money supply. The use of silver could help increase the money supply and bring down interest rates. The Grange supported free silver, the most liberal money standard, which involved silver exchange not based on gold. Generally, the Democratic Party had supported the farmers and the silver issue. McKinley adopted a middle ground in 1880 with his advocacy of bimetallism (use of gold and silver), which was the right approach for mixed farming and industrial states such as Ohio. McKinley's district included a lot of farmers, and their votes often were the determining factor in the local elections. Later, in 1890, Ohio president Benjamin Harrison would make silver part of Ohio republicanism.

The economic theory behind the gold/silver question was never fully defined. The amount of available metals fluctuated with gold and silver strikes in the West. McKinley was not interested in the theory, but the effect. He remained a bimetallist, watching closely to see what might be best for the laborers and businesses, while not hurting the farmers. McKinley always preferred to talk "sound money" versus gold or silver. It was a very polarized issue, with eastern bankers believing in the necessity of gold. This idea came from the need to deal with other countries, which mostly supported the gold standards. Western farmers, rightfully or wrongfully, believed silver was the answer for resolving debt and reducing interest rates.

McKinley's view blunted strong opposition from the Grange. The farmers formed this politically strong organization in 1867, and it functioned as a cooperative able to reduce manufactured products through volume buying. Grange members formed cooperative mills and grain elevators, and they even founded banks and insurance companies. Their real focus, however, became the abuses of the railroads. The Grange would be a political force throughout McKinley's career. Though he frequently won the organization's support for his railroad reform and bimetallism, his protective tariff stands often cost him significant farm votes in a district where he could ill afford any bloc opposition.

The farmers had united with laborers in 1878 to form the Greenback-Labor Party in Toledo, Ohio. In 1880, the party put together a platform endorsing free silver coinage, women's suffrage, regulation of railroads, and restrictions on Chinese immigration. Members nominated James Weaver of Iowa as their candidate for president in 1880. The Greenback-Labor Party was a splinter group but one large enough to affect the presidential elections. Its platform favored the radical wing of the Democratic Party and took votes away from the Democratic candidate, so it strengthened Ohio Republicans. But McKinley favored much of the Greenback-Labor Party's agenda.

The National Republican Convention of 1880 became split and deadlocked. On the 34th ballot, James Garfield took the nomination as a compromise candidate with the help of future presidents Benjamin Harrison and William McKinley. Garfield was middle-of-the-road on protection, but

McKinley, the party loyalist, came in line for the election. Garfield, like Hayes, realized the East Coast branch of the Republican Party controlled the money. Garfield supported tariffs but favored tight money via gold. McKinley still was able to compromise and actively support the party candidate. While the Republican Party often compromised on tariffs, tariffs remained a core value for the Ohio republicanism movement and William McKinley.

McKinley stumped the state for Garfield, who was running against General Winfield Scott Hancock, the hero of Gettysburg. Hancock opposed any tariff, and McKinley became worried should Hancock win. Nationally, it was another close fight, with Garfield winning by only 7,018 votes. McKinley was instrumental in Garfield's selection of James Blaine as secretary of state. The Republican platforms were pro-gold, anti-immigration, and pro–higher tariffs. Seeing his own party split on protective tariffs, McKinley started to work on his concept of reciprocity in trade deals,[6] which President Benjamin Harrison had proposed. McKinley started a labor branch of the party with his tariff views.

McKinley was moving into areas of railroad safety and rate controls as tariff opposition temporarily subsided. Here again, he was at odds with the J. P. Morgan wing of his party. It was during this time that McKinley met George Westinghouse, inventor of the railroad safety air brake. Westinghouse didn't fit the robber baron label of the time; he was manufacturing the air brake and other railroad safety devices. When McKinley asked him to testify on the need for railroad safety, Westinghouse came from Pittsburgh in his special Pullman car to pick up McKinley and go to Washington. The men shared a deep Christian faith, an interest in the YMCA, and a belief that labor and capital should cooperate for the success of the nation. They would become railroad safety crusaders and friends over the years. Westinghouse was known for his humane treatment of workers. For his part, McKinley strengthened the unusual alliance of workers and national capitalists. He was a member of the lower middle class and had little money for luxuries. McKinley, however, would make George Westinghouse a wealthy man with the passage of the 1892 Railroad Safety Act, which required the use of the Westinghouse air brake. McKinley, however, had little financial benefit from the measure.

McKinley had few resources to buy or rent a home in Washington; furthermore, he and his wife were absent from the social scene. They rented two rooms at the Ebbitt House. The cramped quarters consisted of a bedroom and a workroom, as well as a parlor downstairs, which the couple used for social meetings. The family's poor financial health and Ida McKinley's delicate physical health meant that their socializing was almost nonexistent. William McKinley's assets were mainly mortgaged property back in Canton, and he was often short on cash between paychecks. Ida's condition remained poor, and her medical bills were a clear burden on the congressman's salary. McKinley sent notes while he was at work in Congress to make sure Ida was fine, but generally she passed the time in solitude. During the Hayes and Garfield administrations, the couple was often invited to the White House. The Hayeses, in particular, lived a sober, cloistered existence and welcomed the quiet visits of the McKinleys. The McKinleys cherished the out-of-session periods back in Canton, where they lived at the Saxton house, and they could be seen daily sitting on the veranda talking and greeting passersby.

The year 1882 turned out to be a major challenge for McKinley. Initially, things looked bright as state Republicans returned Stark County (Canton) to its old district with (Niles) Mahoning and Columbiana, but the threat came from within McKinley's own party. Tradition, at the time, was that a congressman should step down after two terms. In addition, Ohio congressional districts rotated candidates between representatives of the counties in the districts. The Republican chairman of Columbiana County challenged McKinley to resign and let a candidate from Columbiana take the nomination. The battle against tradition dragged into the fall elections of 1882.

President Arthur, who had succeeded Garfield after his assassination, was very unpopular at the time, and the election trend was Democratic. As a result, McKinley won by only eight votes. A large part of this narrow victory owed to McKinley's anti-liquor temperance stand based on his moral beliefs. It cost him heavily with the Germans and Irish that dominated his district, and he had nothing to gain politically from it. The Republican-controlled state legislature certified McKinley, but his opponent Jonathan Wallace took the contest to Washington, where the Democrats were in control. A committee was formed to look at the election results as McKinley took his seat in Congress and on the Ways and Means Committee. The investigation would drag on for political reasons and be used to block his tariff bills.

In early 1882, McKinley realized the tide was turning against protective tariffs and his brand of national capitalism, known at the time as Henry Clay's "American System."[7] The Democrats, seeing the division in the Republican Party and having control of the House, felt the time was right for tariff reduction. McKinley needed the Democrats to avoid a tariff decrease. He adroitly moved for a House committee to study the matter, feeling any hard look had to be favorable. McKinley stated: "I have no fear of an intelligent and businesslike examination and revision of the tariff by competent civilians who shall be known as Americans and favorable to the American system."[8] He also needed to pacify President Arthur's personal view favoring lower tariffs and the Democratic majority's stiff opposition.

McKinley took a compromise position, since there were also high tariff hard-liners in the right wing of his party. He gave a 35-page speech that supported high tariffs yet promoted a federal commission to control abuses. One of the major points of tariff opposition was the fact that capitalists would profit without investing in increased jobs through plant expansion. The commission heard over 600 witnesses as the tariff issue took center stage. McKinley's speech was well received by Pittsburgh and midwestern iron manufacturers, as well as by coal mining companies in Ohio, Pennsylvania, and West Virginia. This group paid to have McKinley's speeches printed and distributed. His stand against some of his own party was not a result of kickback from industry; it should be noted that McKinley was having financial problems and refused help from even his industrial friends at the time. While East Coast money controlled the Republican Party, the union bosses and farmers controlled the Democratic Party. The press, however, missed a voter coalition of union workers and midwestern industrialists. This alliance would be key to McKinley's new Republican Party in the future and would even resurface a hundred years later in the Reagan Democrats, and again with Donald Trump in the old McKinley districts.

A long-term commission was formed as part of the McKinley compromise to study, report, and protect against abuses by capitalists. Amazingly the results of the commission were extremely liberal, suggesting a reduction in tariffs. Major decreases were advised for tariffs on wool, iron, and steel, which were the major products of a failed filibuster in the House. In the debate, McKinley made one of his most famous retorts. He rose on the floor on January 27, 1883, to denounce the report. Drawing heavily on his belief that free trade ultimately hurt the laborers by initially baiting them with lower prices, he stated: "I speak for the workingmen of my district, the working men of Ohio, and of the Country." Democratic congressman Springer yelled out, "they did not speak for you very largely in the last election." McKinley calmly but forcibly replied: "Ah, my friend, my fidelity to my constituents is not measured by the support they give me. I have convictions upon this subject which I would not surrender or refrain from advocating if a ten thousand majority had been entered against me last October."[9] McKinley faced powerful Republicans like John Sherman of Ohio who were weakening in the support of protective tariffs. I don't believe that even his enemies doubted his belief in the good of high tariffs.

With the conference report accepted, the Democrats moved for a bill with a 20 percent across-the-board reduction. Known as the Morrison Bill, it probably overplayed the Democratic hand by extending the reduction across the full list of protected products. The universal approach allowed McKinley to build support with Democrats in manufacturing districts. His speech against the bill cut to the heart of the matter:

> It has friends today that it never had in the past. Its adherents are no longer confined to the North and the East, but are found in the South and in the West. The idea travels with industry and is the associate of enterprise and thrift. It encourages the develop-

ment of skill, labor, and inventive genius as part of the great productive forces. Its advocacy is no longer limited to the manufacturer, but it has friends the most devoted among the farmers, wool-growers, the laborers, and the producers of land. It is strong in the country as in the manufacturing towns or cities; and while it is not taught generally in our colleges, and our young men fresh from universities join with the free-trade thought of the country, practical business and every-day experience later teach them that there are other sources of knowledge besides books, that demonstration is better than theory, and that actual results outweigh an idle philosophy. But while it is not favored in colleges, it is taught in the schools of experience, in the workshop, where honest men perform an honest day's labor, and where capital seeks the development of national wealth. It is, my judgment, fixed in our national policy, and no party is strong enough to overthrow.[10]

In the end, McKinley prevailed with a 156–151 vote in the House, and he succeeded in bringing over 41 Democrats who represented industrial areas.

McKinley's leadership and speaking ability had become a significant problem for the Democrats, and his success in defeating the Morrison Tariff Bill was short-lived. A few weeks later, the House Elections Board recommended McKinley be unseated, and the strongly Democratic House delivered a 158–108 decision to do so. He accepted the ruling, and Jonathan Wallace took the seat on May 27, 1884. McKinley returned to a hero's welcome in Canton, but he had reached a low point in many ways. When McKinley went to Congress, he had had $10,000 and a practice worth $10,000 a year. After leaving Congress, he had neither. The local crowds hailed him as the "Napoleon of Protection." Workers in Ohio, Kentucky, Indiana, West Virginia, and Pennsylvania marched in support. Still, McKinley was near personal bankruptcy, and his political career seemed in doubt.

McKinley was made chairman of the Ohio Republican Convention in 1884. In addition, he went to the National Republican Convention as a delegate, then was promptly made chairman of the Resolutions Committee, making him responsible for the national platform. McKinley worked hard on the party's policy, which stood for high tariffs with a scientific look at reform, railroad reform, bimetallism, curbs on Chinese immigration, and the eight-hour day. The convention was a wild one, and fistfights were common. McKinley opposed his own Ohio delegation, which supported John Sherman, by voting for James Blaine. As always, McKinley's backing depended on the tariff issue, and Sherman, though an Ohioan, was weak on tariffs in McKinley's view. Blaine won the nomination, and McKinley's platform gave the Republican Party a labor plank to stand on. It was an amazing program that addressed most of the problems of the emerging middle class, laborers, and farmers.

The addition of a call for the eight-hour day was particularly friendly to labor, but it again found opposition in the East Coast wing of the Republican Party. McKinley, however, had always maintained management was part of the labor problem, and he often spoke in support of better management, building a voting coalition of workers that the Republicans had never seen. McKinley would leave his mark on the Republican platform against those of Republican donor class. This platform was, however, representative of his middle-class following. The eight-hour-day plank was visionary, but it seemed doubtful that the Republican Party could fully endorse it. In most manufacturing facilities, the twelve-hour day was standard. McKinley believed in the eight-hour day, pointing to the work of plant manager Bill Jones of Carnegie Steel. Jones had implemented the eight-hour day in the early 1880s over the objections of his boss, Andrew Carnegie. To everyone's surprise, the Braddock plant rose to become the world's most productive factory. Years later, thousands of workers would make a train trip from Pittsburgh to Canton, Ohio, to support his presidential run. Another Pittsburgher and Republican friend, George Westinghouse, had also shown productivity increases with the eight-hour day. Also, the Republican Party still had substantial support from the trade union leadership because of its strong protectionism stand. McKinley had triumphed over the eastern bankers with a bimetallism plank. East Coast Republican power broker J. P. Morgan was particularly upset with the Republicans taking steps away from the gold standard.

McKinley's platform was probably too liberal for the eastern Republicans to embrace, but it reflected where he was with regard to policy. The Grange particularly applauded McKinley's support of railroad reform. He had often, as a congressman, introduced bills for the Grange, and such bills were in opposition to the big-money wing of the Republican Party represented by the likes of J. P. Morgan. The same wing opposed McKinley's support of bimetallism. McKinley's work on the Republican platform was representative of the overall population. It was a tough presidential election because scandals haunted the Republicans. James Blaine had a suspect record, having been named in some scandals. That problem, coupled with his support of railroads and the gold standard, caused many Republicans such as George Westinghouse to vote Democratic. These Republicans were known as Mugwumps. Blaine had been prevented from getting the Republican presidential nomination during the previous two elections because of the stigma of the Mulligan letters in 1876. The Ohio Republicans opposed Blaine on moral issues, but, as always, tariffs were the issue. And Blaine, while not strong on tariffs, was better than the antiprotectionist Democrats. While Ohio Republicans held for Blaine, the Republican donor class and eastern bankers supported the Democratic nominee.

The Democratic Party nominated the conservative Grover Cleveland. Cleveland was a middle-road Democrat with business support from the likes of Charles Goodyear and George Westinghouse. Cleveland actually counted the "Prince of Capitalism," J. P. Morgan, as a friend. They frequently lunched together in downtown New York. The Democratic Party avoided the gold issue while Cleveland supported the gold standard privately. Grover Cleveland, in many ways, looked more like a Republican than Blaine. Cleveland ran on a reform platform, pointing to the endless scandals and abuses in the business community. In particular, Cleveland had the strong support of the Grange and farmers, who were particularly upset with railroad abuses and high tariffs. The Republican platform addressed the issue, but the Republicans lacked the record of addressing it.

McKinley's congressional district was gerrymandered in 1884 and included Stark, Summit, Wayne, and Medina Counties, which tended to vote Democratic. McKinley lost the seat, which suggested this effort to take it back would be easily defeated, especially as the national voting trend was once again Democratic. McKinley, however, reversed the trend in 1886 and carried the district by 2,000 votes. His return to Washington was a great personal victory and established him nationally as a leader. In many ways, it was his greatest victory, since Cleveland had carried Ohio and the district. McKinley's stand and victory against the Morrison Tariff Bill had strengthened his political base and national recognition. Still, McKinley and his wife, Ida, returned to their somewhat monastic routine in Washington.

McKinley had some rental income besides his congressman's salary. He also received some money from the law firm in Canton that his brother maintained. Ida McKinley's medical and care expenses were surely a great burden, and there is evidence that McKinley even considered another line of work because of the financial strain. Ida did improve, or her nervous condition at least became more manageable. Also, with the death of her father in 1887, she received a generous inheritance. Over the years, that inheritance would be eroded by continuing financial problems.

Living in a small Washington apartment, McKinley rose early and shaved while reading the newspaper and letters. As a soldier, he had learned to shave without a mirror. McKinley and Ida breakfasted at the Ebbitt House after he had done a few hours of work. Ida always wore black dresses, even for breakfast. McKinley was always well dressed and wore a Prince Albert coat with a red carnation. In good weather, he walked to the Capitol; and in bad weather, he took the horsecar. He arrived promptly at his seat in Congress every morning. McKinley telephoned his wife or sent notes to her throughout the day; he was stoic in his care and commitment to her. They would dine at the Ebbitt House in the evening, and McKinley would then spend time smoking in the parlor with other residents or taking a short walk, as Ida hated cigar smoke. As a congressman he was noted as a heavy smoker, and he also took up chewing tobacco. The McKinleys often passed the evening with William reading the Bible to Ida or by playing a game of cribbage. When the Hayeses were in the White House, The McKinleys often played euchre with them. While he had emerged on the national scene and campaigned in the East for Blaine, McKinley stayed close to Washington, probably because he was the primary, if not sole, caregiver for his invalid wife. He did have a maid/nurse who stayed with Ida when he was gone, which strained his budget.

In 1885, McKinley made one of his famous protection speeches in Petersburg, Virginia. In the address, he responded to the rural Jeffersonian who talked of factories bringing cholera: "I tell you, manufactories do not bring cholera—they bring coin, coin: coin for the poor man, coin for the rich, coin for everybody that will work; comfort and contentment for all deserving people. And if you vote for increasing manufactories, my fellow citizens, you will vote for the best interests of your own State, and you will be making iron, and steel, and pottery, and all leading products." McKinley was not just a great orator; he was a student of economics. He often studied journals and statistics into the early morning. He built a small library on trade and economics, and few were as well versed in those subjects, even at our best universities. He was always well prepared for even minor debates. Democrats feared McKinley because he had the ability to persuade opponents, and it was a necessary skill, since he mostly faced a Democratic majority in his career.

The spring of 1886 shocked America with the famous Haymarket Riot in Chicago. The Haymarket Riot was different because it was more of a populist movement than a general strike. Prosperity brought labor tension in America's industrial centers. The socialists were also in a position to exploit the problems. In Cincinnati, there were May Day parades for the eight-hour day with plenty of red flags. In Chicago, labor problems at McCormack Reaper Company and Pullman Company mixed with parades for the eight-hour day, and the anarchists and socialists rallied as well. Riot turned to a bloodbath as Cleveland sent federal troops to the city. It was later speculated that Leon Czolgosz, McKinley's assassin, was at the riots, but it seems unlikely. The trial and hanging of the Chicago anarchists for the Haymarket Riot did impact Czolgosz's belief in class warfare. It would also impact a young Theodore Roosevelt, who also saw America heading toward class conflict and socialism.

McKinley did not fear socialism or anarchy. He believed they could only prosper with the failure of capitalism and democracy. In addition, he believed that fair wages, industrial growth, better work conditions, tariffs to protect American wages, and mobility to the middle class were the answers. In his defense, the Ohio coal miners came to McKinley's support in elections. They remembered how, as a young lawyer, he had helped them in a lawsuit against the mineowners. Earlier in his career, he had learned how poor working conditions could lead to labor discontent. Thanks to McKinley, the Republican platform had put the steelworkers in the forefront, with the eight-hour-day issue being addressed in the platform.

In 1886, Congress prepared for new battles on tariffs as Grover Cleveland was determined to reduce them. McKinley prepared by lining up his support from the unions and manufacturers in Ohio, Illinois, and Pennsylvania. He had strong support from union leaders, which gave the Democrats pause at the local level. In early 1886, William Morrison of Illinois drafted a bill for tariff reduction. Morrison was, at the time, chair of the Ways and Means Committee. McKinley once again built a floor alliance with the protectionist Democrats and defeated the measure. The Democratic Party remained split while the Republicans remained united. Grover Cleveland, however, continued to push for tariff reductions against the McKinley House alliance.

Congress was also split on the need to regulate the railroads, which were increasingly coming under public pressure for reform. The railroads and East Coast banking were interconnected, which was a problem for Ohio Republicans. McKinley supported the passage of the Interstate Commerce Act, which regulated such practices. It was yet another example of McKinley breaking from the big business Republican wing.

The 1886 election went well for McKinley, who carried the district by 2,559 votes. The 1887 annual presidential address to Congress focused on one topic—tariff reduction. The Congress was again Democratic, and Cleveland was confident in victory. The government had a surplus, so the Democrats argued tariff revenue was unnecessary. The battle was building, and McKinley was building statistics and rallying industry and labor leaders. This time McKinley's opposition was Roger Mills of Texas, who was now chairman of the Ways and Means Committee. Mills was representative of the southern Democrats who opposed tariffs because of their negative impact on the cotton industry. There was still a protectionist wing of the Democratic Party that McKinley could ally with, but President Cleveland was applying pressure for a party vote. McKinley's effort to kill the bill in committee failed, and the Democrats moved it to the floor.

This time McKinley met the full force of the Democratic administration. Cleveland lobbied the protectionist Democrats by using special favors. Cleveland used the government excise to have the Democrats load the bill with pork barrel amendments. Mills lined up America's best academic minds to testify for free trade. McKinley looked for middle ground, but Cleveland wasn't interested. The eastern protectionist Democrats weakened in their opposition. The floor debate started on April 17, 1888, but McKinley sized up the turning tide and didn't rise to speak until May 18. The Republicans added amendments and moderated the rate reduction level. McKinley had a very effective grassroots operation even beyond Ohio. He was becoming a national figure, and he had the necessary popular support, but Cleveland had bet the House. When McKinley did speak, he spoke to the people more than to Congress. He asserted that he would rather have his political economy founded on the everyday experience of a union steelmaker or a potter than on the learning of the professor, or on the experience of the farmer and factory hand than that of the college faculty. McKinley realized the fight was lost on the floor, but he extended the debate. In early summer, the Mills bill passed the House, but the Senate tied it up until the fall elections.

McKinley had lost his first big floor battle on tariffs, but he gained the American people's support. The floor fight was well covered nationwide, making tariffs the key issue in the 1888 presidential elections, and McKinley was now a national figure. Grover Cleveland's popularity was hurt with his push to end protective tariffs. The election issue would now center on tariffs. Even a weakened President Cleveland had the Democratic nomination assured, but the Republican nomination was up for grabs. McKinley supported Ohio's native son John Sherman, but James Blaine had big-money support. There was also an array of others; even McKinley's name was coming up. Blaine, who was vacationing at Andrew Carnegie's castle, refused to run. John Sherman withdrew as well. The nomination was wide open, and McKinley was even being considered as a dark horse. He declined consideration, knowing he was not ready and not sure he wanted to be. The Republicans did have one divisive issue—that of the gold standard again. The Republican money favored gold, and McKinley's history of bimetallism ruled him out, but the party needed to defeat the pending Mills bill in Congress. Benjamin Harrison offered the compromise of being strong on tariffs and the gold standard.

The famous McKinley Tariff of 1890 was the peak of decades of protectionist policy of the Republican Party and the Whig Party prior to that. The Tariff of 1890 was a specific bill passed by then chairman of the Ways and Means Committee and future president of the United States William McKinley. It also represented a political policy of protection of American industry that was argued for almost 100 years in America. The Tariff Act of 1890 centered on the economic cornerstones of Ohio republicanism—trade reciprocity, protection of the American workers and industries, oversight of profits, and assurance of those profits going into job growth. The act focused on the protection and development of infant industries of the Midwest such as aluminum, tinplate, and electrical products, as well as the basic industrial core of steel, iron, processed food, and glass. It was a follow up of decades of work by Congressman McKinley. McKinley's 1890 bill was the best researched ever, using science and statistics to apply the tariff rates. First, McKinley argued that the revenue tariff approach was the real problem, not protective tariffs.[11]

McKinley also was innovative in his 1890 bill, which included a special reciprocity clause. The bill allowed for 99 percent of the product to be free of the duties collected on raw materials imported such as iron ore, then exported as finished goods such as steel to foreign markets. This allowed industrial materials to enter the country free of the tax and not added to manufacturing costs. South American wool and raw sugar could flow in and be converted by American manufacturers into clothing and refined sugar without duties to South America. The industrialists rallied around McKinley, but eastern bankers offered stiff opposition, enjoying the profits of trade. McKinley built an unusual alliance of capitalists, laborers, middle-class citizens, and immigrants to push the bill through. President Benjamin Harrison went a step further, convincing Republican senators to insert a provision permitting the president to raise duties to match foreign rate hikes, and to sign agreements to open foreign markets without congressional approval. Unfortunately, the timing was particularly bad. The nation was heading into an unrelated depression, which made it easy for the Democrats to target the Tariff Act. One reason for the depression was in the congressional compromise McKinley and fellow Ohio senator John Sherman used to pass the Tariff Act. Farmers and the Democrats opposed the cost of tariffs on purchased goods or retaliation on farm exports. Even though McKinley's bill prevented this, to a large degree, representatives from farm districts hesitated to support the Tariff Act. McKinley and Sherman moved to help the farmers with the Sherman Free Silver Act in 1890, which used a silver base to dramatically increase the money supply, and to reduce interest rates for the farmers.

While McKinley made his mark in 1890 with his famous Tariff Act, his bigger political accomplishment is often forgotten. In 1893, Congress required the Westinghouse air brake and automatic coupler on all trains by passing the Railroad Safety Appliance Act. The act resulted from the work of chairman of the Ways and Means Committee William McKinley and his friend George Westinghouse, inventor of the railroad air brake. The two had been working on railroad safety since the 1870s. Westinghouse had invented the air brake in 1869, but its adoption had been slow because of the cost to the railroads.

The railroads preferred the hand brake system, which was already in place and required coordination and muscle power. The locomotive engineer would start throttling down the engine as he signaled the brakemen with the whistle (known as the down brakes whistle). A brakeman was assigned between every two cars on the train. The brakemen would begin the process of applying friction brakes on each car by turning a handwheel known as the horizontal wheel on a vertical post at the end of each car. The wheel multiplied the force of the brakemen's muscles, and these men's needed strength was the source of the term "Armstrong system." The handwheel pushed brake shoes on each car against the wheels. After the brakes were applied to one car, the brakemen jumped to the other car to apply the brakes. Poor coordination between the men could cause locking and serious jolting to the passengers. Luggage was often thrown wildly inside the passenger cars, injuring the occupants. The danger to the brakemen was unbelievable. The average life of a brakeman on the job was estimated at seven years. The men had to race from car to car, often on roofs slippery with ice, snow, and rain. Even on the best days, the swaying, bobbing, and jolting of the cars caused a loss of footing. The statistics of the time were just as unbelievable. An estimated 1,000 brakemen were killed each year and another 5,000 injured. The Railroad Safety Act of 1892 would make the air brake mandatory and make Westinghouse one of the nation's wealthiest industrialists. Westinghouse's friendship would be behind McKinley's getting the presidency. But before McKinley won the election, President Harrison, the Republicans, and Ohio republicanism would suffer a major setback.

Chapter Eleven

Ohio Republicanism Challenged

The McKinley Tariff Act of 1890 passed in the middle of a recession and upcoming midterm elections. This financial failing caused investment to dry up in America, and America spiraled into recession. In 1890, the famous British investment firm Baring Brothers went bankrupt. Baring Brothers was a major stockholder in American firms, especially railroads. Another part of the problem was that Europeans pulled money out of America because the Sherman Silver Act caused them to lose confidence. Europeans were moving from bimetallism to a gold standard. Regardless of the reasons for the recession, the Sherman Silver Act and the Tariff Act were blamed and would impact the 1890 congressional elections and the 1892 presidential election. The McKinley Tariff Act would be the engine for America's industrial future. But its timing at the beginning of an economic recession and the Homestead Strike allowed the Democrats to use the act against McKinley. In the 1890 election, Republicans lost their majority in the House; the number of seats they won was reduced by nearly half, from 171 to 88. The Tariff Act and a national effort by the Democrats to destroy the bulldog of tariffs cost McKinley his seat.

For 1890, the Democrats gerrymandered McKinley, placing Stark County and Canton, Ohio, in the same district as one of the strongest pro–Democrat counties, Holmes County, which was populated by solidly Democratic German farmers. The new boundaries seemed good, based on past results, for a Democratic majority of 2,000 to 3,000. The McKinley Tariff was a main theme of the Democratic campaign nationwide, and there was considerable national attention and money paid to McKinley's race. The Republican Party sent its leading orators to Canton, including James Blaine (then secretary of state), House Speaker Reed, and President Harrison. The Democrats countered with

An 1889 engraving of the Inaugural Ball held for Benjamin Harrison in Washington, D.C., in the Pension Building. Library of Congress.

their best spokesmen on tariff issues. To drive their point home, the Democrats hired young partisans to pretend to be tinware peddlers. These individuals went door to door offering 25-cent tinware to housewives for 50 cents, explaining that the rise in prices was due to the McKinley Tariff of 1890. The tinplate issue was completely bogus, and a Grange member noted: "I do not know of a single article that is higher than a year ago. Of course, it was less political than to say so from the stump."[1] Historical statistics support the contention that there was no evidence of price increases.[2]

Sugar provisions were actually excluded from implementation (for six months) in 1890. The exclusion of the sugar tariff hurt the Republicans because it was not immediately implemented. This duty and its resultant higher prices were resented by consumers across America. Interestingly, the McKinley Tariff on tinplate did establish the American tinplate industry, with over 200 mills producing 5 million boxes of tinplate by 1901. Still, tinplate would be the focal point of the Democratic attack in McKinley's home district.

Mark Hanna was aware of the attack on McKinley and the Ohio congressmen that had supported the tariff. The distortions required an expensive educational campaign, and Hanna gathered the necessary financial resources. He was having trouble amassing the usual war chest, as many industrialists felt the Sherman Silver Purchase Act had sold them out. Eastern bankers were moving to the Democrats. Even with the McKinley amendments to favor agriculture, the farmers were being taken in by fear. It was the first campaign that industrialist Mark Hanna was highly involved in.

Another problem was the perception that President Harrison was unfriendly to laborers and farmers, the very foundation of the old Greenback-Labor Party. In 1888, the Republicans had made inroads into the labor and Irish Catholic vote. Harrison was not McKinley; he took a hard line on Catholics and labor, and he helped erode what the Republicans had gained in the 1888 elections. With his stand on gold, Harrison had no friends among the farmers either. Clearly, some of the Republicans' problems in 1890 were directly attributed to the backlash against Harrison. Democrats, still smarting from the takedown of their free trade representatives, targeted McKinley from a national perspective.

McKinley was aware of the Democratic effort in the 1890 midterms, and he ran one of his most active campaigns, making 30 speeches in 14 days. Beds were set up in railroad cars as he traveled the district. Still, he was at a large registration disadvantage and caught in a huge national Democratic trend. There was no question that had McKinley been in an industrial congressional district such as Pittsburgh, he would have had a lifetime seat. However, his Democratic-leaning district dogged his whole career. The 1890 election lived up to the name "farmer's revolt." In a Democratic landslide, 78 of the 166 Republicans were defeated, and the Democrats held their seats, leaving 88 Republicans against 235 Democrats in the House (with 9 Populists). All Republicans in farm districts lost. The "Farmer's Alliance" of congressmen, or what we would call a caucus, consisted of 50 Democrats. McKinley lost by only 302 votes, a truly heroic effort. Ohio elected 14 Democrats versus 7 Republicans. Newspapers, Democrats and Republican Party insiders called the 1890 election a national rejection of tariffs and Ohio republicanism.

McKinley tirelessly stumped in his new district, reaching out to its 40,000 voters to explain his tariff; but in the end, he lost by 300 votes. Yet this defeat would forge the sword of victory as McKinley took on a national stage. Harrison was also supporting McKinley, and the loss would augur Harrison's own defeat in 1892. The 1890 loss was a stinging defeat for the architect of 20th-century Ohio republicanism. McKinley had to endure with dignity the celebrations and taunts of Democrats on the floor of Congress. After the close of session, he took his wife to Chicago for a vacation. Newspapers in Ohio almost immediately started to suggest that McKinley run for governor. Harrison's popularity was also in decline as the recession gained momentum, and the 1890 midterms were a referendum on the Harrison presidency.

The Democrats had done a masterful job of blaming the tariffs for just about every problem. The presidential election of 1892 devastated Republicans, who lost all three branches of government. Losing the presidency was an extension of the 1890 congressional losses. In addition, the Republicans lost farm and western support with the rise of the Populist Party. The Populists nominated James Weaver of Ohio, who had left the Republican Party. He would get 300,000 votes in the election. Traditional Republican support faltered as the eastern bankers supported Grover Cleveland, a gold supporter and friend of J. P. Morgan's. The election followed the Republican setback of 1890. Grover Cleveland won by over 100,000 votes and carried the Electoral College 277–145. There were Democratic majorities in the House (218–127) and the Senate (44–38). But the Democratic celebration would be short-lived, as the Panic of 1893 started to reach the factories of America. Cleveland set his sights on the successful repeal of the McKinley Tariff.

McKinley returned to Canton, and Mark Hanna set him up for a run for governor in 1892. In the end, McKinley ran a tough, clean campaign based on the issues. He depended on the state organization, having almost no money of his own, but he did have donations from Hanna's industrial group. McKinley carried the state by 21,511 votes, and the Republicans took a majority of 50 in the state legislature. Thus Ohio bucked the national trend of 1892. Industrial towns such as Pittsburgh, Chicago, and Buffalo saw Republicans' Ohio victory as a national victory. With John Sherman over 70 years of age, and making his last run for Congress, McKinley certainly was a national Republican figure. He had a solid labor vote in the Cleveland-Pittsburgh corridor that no Republican before or since could count on. McKinley was from this area, and he understood its people. And as governor, he had addressed their needs first.

Democrats fought McKinley on his perceived weakness on tariffs. During the 1892 governor's race, McKinley's Democratic opponent, James Campbell, made an unresearched claim that the tariffs had favored foreign aliens in the Ohio glass industry, not Americans. The northwest Ohio glass industry was booming, and it required skilled craftsmen from key parts of Europe. In the early 1800s, American glass manufacturers actually had to smuggle master glassmakers in from Europe, which made it illegal for glassmakers to immigrate to the United States. The cylinder glass towns of northwest Ohio, such as Maumee and Findlay, needed some of the world's most skilled glassworkers. In particular, Campbell was referring to the Belgian cylinder glassblowers, many of whom were unnaturalized aliens at the time. McKinley correctly pointed out that the wages of American cylinder glassblowers were six times as high as those of Belgian workers. The difference had allowed American companies to readily get these skilled blowers, who made up a small percentage of the overall workforce created by the tariffs. Campbell had ignorantly focused on one of the success stories of the McKinley Tariffs. McKinley won handily.

As governor, McKinley exhibited adept executive abilities, which he had honed in the military. Furthermore, he demonstrated that the governorship was not just a stepping-stone, but also a position with which to leave his mark on Ohio. He worked hard behind the scenes on many controversial issues, often going against his own party. He reached his hand to the Democrats in a conciliatory manner to advance his ideas. McKinley's behavior was far from that of a political puppet of the industrialists, despite his critics' attempts to frame him as such. In fact, he always adhered to simplistic middle-class values. His vision included good industrial jobs with wages that could give workers a future. McKinley wanted to prioritize the twin fears of the middle class—debt and unemployment. Often, he took on industrialists concerning workers' safety and treatment. He wanted an industrial America, not a big-business America. Thanks to Hanna, McKinley was a regional figure in the old Whig country and Transylvania who was fast becoming a national figure.

McKinley's approach to the heavy burden on middle-class taxpayers was yet another demonstration of a middle-class vision for America. Real estate carried most of the state's tax income, while capital and investment carried none. His desire to form a commission to study state taxation found strong opposition from party heavyweight Hanna. Still, McKinley forged ahead with tax reform, and Hanna came around to his view. McKinley had a deep belief that the wealthy should carry the tax burden, but not the middle class, having seen the struggles of his own father to pay taxes in bad times. He took on the tax issue in Ohio like he had addressed the tariff issue on a national level. McKinley wanted a corporate tax as part of his industrial vision. This was far from the vision of the capitalists, whom his critics said he was in bed with.

McKinley maintained an active schedule, dealing with state issues while taking requests to speak in America's industrial districts of old Transylvania. He went to Indiana for the opening of a giant new tinplate mill, to Pittsburgh to talk to steelmakers, to Indianapolis to speak on patriotism, to Kentucky to talk about agriculture, and to Chicago to talk to workingmen. He was drawing crowds of thousands as his national popularity grew. He was a political workhorse for the national party, speaking on behalf of Republicans in almost every state while governor of Ohio. It appears clear that McKinley was thinking about the presidency in the long run, but his plans weren't interfering with his duties as governor. By 1895, McKinley was the clear leader of the Republican Party and on the path to the return of Ohio republicanism.

President Cleveland faired far worse than Governor McKinley in his third term as president. Before the Panic of 1893 ended, a quarter of America's railroads would fail. In addition, 15,000 businesses collapsed, along with 158 banks. Of America's 253 blast furnaces, 116 shut down in 1893. Over 3 million workers were unemployed, or over 25 percent of the workforce, a figure only surpassed during the Great Depression of the 1930s.

Layoffs in the fall of 1893 were approaching 1 million, and 141 banks had failed. The smokestacks of Ohio's Mahoning Valley and Pittsburgh were cold. Two old steel companies—Pennsylvania Steel and Oliver Iron and Steel—went bankrupt. Railroads, which were the nation's largest employer, failed almost monthly, forcing massive unemployment. One of the reasons for this high rate of failure was that the railroads had overextended once again. Unemployment was probably approaching 30 percent. Wage cuts were causing a rash of strikes as well, and the country declined further into a depression. The election year 1894 would be the darkest of the Panic. The unemployment in the old Whig nation and industrial areas was probably near 40 percent. Ohio was hit the worst, and workers rose up.

During what was considered the deepest depression before the 1930s, Jacob Sechler Coxey of Massillon, Ohio, formed the idea of a massive march on Washington to highlight the rising unemployment rates. Coxey had also run for Congress as a Populist candidate in the election of 1892. The depression had idled his mining operation in Ohio for months. Coxey hoped to form a Christian nation based on charity. He called also for an eight-hour day and a minimum wage of $1.50, as well as a national bond issue to support the unemployed. Coxey suggested a massive influx of money and public works for the unemployed, but it was the idea of a national march that struck fear in the heart of Congress.[3]

The idea of an army of tramps, socialists, and anarchists marching through the country struck a nerve with the nation. Politicians remembered the railroad worker revolt of 1877 and the more recent riots in Chicago and Homestead. Many believed the country was ripe for a socialist revolution like those seen in Europe. The concerns were further stirred by the Chicago press, which descended on Massillon, Ohio. While editorials denounced the march, the headlines promoted fear to move Congress. Money and support started to pour in from labor unions, Populists, and probably a few Republicans. In the midst of the Coxey cry, then governor William McKinley was dealing with an outbreak of worker violence. Coal miners from Stark County (including Massillon) were remnants of a settled national miners' strike. The strikers were attacking trains carrying coal into Ohio from West Virginia. Rails were being torn up, trains shot at, and bridges burned. McKinley summoned John McBride, the president of the United Mine Workers, to his office. McBride had noted he had "fourteen cannon pointed on one mine." His cajoling failed, and McKinley ordered a massive call-up of the National Guard. The show of overwhelming force ended the violence; one train alone carried 12 men and two Gatling guns.

The body of the march reportedly reached 20,000 in western Pennsylvania. Coxey and his "officers" rode horses at the front of the column as a band marched alongside. Hugh O'Donnell, one of the Homestead principals, led the way. Headlines seemed to rally more people from all parts of the country. Coxey's Ohio army roughly followed today's Route 30 to Pittsburgh. Towns offered food as the armies passed through. As the army reached Pittsburgh, it swelled to 300,000 in the city.[4]

Hobo towns lined the great railroads leading into Washington, and the streets were filled with beggars that joined the march. Immigrants living in tent cities struggled to stay warm and eat. The rich suburbs of Chicago, New York, Pittsburgh, Baltimore, and Washington lived in constant fear of looting or attack. Residents of these areas hired their own guards to protect their neighborhoods as the great march moved on. In Maryland, roads were muddy from a rainy spring, and the army bogged down. Food became scarce and towns less supportive. Mounted police had an easy time intimidating the weary army in Washington, D.C. Populists in Congress read Coxey's petitions, and a bill was unsuccessfully introduced in the Senate. The New Deal in the thirties would finally see many of Coxey's ideas implemented, and his march would be a model for the civil rights movement.

As Coxey marched on Washington, violence escalated in Ohio. McKinley worked hard to bring compromise and help. Still, he was forced to control riots in Cleveland and Akron. His work during the crisis won him national praise and renewed support from the workers.

The Panic of 1893 was nearing its peak in August as Coxey's army died out. The American Treasury's gold reserve was below the mandated level, forcing the government to borrow from other foreign governments. Without a Federal Reserve, the American government needed the help of big bankers like J. P. Morgan for money. The United States was approaching bankruptcy.

Grover Cleveland was secretly dealing with Morgan to put together a pool of banks by August.[5] Morgan would have to pool with the only other power remaining, the banking house of August Belmont. In all, 158 national banks failed, 177 private banks failed, 47 savings and loan associations failed, and 177 state banks suspended operations, representing America's greatest depression to that point. The new "Morgan-Belmont syndicate" would ultimately spare the United States from bankruptcy.[6] Morgan would gain the title of Pierpontifex Maximus for his diversion from trust building to save his nation's Treasury, but politically it was too late for the Democrats.

Violence would again erupt in Chicago in 1894. The once-hailed utopian Pullman Company and town would be the location of the breakout. The trouble started in June with a layoff of 3,000 of Pullman's 5,800 employees at the Chicago plant. In an effort to save jobs, George Pullman cut the wages of the remaining employees by 25 percent. At its peak, the strike would involve over 250,000 in 27 states and last three weeks. The violence resulted in the death of 13 strikers, the wounding of over 60 people, and property damage worth over $340,000 (about $9 million today). The strike was the effort of the American Railways Union headed by socialist Eugene Debs.[7]

George Pullman was labor friendly, but he was hardheaded and a poor communicator. Members of the American Railway Union asked that the rents in Pullman's worker town be reduced. Pullman ended up firing the union representatives, which brought union president Eugene V. Debs into the disagreement. Things escalated quickly to a strike, as Pullman announced a regular dividend to its stockholders. The strike slowly started to evolve along related railways, as three-quarters of the rails moving in and out of Chicago closed. The combination of rail lines was managed by the General Managers Association. The association had strong ties in the Cleveland administration as well as with J. P. Morgan, both of which would tie the Pullman strike to the Democrats.

President Cleveland got involved with hiring 3,600 special deputies, who had the full protection of the United States government. President Cleveland thought these hires were less offensive than sending in federal troops. The newspapers' initial support for President Cleveland was short-lived. Federal involvement inspired more rioting by the workers, and the strike started to spread across the country. Cleveland was forced to get an injunction against the strikers, who stood their ground against all troops and legal efforts.

Chicago began to attract socialists and anarchists to "help" out. Ray Baker, second-in-command of Coxey's army, showed up in Chicago. The country seemed split between fear and outrage. Pullman refused arbitration, but New York and other large cities supported him, characterizing the strike as an attack on society. As famous socialists and anarchists such as Emma Goldman joined the effort, many feared a rebellion in our large cities. The

John Sherman (1823–1900) in 1894. Sherman held the following offices: Republican representative from Ohio, 1855–1861; senator, 1861–1877, 1881–1897; U.S. secretary of the Treasury, 1877–1881. Retrieved from the Library of Congress, https://www.loc.gov/item/2004667569/. (Accessed June 23, 2017.)

timing was poor for the strikers, as the president of France had just been assassinated by an anarchist. Mark Hanna, however, supported the workers, calling Pullman a "damn idiot."[8] Hanna would be one of those to expose Pullman's utopia, which would help gain more support for Republicans and the presidential run of William McKinley in 1896. Pullman charged rents 25 percent higher than those in surrounding neighborhoods. In addition, he purchased water from Chicago at four cents per thousand gallons and sold to his town at ten cents. Emma Goldman would later inspire Leon Czolgosz, McKinley's future assassin. Goldman was an anarchist, socialist, Russian immigrant, and revolutionary.

Meanwhile in Ohio, Governor McKinley sat by as industrial activity further declined due to shortages created by the Pullman strike. McKinley would have forced arbitration, but his support was also with the strikers. Mayors from over fifty cities asked Pullman to accept arbitration. Samuel Gompers, one of the most enlightened labor leaders of the time, tried to mediate a settlement. He telegrammed President Cleveland only to have his assistance rejected. Cleveland commented, "If it takes the entire army and navy of the United States to deliver a postal card in Chicago, that card will be delivered."[9] Cleveland sent in 14,000 federal troops, and the anger now turned toward him. The strike ended, but the courts took over to revenge the upheaval. Cleveland and the Democrats were hurt badly with union voters as well as many business leaders. Workers looked once again to Ohio republicanism.

The result of the Pullman Strike would change the landscape of American politics. Eugene Debs was sentenced to six months in prison and would later form the American Socialist Party. The Sherman Antitrust Act was used to support the conviction, and the Supreme Court upheld its use against labor.[10] Socialists would oust Samuel Gompers as president of the American Federation of Labor. President Cleveland lost the support of his party and would be forced to run as a third-party candidate. The Democratic majority lay in ruins, and the elections of 1894 and 1896 would sweep in a Republican majority. William McKinley's stock boomed as a supporter of labor and prosperity.

While things were starting to improve for Republicans, another divide opened up among party members. Andrew Carnegie in 1894, in an effort to appease the Democratic administration of Grover Cleveland, wrote a letter to the *New York Tribune* supporting the reduction of the 1890 McKinley Tariff.[11] The Wilson-Gorman Tariff of 1894 would pass and lower tariffs. It was the first of many breaks in tariff philosophy by Carnegie. Carnegie's partner, Henry Clay Frick, was angered by Carnegie's willingness to trade capitalistic principles for political favors. Frick would look to 1896 with McKinley in mind.

The Wilson-Gorman Tariff of 1894 reduced the United States tariff rates of the 1890 McKinley Tariff and imposed a 2 percent income tax (which would be declared unconstitutional)[12] to replace revenue loss. The tariff is named for William L. Wilson, representative from West Virginia and chair of the U.S. House Ways and Means Committee, and Senator Arthur P. Gorman of Maryland, both Democrats. The Wilson-Gorman Tariff was a disaster for Americans, and even President Cleveland opposed it but in the end signed it.[13]

Cleveland was hopelessly damaged by the Pullman Strike, tariffs, and the economic depression. He lost donators and voters and finally his own party. Cleveland's relationship with J. P. Morgan and the gold standard had been a sore point with most inside Democrats. His enemies gained control of the Democratic Party in 1896, repudiated his administration and the gold standard, and nominated William Jennings Bryan on a silver platform. For the Republicans, Ohio republicanism had been vindicated, and William McKinley was being looked at as the answer for a return to American prosperity. The nation's brief flirtation with the Democrats' economic policy was over.

Chapter Twelve

Ohio Republicanism at the Summit

Of all the Ohio presidents, William McKinley was the face of Ohio republicanism. He was the linchpin of those that came before and after his presidency. It was under his leadership that the principles of Ohio republicanism were firmed up for the new century. It was under his watch that America became recognized as an industrial power. The United States overtook Britain as the world's largest producer of iron, steel, rubber, and electrical and railroad products. American steel-armored battleships would inflict a major blow to Spain's navy, putting it on equal footing with the British navy. America's new single electrical power plant at Niagara Falls could produce more electricity than the rest of world together. The nation had a huge industrial surplus and now looked to conquer international markets to conquer as it had done with agricultural products in prior decades. Industrial growth would replace the move west as America's Manifest Destiny. The state of Ohio would alone rank among the top five nations in industrial production.

McKinley's view of American industrialism was an evolutionary one deeply rooted in many Ohio politicians and workers. Even before the Continental Congress issued the Declaration of Independence, it passed a resolution for economic independence. John Adams urged in March 1776 "a society for the improvement of agriculture, arts, manufactures, and commerce, and to maintain a correspondence between such societies, that the rich and numerous natural advantages of this country, for supporting its inhabitants, may not be neglected."[1] Jefferson's agrarian society seemed to dominate after the Revolution until Henry Clay, Speaker of the House, developed the concept of national industrialism and capitalism called the American System. This idea was recognition that independence was as much economic as political. In the 1820s, Clay became the apostle of protectionism, which found popularity with America's growing manufacturing segment. He had a strong holding in Ohio, and a growing group of Clay Republicans continued to develop the philosophy of independence and national dominance through technology and industry. The Republican Convention of 1896 presented William McKinley, its presidential nominee, a well-deserved award. It was gavel carved from wood from Henry Clay's homestead and inscribed "The Father of Protection." Like John Adams, New Englanders seemed to expound McKinley's philosophy of economic and technological freedom. Writers like Emerson and Hawthorne found this new McKinley industrialism on a level with Jeffersonian ideals. These roots of technological innovation and economic freedom were at the heart of McKinley's dinner pail industrialism. The Jeffersonian ideal was applied to industrialism and strengthened through nationalism.

William McKinley would arrive at the Republican Convention in 1896 as the people's favorite. But he lacked support from the eastern political bosses, who believed the 1890 and 1892 elections had ended Ohio republicanism. The combine of eastern bosses was a fearful thing. It included Thomas Platt, who controlled everything in New York that Democratic Tammany Hall didn't. Platt was tough and old line, with a history of using his power in the state to control national elections. New York had the biggest bloc of votes at the convention. Platt had a strong relationship with New York bankers such as J. P. Morgan. New York boss Levi Morton was a protégé of Platt. Morton was governor of New York and a banker, and he had been Harrison's vice president. Philadelphia boss Matthew Quay controlled Pennsylvania in a similar fashion and opposed McKinley. Speaker of the House Thomas Reed rounded out the great eastern combine against Ohio republicanism. In the end, Reed and Quay remained favorite sons at the convention and did not pull their votes, but that was probably due to a realization that it was hopeless to do so. These eastern bosses were the main part of the combine, but there were others, such as Russell Alger of Michigan and Senator William Allison of Iowa, who opposed McKinley. Mark Hanna, perceived as a boss himself, put together an anti-boss midwestern strategy.

These bosses supported tariffs generally but feared Ohio protectionism went too far, incorrectly basing this belief on the 1890 and 1892 election results. The gold standard was much closer to their hearts because it linked them with the big bankers. Eastern bosses and bankers wanted the gold standard, but McKinley was not fully convinced and preferred a sound money policy that was open to a mix of silver and gold. McKinley's position on gold had evolved over the years. He had believed in bimetallism as the best compromise for the middle class, farmers, and laborers. However, the global operations of banking and the government by the 1890s did change things. McKinley became convinced that the country needed an international agreement on bimetallism, and that the government should stay with the gold standard until that agree-

President William McKinley (left) and others posing in an open automobile with mountains and rustic structure in the background, 1897. Library of Congress.

ment was reached. McKinley also saw that the country's best productivity occurred from 1882 to 1890 under the gold standard. The idea was to hold steady and try for an international agreement on bimetallism, something that was unlikely. This somewhat vague and middle-of-the-road approach allowed McKinley to avoid the issue. McKinley's view was Ohio republicanism, which was a middle-class approach to American industrialism.

Thomas Platt, boss of the Pennsylvania political machine, was a tough opponent of McKinley. Platt confidently stated: "My opposition to Governor McKinley proceeds almost entirely from my belief that his nomination would bring the Republican party into turmoil and trouble.... McKinley represents the most radical extreme view of protection. I foresee the greatest dangers to the Republican Party as the result of extreme tariff legislation.... He voted once for the free and unlimited coinage of silver.... This should remove McKinley from the list of Presidential possibilities."[2] Platt soon realized that the rank and file was solidly behind McKinley in the urban and industrial areas. McKinley's anti-boss campaign would come back to haunt him in the general election.

More problematic was J. P. Morgan, who was the gold anchor for the Republican Party. The struggle between McKinley and J. P. Morgan remains controversial. It appears now that McKinley's advisor, Myron Herrick, met with Morgan in New York prior to the Republican National Convention.[3] At the meeting, Morgan said he found McKinley's waffling on gold nauseating. Morgan had no time for compromise, but many argued the problem could split the party. J. P. Morgan, for one of the few times in his career, didn't hold all the cards, but he had nowhere to go. The Democrats were the worst case of free silver. In addition, they were making a scandal out of the gold settlement between President Cleveland and Morgan.[4] Mark Hanna, however, wanted full financial backing, and he had Herrick set up a meeting on Morgan's yacht, the *Corsair* (this was Hanna's first ever meeting with Morgan). According to Morgan's biographer Jean Strouse, Hanna reached a deal with Morgan prior to the convention. Later, it was suggested that McKinley submit a draft of the platform to Morgan for his approval or suggestions.[5] Election chronicler Stanley Jones confirms that Morgan was given a copy of the platform stand, but Morgan's response came too late for the convention.[6]

McKinley's preconvention campaign was based on his strength in Ohio—tariffs. He avoided his silver critics in the West and gold critics in the East with sound money. Hanna flooded the nation with sound money pamphlets. The Democrats had turned to free silver and turned against President Cleveland's support of gold. In an effort to save his presidency, Cleveland then turned on the gold standard. The Republicans were more split on the issue, the West for silver, the East for gold, and the Midwest for bimetallism. Democrats' shift to free silver left eastern Republicans with few choices. McKinley believed tariffs and sound money would work. He was counting on the industrial workers and conservative farmers of the Midwest. In the East, it would be the industrial workers that would provide support. Hanna even believed they might carry the Upper South. Even with a convention victory in hand, both McKinley and Hanna realized the eastern moneymen would have to be pacified. McKinley also had gold supporters in his own organization, such as Charles Dawes. Furthermore, the first-tier capitalists such as Andrew Carnegie and Henry Clay Frick were demanding a gold standard. McKinley first looked to winning the nomination, hoping he could then compromise on gold from a position of strength. J. P. Morgan presented another problem to McKinley. Morgan didn't have a strong opinion on protective tariffs. He had not yet formed his steel trust in the 1890s, and he made more money on imports than exports. Morgan had allies on the matter of lower tariffs in the East Coast shipping industries. McKinley and Ohio republicanism had the popular votes for tariffs, but money was going to be an issue.

Even before Harrison withdrew from the race in early 1896, McKinley's strongest opponent was Speaker Thomas Reed. Reed was the candidate of the eastern Republicans and party bosses, and he had the support of powerful party members such as Henry Cabot Lodge. Reed's backing of gold also gained him approval from the eastern bankers, who looked at McKinley as "Wobblie Willie" on gold. Reed was from Maine, which he could count on for solid support; but New England industrial centers were his weakness. Thomas Reed had strong financial support outside of his section. He had the initial backing of Henry Clay Frick in Pittsburgh and of Pennsylvania boss Matthew Quay. Hanna focused a publicity and literature campaign for McKinley in these areas, deciding to battle up from the rank and file. The eastern bosses, however, saw Hanna as an amateur. He focused on the eastern industrial centers where McKinley's tariff had made him near unbeatable. For example, Hanna took cities like Pittsburgh away from Quay, whose real strength was eastern Pennsylvania. Boston delegates went for McKinley over boss Reed of New England. Hanna's plan worked, and by April, Reed's support was weakening. Hanna's educational approach was different, but it worked against political machines. This preconvention success of Hanna's shocked the bosses, who felt unbeatable on their home turf. Political bosses started to hedge their bets with a possible dark horse—Levi Morton, the governor of New York. McKinley's ground support, however, seemed to be everywhere.

The silver Republicans in the Midwest and West supported William Allison of Iowa, who had a strong record on silver. In reality, Allison was a bimetallist, and many believed that the eastern bosses might support him in the end. President Harrison publicly remained neutral, but he was no friend of McKinley's and privately favored Allison. Allison had some support from the Chicago bosses, who were extremely anti–McKinley. But in boss-controlled Cook County, McKinley's grassroots supporters put fear in the party leaders. The main driver in Chicago and Illinois was young businessman and McKinley believer Charles Dawes. McKinley had captured the youth like no politician before. What these loyalists lacked in experience they made up in enthusiasm. In the end, the bosses' combine counted for only 239 convention votes compared to McKinley's 400 plus.

Mark Hanna tried to appease the silver Republicans in the West by suggesting McKinley was a bimetallist and would still remain open to some arrangement on silver. Senator Teller of Colorado read the minority report calling for bimetallism. However, the gold plank was upheld with an 818–105 vote. A number of silver Republicans left for the door, but Hanna would work behind the scenes to bring them back. Back in Canton, McKinley had a war room at his rented house on Market and Eighth Street (where the McKinleys had lived 25 years earlier). The library had a telephone and a special telegraph set up to communicate with Hanna at the convention. Ida was in the sitting room with Mother McKinley, while McKinley manned the library. A mass of reporters was on the porch, and McKinley would appear from time to time to talk to them. Canton residents were at the offices of the *Canton Repository* newspaper listening to news bulletins as the convention approached a vote. The city fathers had a number of company bands ready for the moment of McKinley's nomination.

As the balloting started, McKinley's telephone hookup allowed him to hear the activity on the floor. Alabama started the vote with one for Morton and 19 for McKinley. McKinley steadily built a lead as the vote progressed. Iowa broke the trend with all 26 votes going to Allison, and New York went for Morton. It would be Ohio that put McKinley over the mark. McKinley rose to go to the next room and inform Ida and his mother. The bands began to play, and the crowds moved toward the McKinley residence. The final vote was McKinley 666; Thomas Reed, 84; Senator Quay, 61; Levi Morton, 58; and Senator Allison, 35. Senator Lodge called to make it unanimous, and the decision was approved.[7] Finally, Garret Hobart (1844–1899) of New Jersey was nominated for vice president. Hanna had selected Hobart to add geographical balance without necessarily having an eastern boss surrogate. As trains arrived from the nearby cities of Massillon and Alliance, the crowd swelled to 50,000. McKinley would also make his first "front porch speech" of the campaign.[8]

McKinley owed much of his national success to the innovative advisor Mark Hanna. Hanna proved to be the model for campaign managers. He used new polling techniques, albeit primitive ones, to monitor the pulse of voters, especially in states he thought could swing either way. Hanna produced over 200 million pamphlets, newspaper inserts, and other pieces of literature when there were only 14 million voters in the United States. Much of these materials were issue oriented and targeted to particular market segments such as German Americans or black voters. Hanna hired and dispatched 1,400 surrogate speakers to spread a unified Republican message. His success with big-business donors had its roots in Ohio and western Pennsylvania. Hanna also applied the telephone and telegraph to support the political infrastructure.

Hanna showed adeptness in healing the party for the national election. First, Hanna and McKinley mended the differences with Speaker Reed and turned him into a stump campaigner. Hanna and Reed started to turn the psychology in the East to a positive confidence. Hanna met secretly with boss Platt of New York. With McKinley's approval, Hanna agreed that Platt would run the machine in New York.[9] Furthermore, McKinley met with Matthew Quay of Pennsylvania in Canton in an effort to improve relations. Improved dealings with the eastern bosses, Hanna's cheerleading, and a mounting fear of gold-supporting Democratic nominee Bryan finally opened the purses of Andrew Carnegie, Henry Frick, J. P. Morgan, and John Rockefeller in amounts of $250,000. Estimates were that Hanna raised over $4 million from the East, and it would be needed since expenditures of the Chicago office alone were over $3.5 million, mostly in literature and pamphlets. Rockefeller kicked in over $250,000 as Hanna requested.

Bryan used the whistle-stop train approach to national campaigning. McKinley followed Garfield's front porch campaign but perfected it with the help of Hanna. Delegations and groups numbering from hundreds to thousands came in endless streams to thousands to Canton, Ohio, via train. McKinley's neighbors organized the "Home Guard," horse-mounted guides at the train station. Civil War veterans joined the "Guard" in large numbers to escort delegations, control traffic, and ride ahead to alert McKinley's staff. The McKinley aides were well prepared by Mark Hanna with names, personal details, and hometown statistics. Bands were directed to play the appropriate regional song, such as "Dixie" for southerners. In addition, campaign songs were written to promote protection and prosperity. McKinley and Hanna readied variants of speech themes to address regional concerns. While McKinley was briefed by Hanna to be able to speak informally with the members of the delegation, McKinley himself prepared his more formal speeches. Other speakers were enlisted, and writers drafted material with a final review from McKinley. One day alone, McKinley gave nine speeches. Hanna would set up food tents to feed and entertain large delegations.

The delegations represented workers, trade associations, unions, companies, and sometimes even cities. Hanna lined up big business to pay the fare for workers. Pittsburgh steel and coal delegations flooded Canton on one September day. Moreover, steelworkers from Pittsburgh mills were a common sight throughout the campaign. Trains were set up routinely by the Pennsylvania Railroad, and commercial travelers often found themselves in Canton. Daily crowd totals at the train stations often ran as high as 20,000 to 40,000 supporters. In the meantime Bryan's whistle-stop campaign was bogged down with commercial train schedules; he only got his own railcar at the end of the campaign. Still, Bryan's crowds were massive for the times. If McKinley was struck by the audiences that turned out for Bryan's whistle-stop speeches, Bryan must have feared the sight of laborers pouring into Canton, Ohio.

Hanna proved a true visionary in campaigning. Historian Lawrence Goodwin notes: "In sheer depth, the advertising campaign organized by Mark Hanna in behalf of William McKinley was without parallel in American history. It set the creative standard for the twentieth century."[10] Hanna was one of the first to use political polls, and their use helped him identify an early boom for Bryan. He was also the first to use the telephone extensively, paying for lines where needed. Hanna used news summaries to stay informed on editorial comment. Never before had literature been used so successfully in a campaign. Earlier elections had focused on political stump speakers, but Hanna found pamphlets to be almost as effective. Later in the campaign, public opinion polls clearly defined tariffs as the issue in the Midwest, silver in the West, and gold in the East. Hanna organized his strategy accordingly. He used the millowners and managers to get the pamphlets in the hands of workers. The tariff issue played well with the industrial workers, and pamphlets allowed the campaign to focus on local color, such as by printing materials in German.

Hanna used the religious roots of Ohio republicanism to bring in mainstream religions, including the Democratic-leaning Catholics. Like the old Ohio College of Teachers, McKinley's Republicanism welcomed Catholics into the ideology's moral foundation. While Bryan spoke with the fire of a preacher, mainstream religions trended for McKinley. Catholic leaders feared anarchy and socialism were expressed in the preaching of Bryan. The fact that socialists like Eugene Debs and Edward Bellamy campaigned for Bryan seemed to confirm their suspicions. McKinley's middle-class values crossed all religious lines, and his fairness in appointing government workers regardless of their faith paid dividends. McKinley had a proven record of ecumenicalism, and it was part of the overall "McKinley Realignment."[11] McKinley consistently saw civil rights, equality, and upward mobility as the cornerstones of prosperity. He had strong support from midwestern Catholic bishops, such as Bishop Elder of Cincinnati, Bishop Horstmann of Cleveland, and Bishop Ireland of St. Paul. While a Mason and a devout Protestant, McKinley carried as much as 45 percent of the Catholic vote. Presbyterians and Methodists were strong McKinley supporters as well, and so were German Lutheran farmers, for whom Ohio republicanism's moral base trumped the tariff issue. McKinley proved stronger at bringing farmers to his side than Bryan did in garnering workers' support. A large part of McKinley's success owed to religious values anchored in Ohio republicanism.

The McKinley election of 1896 saw the old roots of abolition surface as support for civil rights for blacks. McKinley also promoted the civil rights plank of Ohio republicanism, which cost him in the South but strengthened him in old Transylvania. McKinley's belief in the need for full civil rights for blacks centered on their fighting during the Civil War.[12] He stated of black service in the war, "they enlisted in our armies and were made soldiers ... they served with distinction in the field, they marched, countermarched, and fought side by side with white soldiers. They were not only soldiers, but see the service they rendered as guides to our armies, as spies to the enemy's camp, and the greatness of all their kindness, sympathy, and assistance to our soldiers' attempting to escape from the prison hells of the south. I tell you there was nothing else to recommend them their services alone should be sufficient."[13] McKinley fought hard to ensure equal treatment for black veterans feeling anything less was un-American. He might have fallen short of the mark politically, but never personally. In southern cities, he changed hotels if management refused to allow blacks to meet with him on the premises. McKinley reignited the civil rights issue that had been at the foundation of the Republican Party and Ohio republicanism. His strong defense of civil rights stirred the old party abolitionists to his side.

McKinley went to vote early on Election Day morning, November 3, in Canton's First Ward. He and Hanna were confident of victory at this point, and McKinley was said to have chain-smoked cigars into the early morning as he awaited returns. By 4:00 a.m. on November 4, 1896, the results showed the greatest presidential victory since Grant's. McKinley got 7,101,401 popular votes and 271 electoral votes to Bryan's 6,470,656 popular votes and 176 electoral votes. McKinley carried the Eastern and Middle Atlantic states, where his labor alliance carried the day. The South and West went to Bryan, but McKinley took the battleground states of the Great Lakes and Upper South (parts of old Transylvania). These states showed McKinley's strength with midwestern farmers by carrying Ohio, Indiana, Iowa, Michigan, Minnesota, and Wisconsin. In the prior election, Grover Cleveland had carried the Midwest, so McKinley's success was hailed as a new realignment. However, Grover Cleveland, while a Democrat, was close to the principles of Ohio republicanism.

McKinley enjoyed a great victory, but there were some disappointments. He carried Ohio by only 48,494 votes (a smaller margin than in Wisconsin and Illinois), and he lost South Dakota by 200 votes and Wyoming by 300. McKinley's effort in the South also fell a bit short, losing him Virginia, North Carolina, and Tennessee by 19,000 votes. He probably would have won all three states had full black voting been allowed. While McKinley carried the industrial immigrant vote, he failed to crack the hold of Tammany Hall on the Irish ballots in the East. However, he did break the Democratic farm alliance. The Republicans took the House as well and established a majority in the Senate. McKinley had proved his protectionism was the will of the people, and he now faced the difficult task of turning the economy around.

The McKinley realignment was really an extension of the 1894 elections, but McKinley also built the labor alliance and broke the farm alliance. This new arrangement brought together the middle class and rising lower class from all regions and occupations. Every state of old Transylvania labeled as part of this new realignment, with the exception of Kentucky, would remain Republican until 1912. McKinley had a simple message of prosperity, equal rights, civil rights, and nationalism. Historians talk about the battle of ideas, but McKinley knew it was the economy and equality of opportunity, not the methodology, mattered to voters. An election was a vote for capitalism versus socialism, which Bryan represented. Labor wanted better conditions and more money, but jobs and employment had to come first. McKinley realized from his own family experience that what workers feared most was unemployment. His victory heralded the end of the People's, or Populist, Party, which never again was challenged at the national level. McKinley was a populist because he was of the middle class and understood it. He saw the link between labor and capital that Ohio republicanism was all about. McKinley had demonstrated his labor support early on with the miners, and they never forgot it. He did the same with Catholics and blacks. America and its principles were always put first, and McKinley became synonymous with the American flag. He had avoided scandals and was a member of the middle class that loved him. He had built a foundation for decades of Republican Party and Ohio republicanism dominance.

McKinley's actual first term ran according to plan as the economy boomed, and America became the industrial leader of the world. McKinley had campaigned solely on domestic issues, but foreign problems quickly became part of the administration's focus. Cuba had been a mounting difficulty for a decade as rebels called for freedom from Spain. The issue of Hawaiian annexation had surfaced first in the tariff debate in Congress because of the islands' strategic position in American trade and sugar production. Furthermore, the Hawaiian Islands were the stopping and coal refueling point between Japan and California. Reciprocity trade agreements with Hawaii dated back to the Grant administration. American merchants and businessmen saw Hawaii as a key to commerce in the Pacific. Germany and Japan also started to use Hawaii, and fears rose of rivalries between navies. Republicans under President Harrison had pushed for annexation, but the effort died under the Cleveland administration. In 1896, the issue was put back in the Republican platform. McKinley fell short of pushing the Hawaiian annexation until the Spanish-American War.

Action on the Spanish-controlled island of Cuba, however, was being pushed on McKinley from all fronts. The press, led by Hearst in the West, was constantly running stories of Americans being beaten and tortured in Spanish Cuba. Thus Americans supported the rebel cause to overthrow what appeared to be oppressive Spanish rule. McKinley was trying to hold down expansionists in his party just as eastern Republicans, Henry Cabot Lodge and Teddy Roosevelt, were following the drumbeat of the press toward war. The expansionist drive had really started under the Harrison administration with the rebuilding of the American navy and growth of the merchant marine. Economic pressure was also building for expanded trade in the Pacific as a means of relieving production surplus. The Republican and Democratic Parties had called for support for Cuban independence in the elections. McKinley came into office with all ingredients in the pot being stirred. Annexation offered no problem for him, but he fiercely opposed war or use of the military.

Early 1898 brought more problems; rebel violence increased in Cuba, and the insurgents tried to pull the United States into the struggle. In early

February, Hearst's yellow press published a letter from a Spanish minister calling McKinley a weak abider for the admiration of the crowd. Then on February 15, 1898, the American warship *Maine* was blown up in Havana Harbor. McKinley again kept his powder dry, as the press screamed for the United States to take action with headlines like "Remember the Maine." A naval commission was assigned to inquire into the nature of the explosion. The source of the blast remains unknown to this day, but the press and public assumed it was Spanish loyalists. McKinley did everything to avoid war, even trying to buy Cuba. McKinley negotiated with Spain until April 11, when he sent a war message to Congress. In the meantime, McKinley sent an ultimatum to Spain for an end to its control over Cuba. War was declared on April 24 (it was backdated to April 21).

The declaration caught Spain a bit off guard. Spain was 5,000 miles from Cuba, but its fleet was even farther away, tied up in another insurrection in the Spanish Philippines. While sizable, the Spanish Navy lacked firepower and included many obsolete ships. America, on the other hand, had a new and retooled navy. In addition, the main American fleet was ideally located in Japan, thanks to the foresight of assistant secretary of the navy Teddy Roosevelt. Roosevelt had sent the ships there to be close to the Spanish main fleet in the Philippines, just in case. The American army faced a much different problem; it only had 28,000 soldiers, while the Spanish had 155,000 soldiers in Cuba alone. A call went out immediately for volunteers, and 200,000 poured into the army. The press had created a surge in nationalism.

McKinley ordered the navy to attack the Spanish fleet in the Philippines as Spain launched another fleet toward Cuba. Admiral Dewey and the American fleet engaged the Spanish at Manila Bay on May 1, 1898. Within five hours, every Spanish ship was sunk, and 381 Spaniards were killed. The victory was a triumph for American steel-armored ships, which had cut down the Spanish wooden ones. The vessels' steel armor was a product of the Homestead Steel Works. On May 19, the other Spanish fleet reached Santiago, Cuba. Here the Americans blockaded the ships as they prepared to mount a land attack on Cuba. United States troops landed on June 30, proceeded on two fronts, and quickly won two battles. Teddy Roosevelt's volunteers, known as the Rough Riders, made a name for themselves. The Spanish fleet, sensing defeat, made a run for it on July 3. Subsequently, the American fleet quickly engaged and destroyed every Spanish ship, killing 474 Spaniards. The Spanish Army surrendered on July 17 in Cuba, then in Guam Island and Wake Island in the Pacific. Insurgents took Manila in late July, and the war was over.

America's attack on the Spanish fleet was the type of war that armchair commanders dream of—quick and flashy victories with low casualties. The war lasted less than four months and resulted in only 385 battle-related deaths, although 2,500 additional soldiers died of disease after the August cease-fire!

The peace treaty in December forced Spain to give up Cuba, Puerto Rico, Guam, Wake Island, and the Philippines. The United States offered $20 million to cover property damages, and the injury to Spain's national pride.

In the fears of another war, McKinley successfully pushed Congress to annex Hawaii. The war's political impact on McKinley was probably more positive than negative. Secretary of War Russell Alger took some of the heat out of the medical crisis that cost so many nonbattle causalities. McKinley replaced him with Elihu Root, a moderate on expansion and a man of solid administrative skills. Root's appointment helped calm anti-imperialists for the short term. McKinley was able to convince labor interests, including opponents like Samuel Gompers and the American Federation of Labor, that he was not planning to import cheap workers from the Philippines.

While the war had little effect on the booming economy and Republicans feared backlash against the poor management of the troops, nationalism overwhelmed all issues. The midterm elections defied the usual swing against the incumbents. Republicans increased seats in the Senate and held a majority of 53 to 36. In the House, they lost a few seats but held a majority of 185 to 163. McKinley tried to take some short vacations as a rest, but the problem of the Philippines dogged him. The Filipinos resisted the American occupation for over three years. While not considered a war or part of the Spanish-American War, this period of fighting resulted in 4,230 American casualties.

Chapter Thirteen

McKinley's Final Days and the Setting of a Vision

McKinley's popularity continued to increase during his first term. He remained consistent on trade and tariffs while looking to find ways to increase exports, such as by expanding the merchant marine and committing to the Panama Canal. Ohio was where cornfields surrounded steel mills and Wall Street finance clashed into western speculation. Ohio bimetallism was sandwiched between the East Coast gold standard to prevent inflation and the western silver standard to support growth. With other Ohio Republicans, McKinley forged a gold standard within a silver-equivalent framework known as buckeye bimetallism. He worked with western Democrats to pass the Sherman Silver Purchase Act of 1890 as a compromise. McKinley's bimetallism would help him win some of the Border States in the presidential elections of 1896, which had voted Republican. He approached the election of 1900 with the wind behind him.

The McKinley decade of 1890–1900 speaks for his popularity. Statistics for these years support the conclusion that prices came down, profits rose, capital investment went up, and wages held or slightly increased (real wages clearly rose). Average annual manufacturing income went from $425.00 a year and $1.44 a day in 1890 to $432.00 a year and $1.50 a day in 1900. The average day in manufacturing remained around ten hours long, but inroads were made for a national eight-hour day. Heavily protected industries such as steel fared slightly better with wages. The cost-of-living index fell during the decade from 91 to 84, or about 8 percent. The clothing cost of living dropped even more from 134 to 108, or 19 percent. Food stayed about the same, but the cost of protected sugar dropped around 25 percent. The bottom line is that the real wage (adjusted for cost of living) index rose from $1.58 a day to $1.77 a day in 1900, or about a 12 percent increase. The success of this period of managed trade depended on government oversight, business cooperation, and labor support. Steel production went from 1.3 million tons in 1880 to 11.2 million tons in 1900 to 28.3 million tons in 1910. In 1898, the American steel industry surpassed Britain in pig iron production. The U.S. gross national product grew from an estimated $11.0 billion in 1880 to $18.7 billion in 1890 to $35.3 billion in 1910. The American glass industry was another struggling industry in 1880. Due to imports by 1910, the glass industry had increased its output five- to tenfold. During the peak tariff years of 1896 to 1901 under President McKinley, steel production increased 111 percent, electrical equipment production increased 271 percent, and farm equipment production increased 149 percent. During the same period wages increased 10 percent and employment 20 percent. Maybe just as important was a belief in American exceptionalism and healthy nationalism.

The stock market rose 70 percent from 1896 to 1899. The government ran a surplus, and in 1899, exports were double the amount of total imports. McKinley won both national elections by a wide margin. His coattails carried the Republican Party, controlling both houses and winning both midterm elections. The Republicans held or captured all the nonsouthern governorships as well. The only comparable electoral revolution was that of Franklin Roosevelt's New Deal. McKinley would unite and define the heart of Ohio republicanism.

Consumerism, coupled with protected industries, allowed for the rise in the middle class. Consumer-driven industries, such as all textile makers, employed 112,900 in 1890 and 324,000 in 1900. The leather industry employed 6,000 in 1890 and 13,200 in 1900. Even more dramatic, foundries and machine shops employed 15,500 in 1889 and 145,400 in 1899. The depth of this economic boom was nothing short of amazing—the consumer market of America was the greatest in the world. The upward spiral of factories and consumers built a middle class that was rich compared to that in most countries.

McKinley defined Ohio republicanism as American-centric trade, civil rights, government reform, job creation and full employment. His policy was America first in trade deals. To this end, McKinley applied a scientific approach balancing import tariffs with reciprocity. The approach protected jobs, expanded industry, held consumer prices steady, and prevented profiteering.

It's not a small point that managed trade of the McKinley type can be abused as capitalism itself. Such commerce success depended on American capitalists' reinvesting in American plants, not pocketing profits. McKinley's establishment of a permanent congressional Tariff Commission to ensure that profits went to job creation was the heart and genius of his system. Early in 1882, Congressman William McKinley, also the chairman of Ways and Means, had formed a review board in Congress to access the ongoing impact of the tariffs. This oversight and limited regulation was the final piece of the puzzle, preventing the abuses many feared. McKinley had taken the trade policies of Clay and Lincoln, making them the cornerstone of the party until 1930.

McKinley's basic belief in the American System was deeply personal. He was not a friend of the robber barons or the New York bankers of the time, even though many tried to tie him to them. J. P. Morgan had reluctantly financially backed McKinley, but he feared the candidate's weak commitment to the gold standard. Morgan also favored free trade and supported Democrat Glover Cleveland. Moreover, McKinley believed that government should act more as a referee than as a judge or law enforcement arm. His vice president (in his second campaign) Teddy Roosevelt had a much different view. He believed in trust-busting and favored lower tariff trade. J. P. Morgan believed he could control Roosevelt on trusts and use him on trade issues.

McKinley's dream of an industrial empire had come true by 1900. It was followed by a rise in patriotism and nationalism with the victory in the Spanish-American War. Americans were proud of their economic might. One magazine deemed it "Almost incredible that we should be sending cutlery to Sheffield, pig iron to Birmingham. Silks to France, watch cases to Switzerland ... or building sixty locomotives for British railroads."[1] National pride and consumer confidence could be seen everywhere. Production was at record levels, and prices had fallen. Our exports were at record levels as well. Our art reflected our industrial empire. Free traders and silverites were both at a loss as to how tariffs had led to such an economic boom. Had McKinley found the Rosetta stone to the economy? Even today economists scramble for reasons to avoid crediting scientific tariffs, yet the McKinley boom had delivered the full dinner pail and more. McKinley's biggest problem was how to sustain the boom. The issue of large trusts was just starting to be seen in the headlines in the early 1900s.

In his 1900 annual address in January, McKinley addressed head on the growing problem of trusts: "Combinations of capital organized into trusts to control the conditions of trade among our citizens, to strike competition, limit production, and determine the prices of products used and consumed by the people, are justly provoking public discussion, and should early claim the attention of Congress.... There must be a remedy for the evils involved in such organizations. If the present law can be extended more certainly to control or check these monopolies or trusts, it should be done without delay. Whatever power the Congress possesses over this most important subject should be properly ascertained and asserted."[2]

The rise of the trusts was not a fully unexpected event. McKinley had studied the problem for years, as tariff critics had used it since the 1880s to attack legislation. However, the real rise of problematic trusts occurred in the last months of the 1890s and the early 1900s. Though public attention through most of the 1890s was sporadic, McKinley, Dawes, and Hanna anticipated the problems. McKinley's comptroller of the currency and campaign manager, Charles Dawes, noted the following about a March 28, 1899, meeting: "I talked over the matter of the unprecedented growth of trusts with the President and the position in reference to them and their evil tendencies which our party should assume. He told me he expected to call the attention of Congress to the matter in his next message and would lead the movement for their proper restriction."[3] Dawes and McKinley had a number of conversations in early 1899, and McKinley did follow up with his address to Congress that year. The president, however, did not see trusts as systematically evil. In his mind, they could just as easily be good. He was slow to move, in any case, seeing some value to the overall economy. As the combinations increased, McKinley tried to put public pressure on their behavior, but the matter would become a point of an attack by the Democrats in the upcoming elections. The formation of United States Steel took the headlines in 1900, creating new interest by the press. In addition, the popular press had taken up the idea of antitrust legislation in late 1898. The Republican platform of 1900 took on the trusts, stating that the Republicans favored legislation that would effectually restrain and prevent all such abuses.

McKinley did not wait for the summer platform for the 1900 election to address the issue of trust abuse. Instead, he pushed Congress to hold hearings and establish an industrial commission. Unlike Roosevelt, who followed him, McKinley did not see a role for the executive in attacking the trusts or using aggressive legal action. McKinley did discuss his role with his attorney general to review the available legal recourse. Attorney General John Griggs felt the Sherman Antitrust Law of 1890 had little application in this case; the 1895 Supreme Court ruling (*United States vs. E. C. Knight*) had determined that legal action required both the monopoly of manufacture and a monopoly of interstate commerce. Griggs felt the ruling even prevented action against Standard Oil. McKinley, who adopted a minimal legal policy and opted for a legislative strategy, accepted Griggs's advice.

The Republican Convention found a strong and popular president in the White House with McKinley, but the question was the vice presidency. Vice President Hobart had died in November, so there were new opportunities for up-and-coming Republicans. Teddy Roosevelt was popular with the rank and file and had the support of some key easterners such as Senator Henry Cabot Lodge. Also, eastern machine bosses like Senator Platt wanted him out of New York. McKinley didn't really want Roosevelt, but he remained neutral and at odds with Hanna, who wanted nothing to do with Roosevelt. Corporate interests feared Roosevelt's antitrust stand and threatened to withhold campaign support. Hanna therefore tried to mount several anti-

Roosevelt efforts against the wishes of McKinley. Though Hanna was national chairman, the pre-campaign state of affairs was not what it had been in 1896. The bosses again had control.

Hanna became obsessed with keeping the "damn cowboy" away from the White House. McKinley rebuked him a couple of times, but he persisted and split the administration's cabinet. Charles Dawes became concerned about this division. Hanna worked directly with Roosevelt to get him to pull out, but the draft movement on the convention floor was huge. Finally, McKinley had to be perfectly clear with Hanna by telephone. After the conversation with the president, Hanna angrily stated: "McKinley won't let me use the power of the administration to defeat Roosevelt. He is blind, or afraid, or something."[4] The politics were complex, but bosses like Tom Platt and Mathew Quay actually did care personally for Roosevelt; they just didn't want him in New York politics. McKinley had always been willing to accept the will of the Republican Convention, so he brought Roosevelt in with grace. McKinley was much more interested in directing the platform. Again, Hanna and McKinley had differences, with Hanna wanting a more positive framing of trusts. McKinley was clear that he was going to take on abuses of certain trusts, and he wanted campaign policy to reflect that approach.

The arguments and differences of McKinley and Hanna are interesting. They clearly show that McKinley was in charge and that their disagreements were not great. Hanna might have even seen Roosevelt as a long-term threat to his own future run for the presidency. McKinley didn't care for Roosevelt, but he didn't care for playing political boss either. Roosevelt was also given a free rein by McKinley to attack the abuses of trusts in his speeches. As to the trusts, Hanna had come to see the positive side much like J. P. Morgan had. Hanna didn't care for the trusts' methods, but he had, years earlier, seen no way to prevent their growth. Still, his reasoning that trusts were a natural outgrowth of prosperity was really hopeful thinking. He had agreed with McKinley that abuses existed. Thus Hanna was a friend and a loyalist who did what he could to give McKinley the platform he wanted.

The Democrats went back to Bryan as their candidate almost conceded the election. Apathy remained a problem for McKinley, while Bryan searched for an issue to attack him on. Bryan probed the silver issue of the 1896 election in a western campaign swing and found no interest, even in the silver states of old. The economy was just too good for both the urban and rural areas. Bryan found some interest in the trusts, especially in the large cities; but Socialist Party candidate Eugene Debs was more likely to get most of these votes. Labor unrest and strikes were building, but it was too soon for great public concern. Bryan did hold the South by opposing black civil rights. America's continuing military involvement in the Philippines and the mounting death toll could have been possible if he could have garnered the support of the press. Amazingly, the death toll of over 4,000 American soldiers was lost to history because of journalists' lack of interest. Press giants such as Pulitzer and Hearst were imperialists who downplayed the Philippine Insurrection. Imperialism struck a note, but it never overcame the McKinley prosperity. In addition, the nation as a whole was a bit more to the imperialist side. Andrew Carnegie and Grover Cleveland had formed an Anti-Imperialist League to counter McKinley, but it never really mounted a serious threat to McKinley's campaign, except for Carnegie's money. Money was the least of McKinley's problems, even without Carnegie, as the Republican fundraising machine was unstoppable. McKinley even stunned Rockefeller by returning $50,000 of unused funds.

McKinley basically stayed at home, not launching a front porch campaign as he had in 1896. Roosevelt and Hanna did most of the canvassing, and McKinley assigned future president William Taft to manage the territory of the Philippines and calm concern. The Taft Commission report in September was very positive, and it took the wind out of the sails of Bryan's attack on the war. Hanna did seem to tire of his role, and disagreements between him and McKinley were common. Roosevelt was a huge asset, as crowds came to see him and his touring Rough Riders. Roosevelt's enthusiasm seemed driven by his belief that he would be the presidential candidate in 1904. People began to joke about Bryan's chasing any cause to become president. Hanna mounted a special train campaign and turned out bigger crowds than Bryan, who had made whistle-stop campaigns famous. Most Republicans were confident that nothing could beat the McKinley prosperity.

Hanna took no chances, however, mounting an expanded publicity campaign. He refined his news releases, sending 2 million of them to 5,000 newspapers each week! In total, he published 125 million documents and sent out 21 million postcards. Hanna also mastered the concept of segmenting the vote. His organization had departments to focus on voting blocs such as German Americans, Catholics, blacks, organized labor, unorganized labor, farmers, and Protestants. In addition, he printed documents in German and Polish for the nationality papers in cities like Chicago. This effort dwarfed the document campaign of 1896. Speakers were in the traditional campaign mode, and Hanna organized over 600 of them for 1900 to cover various cities and voting groups. Bryan lacked the money and issues to counter Hanna.

The election of 1900 confirmed McKinley's domestic and foreign policies. He became the first president since 1872 to win reelection, and his margin of victory was 200,000 votes higher than in 1896. This time McKinley carried six of the western states, as Bryan held the Democrats of the Solid South and added Kentucky. Northern Kentucky and old Transylvania stayed with McKinley. McKinley won the electoral vote 292 to 155 (a margin of victory 21 votes higher than in 1896). His coattails were extremely long—Republicans increased their House majority from 151 to 197 members, and their Senate majority from 35 to 55 members. McKinley gained support among all economic classes of voters as well as in the large ethnic groups. Yet while the McKinley realignment seemed complete, there was one signal of a problem for the future. Socialist Eugene Debs collected an amazing 900,000 popular votes.

McKinley did realize in his second term that the American System might need to be modified to meet the emerging international role of America and the booming surplus of American industry. In his Pan-American Exposition speech a few days before his death, McKinley proclaimed, "Isolation is no longer possible or desirable." In addition, the McKinley Tariff had built a robust American industry with high capacity and an excess of production. Again he noted in his exposition speech, "Our capacity to produce has developed so enormously and our products have so multiplied that the problem of more markets requires our urgent and immediate attention."[5] In his new administration of 1900, McKinley looked into opening up trade to further stimulate American industry and productivity. His own success had created some inherent blockages to selling the mounting American industrial surplus. The country's shipping and merchant marine industry was all but dead. He needed a mechanism to open trade without causing an import flood, and an Isthmian Canal was needed to expand shipping and trade. Furthermore, McKinley wanted to expand the merchant marine. In 1900, 90 percent of our exports were shipped on foreign ships, leaving the greatest manufacturing nation hopelessly dependent on other nations.

In the late 1880s, McKinley had started a policy of trade reciprocity, but now he was in a position to guarantee it. The program would be based on the minimum requirement of equality in trade, and it would offer a means to lower tariffs and increase exports. Reciprocity, in McKinley's view, was to be economic, not political. He actually appointed reciprocity commissioner John Kasson to work directly on trade relationships after the passage of the Dingley Tariff Bill of 1898. There were agreements made with Argentina and Jamaica. In Argentina, American wool manufacturers got lower duties, while Argentinean farmers got lower duties on their citrus fruits. Overall, McKinley had limited reciprocity agreement successes, but he forged a new and pioneering approach. The policy alone helped prevent retaliatory trade wars.

McKinley set his new modification on trade in his final speech of his presidency. He roared with pride:

> My fellow citizens, trade statistics indicate that this country is in a state of unexampled prosperity ... they show that we are utilizing our fields and forests and mines that we are furnishing profitable employment to the millions of workingmen throughout the United States, bringing comfort and happiness to their homes and making it possible to lay by savings for old age and disability.... Our capacity to produce has developed so enormously and our products have so multiplied that the problem of more markets

requires our urgent and immediate attention.... By sensible trade arrangements which will not interrupt our home production we shall extend the outlets for our increasing surplus.... Reciprocity is the natural outgrowth of our wonderful industrial development under the domestic policy now firmly established.... Reciprocity treaties are in harmony with the spirit of the times; measures of retaliation are not.[6]

Just as important were the social and civil rights programs that were always part of Ohio republicanism. McKinley had crafted the 1900 Republican platform to address the abuses of Democratic Party–controlled southern states. These states, which had been returned to state governance over two decades after the Civil War, had reverted to a violent and repressive form of government. Southern Democratic legislatures passed laws of racial segregation that were directed against blacks at the end of the 19th century; these statutes became known as Jim Crow laws. McKinley's 1900 platform stated clearly: "It was the plain purpose of the fifteenth amendment to the Constitution to prevent discrimination on account of race or color in regulating the elective franchise. Devices of state governments, whether by statutory or constitutional enactment, to avoid the purpose of this amendment are revolutionary and should be condemned."[7] This strong civil rights program was not favored in the East because McKinley's campaign officials believed it would permanently put the South in the Democratic column.

The Republican platform further addressed the abuses of child labor, the restriction of cheap immigrant labor, and the expansion of veteran benefits. McKinley that, felt with the return of prosperity and the world preeminence of American manufacturing, it was time to look inward to the social planks of Ohio republicanism. The civil rights of black voters were under attack, and lynching was on the rise. The press of the time was far more interested in trust abuses and union struggles. Unfortunately, with McKinley's untimely death, the social vision of Ohio republicanism would move to the background.

Chapter Fourteen

Progressivism's Back Door

McKinley's death achieved what the vote could never do—bring an eastern progressive Republican to the presidency. His passing would reopen the old divide going back to the Whigs. McKinley had become the pinnacle of Ohio republicanism, which favored business and manufacturing while the eastern progressives favored big banking. These roots ran deep. McKinley was often called a populist, but, in reality, he was committed to his Ohio ideology, as reflected by the voters. Roosevelt would be much harder to define. His political character was popular, and it dominated how he was viewed. The Rough Rider, trustbuster, hunter, and fighter was the ideal image of America. Still, Roosevelt had stronger ties to big bankers than his public image might suggest. During the Panic of 1907, he would cut a deal with J. P. Morgan that would further enlarge the nation's biggest trust—U.S. Steel.

Roosevelt's approach would mean years of being in the wilderness for Ohio republicanism. He came to office with conservatives fearing his progressive attitude on economic and social issues. Progressivism emerged as a political movement in the 1890s in response to significant economic, social, and political inequalities, as well as the rise of socialism. These emerging progressives favored big government but had little interest in social issues other than big-business abuses. On civil rights, Ohio republicanism had really been on the progressive side. Ohio republicanism had always had a deep belief in social issues such as abolition and civil rights. After all, slavery had been the reason for the Republican Party's birth. Slavery had divided the Whig Party, moving conscience Whigs to form a new party. Educational and abolitionist movements in 1820s Ohio had set the voter base to end slavery. Presidents Grant, Hayes, Garfield, Harrison, and McKinley were all from abolitionist families and were Civil War veterans who knew the horrors of slavery. McKinley would be the last Civil War veteran to serve as president. Ohio republicanism in 1900 still saw the civil rights and slavery issues as far from settled.

Photograph showing President Theodore Roosevelt (front left) standing with men at a Panama Canal ceremony, 1906. Library of Congress.

Interestingly, the civil rights of former slaves were not embraced by progressives.

Ohio republicanism and the Republican Party were really born as a progressive movement supporting abolition and temperance. It was therefore unsurprising that progressivism would evolve out of the Republican Party. Roosevelt's and America's progressivism in the 1900s was different than that of today. "The progressive phenomenon was not merely a rerun of the Populist crusade of the 1890s, although a strain of it was certainly evident in the West and Midwest. It included many new recruits from the urban middle and upper classes who felt threatened by the new barbarians of corporate wealth who were fast replacing them in influence and status across the country. Not only did progressives push for a new relationship between national government and business in which private greed would be subordinated to public interest, but were responsible for a bewildering array of proposals."[1] These new progressives saw the national government as a regulator of behavior.

Progressives advocated for many reforms that Ohio republicanism had put in the forefront, but others, such as civil rights, were ignored. McKinley supported limited government involvement in economic and socioeconomic issues, but he believed the full force of federal government should be used in civil rights. Previously under Ohio republicanism, the general consensus was that economic ills were best solved through private efforts. Abuses of capitalism should be addressed through the courts. The main difference between Ohio republicanism and Republican progressivism was in the priority of social problems. Progressives followed the headline issues such as trust abuses, corporate corruption, the opulence of the wealthy, and unionism, while Ohio republicanism was centered on civil rights, educational opportunity, and jobs. Muckraking and yellow journalists and intellectuals publicized progressive issues through newspapers and lectures, and protesters and activists began to effect modest change across the country. But with McKinley's death, progressives had a champion in the White House. Civil rights moved to the background as the press and progressives found socioeconomic issues taking the headlines and political glory of being a reformer. In its earlier days, Ohio republicanism had been a church- and school-based movement, often at odds with the more progressive press. Unfortunately, the "Big Press" would become the political driver versus the churches and community leaders. Of course, at times, these groups would find mutual ground.

It was a symbiotic relationship between Roosevelt and the national press that threatened Ohio republicanism the most. Not long after Roosevelt took the oath of office, he started what was then the unusual practice of press meetings on an informal basis.[2] Journalists had made Teddy Roosevelt a national figure with his charge up San Juan Hill. The Spanish-American War had been, to a degree, the vision of the press; in fact, the conflict was often referred to as the first media war. During the 1890s, journalism that oversensationalized and sometimes even made up dramatic events was a powerful force that helped propel the United States into war with Spain. Led by newspaper owners William Randolph Hearst and Joseph Pulitzer, yellow journalism of the 1890s used melodrama, romance, and hyperbole to sell millions of newspapers. Teddy Roosevelt was the perfect bigger-than-life character to sell papers. Roosevelt also realized that the press could be used as a powerful political tool. He was driven by the press, and drove it. McKinley, though, was low-key, preferring to handle problems behind the scenes.

The problem in 1900 was that yellow journalism had moved the evils of big business, any poor treatment of workers, health issues in the food industry, and the opulence of the wealthy class to the front page. The excessive lifestyles of the robber barons were making headlines. J. P. Morgan's and August Belmont's great banking trusts seemed to have given the ownership of America's industrial assets to a handful of bankers. Bankers and the trusts did present a need for regulation. McKinley united these groups in the need for a protective tariff, but he was never personally close to them. In 1901, 65 percent of America's wealth was controlled by the trusts, but the trusts were also feeding over 10 million people. Even with relatively high tariff protection, these trusts had pushed prices down through economies of scale and technology. McKinley's approach found common ground. The capitalists wanted protection as much as labor. Trusts had exploded in the late 1890s, and McKinley had been well aware that new regulation would be needed.

McKinley rarely applied the Sherman Antitrust Act in his administration, but he had been key to its passage in 1890. As chair of the House Ways and Means Committee in 1890, McKinley forged a compromise that passed both the Sherman Act and the Tariff Act of 1890. He realized that the public had a negative opinion of trusts, and the passage of these two measures helped to dampen criticism and unite the Republican Party. McKinley was also well aware that trusts could readily be tempted to abuse their position. McKinley's industrial employment plans ushered in the great technological advances of the period; but ambivalence toward trusts is a fair criticism, and he favored anything that expanded or favored American trade. Trusts and monopolies grew because technology actually allowed for increased competition.

Mark Hanna came to believe, like Morgan, that large combinations resulted in efficiencies and were good for the country. By 1898, Hanna had showed little concern for the growth of trusts, while a worried McKinley counseled and disciplined him on the subject a number of times. McKinley had clearly supported the Republican platform that called for legislation against the trusts, but he resisted the use of executive action to limit them. The result was robust debate within the administration.

McKinley, Treasury Secretary Gage, and Comptroller of Currency Dawes all became aware of the rapid rise of trusts in 1898–1899. Gage and Dawes had long been advocates of trust monitoring and restrictions.

Artist rendering of Senator Mark Hanna being interviewed by reporters in March 1897. Library of Congress.

While Secretary Gage felt there was no method to control the trusts, Dawes argued for legal action. He had noted in his journal several discussions with the president on the abuses of the growing trusts. As early as March 1899, McKinley and Dawes had come to this conclusion: "the enormous capitalization of industrial concerns and combinations in apparent effort to control and raise prices is deeply stirring the people, and will force the question of further legislation on this subject into the next campaign."[3] McKinley pushed Congress for review and legislation. He did not pursue aggressive legal action because his attorney general, Philander Knox, felt recent court rulings on the Sherman Antitrust Act had precluded it. Even on the legislation front, Senator Mark Hanna did not see too much of a role for Congress. Yet McKinley was not persuaded. He challenged Congress in his annual address, then in a call for legislation in the 1900 Republican platform.

Just back from McKinley's funeral, Roosevelt had his first informal press meetings. "According to one source, he put Knox to the test right away by using the meeting to deliver a scathing indictment of the old guard in his party. 'If you even hint where you got it,' Roosevelt warned when he had finished, 'I'll say you are a damned liar.' He would do more than that. Roosevelt told the wire representatives that a reporter who violated his trust would be mercilessly cut off from further access to news. He would even take steps to deny legitimate news to the paper or agency that employed the offending reporter. The ground rules could not have been made clearer. 'All right, gentlemen, now we understand each other,' the president said in adjourning the meeting."[4]

The timing was also poor, as economic prosperity had brought an explosion in trusts. With the McKinley filled lunch pails, the population could be more outraged by the spending of the rich and by social issues. The national press was able to lead the outcry, and Roosevelt saw it as a new cause to take up. Trusts appeared to be an excellent target for the progressive new president. He also took on the regulation of railroads, as well as pure food and drugs. Roosevelt demonstrated that government was the defender of the people against greed and corruption. In early 1902, the national Anthracite Coal Strike gave him a chance to show the power of the executive branch.

The Anthracite Coal Strike threatened the heating supplies of most homes, and the public was worried. Jobs in other major industries such as steel were also threatened. Roosevelt forced an end to the strike when he threatened to use the United States Army to extract the coal and seize the mines. Republican presidents had used the army to limit violence in previous strikes, but they had never used it as a workforce. By bringing representatives of both parties together, Roosevelt was able to facilitate the negotiations and convince both the miners and the owners to accept the findings of a government commission. The labor union agreed to cease being the official bargainer

President Theodore Roosevelt (left) conferring with Senator Mark Hanna while on the way to the Milburn house in Buffalo in 1901. Library of Congress.

for the workers, and the workers got better pay and fewer hours. The problem for the conservative followers of Ohio republicanism was that Roosevelt made the government the de facto bargainer for the workers.

On trusts, Roosevelt avoided attacking manufacturing and banking combines that had brought jobs and prosperity, focusing on the press-driven bad boys—railroads and meat-packing. In 1902, President Theodore Roosevelt directed Attorney General Philander Knox to bring a lawsuit against the "Beef Trust" by using the Sherman Antitrust Act of 1890. The evidence at trial demonstrated that the "Big Six" leading meat-packers were engaged in a conspiracy to fix prices and divide the market for livestock and meat in their quest for higher rates and profits. The United States Supreme Court ruled that the Commerce Clause allowed the government to regulate monopolies if they had a direct effect on commerce. This decision marked the success of the presidency of Theodore Roosevelt in destroying the Beef Trust. In 1906, Upton Sinclair published his classic muckraking novel *The Jungle*, which exposed labor and sanitary conditions in the U.S. meat-packing industry. The ensuing public uproar contributed, in part, to the passage a few months later of the 1906 Pure Food and Drug Act and the Meat Inspection Act. Roosevelt had become a popular crusader with the victory. The railroad was another easy target for trust regulation. The Midwest, including Ohio, had suffered much from railroad rate fixing. Roosevelt found willing conservative Republican allies in Congress.

By 1904, it was becoming clear that Roosevelt had shifted the Republican Party to progressivism without the necessary electoral support. Personally, Roosevelt was a bigger-than-life figure who owed his popularity to the press. His trust-busting fit journalists' view of the nation's biggest problem. While Teddy tapped into a progressive swing in the nation, he was not rooted in any true political philosophy such as Ohio republicanism. To remedy this, he created a simple label for his view of progressivism called a "square deal." Teddy defined the square deal as follows: "When I say that I am for the square deal, I mean not merely that I stand for fair play under the present rules of the game, but that I stand for having those rules changed so as to work for a more substantial equality of opportunity and of reward for equally good service."[5]

Notice that while Roosevelt's words seemed nonthreatening enough to conservatives, it was his actions that better represented progressivism. Progressivism was a true shift from Ohio republicanism, one that focused on perceived fairness more than equality. The press had presented the public with a view in which abuses of corporations increased and the progress of workers declined. There was no doubt about the abuses and opulence of wealth in America. McKinley had agreed with this contention, but Roosevelt's methodology was far different. McKinley and the federalism of Ohio republicanism looked to legislation as the regulator of these abuses. Roosevelt felt it was the executive that had to act forcefully to regulate and even punish offending corporations. Thus he broke directly with the root of Ohio republicanism, limited government.

Roosevelt went hard left with the press on corporations as abusing entities. This view weakened what had been a successful alliance of capital and labor under McKinley. The linkage of corporative growth with jobs and wages was lost. Roosevelt's very success at highlighting corporative opulence and, at times, corruption worked against the Republican Party in the long run, leading to an internal and long-term split. His eventual break with the party would allow the Democrats to label the Republicans as the party of big business, destroying the McKinley worker alliance for six decades. Ronald Reagan would eventually tap back into it. The year 1907 was the peak of the McKinley labor coalition. A labor historian notes: "Most of Pittsburgh steel workers vote the Republican ticket, because they see no immediate hopes of success through the Workingmen's party; but they are ready to accept any political theory that promises something worthwhile for labor."[6] This alliance of labor would start to weaken with public resentment of corporations, Roosevelt's nonsupport of labor unions, and the growing allegiance of union workers to the Democratic Party.

Roosevelt's management of the coal strike, which affected jobs and consumers, was popular with the public, but it hit the unions hard. This again was a break with Ohio republicanism, which tried to keep government out of these disputes. Interestingly, Roosevelt kept government out of major civil rights issues in the South that Ohio republicanism begged to be addressed. He made popular headlines attacking trusts and their abuses. He further framed his views on conservation as a struggle between natural-resource companies and the public. In both cases, Roosevelt ignored the linchpin of jobs that had balanced Ohio republicanism and big business.

Even with these popular victories, Ohio republicanism hoped to challenge the nomination of Roosevelt in 1904. The hope was that Mark Hanna, now a senator, would mount the challenge. Roosevelt, in November 1903, asked Hanna to run his reelection campaign. Hanna understood this as an unsubtle attempt to ensure that he would not oppose the president, and he was slow to respond to this request. In the interim, Hanna allowed talk of his potential campaign for president to continue, although his health prevented him from running or serving. Hanna's death in 1904 assured the nomination for Roosevelt. The Democrats offered a conservative to counter him and pick up some supporters of Ohio republicanism. In 1904, both William Jennings Bryan and former president Grover Cleveland declined to run for president. Since the two Democratic nominees of the past 20 years did not seek the nomination, Alton B. Parker, a Bourbon Democrat from New York, emerged as the candidate. Roosevelt easily defeated Parker, sweeping every region in the nation except the South.

Teddy Roosevelt, the trustbuster, actually got over $600,000 from J. P. Morgan and his associates. Roosevelt also got $500,000 from George Gould in 1904. Roosevelt's array of New York donators was actually larger than McKinley's. Still, while Teddy Roosevelt gets credit for the "progressive era" that broke up the trusts, it was McKinley who set the groundwork for this era. Many progressives such as Teddy Roosevelt, Roosevelt's vice president Charles Fairbanks, and Republican senator Robert La Follette were first McKinley lieutenants. McKinley's selection of Gage as secretary of the Treasury showed his opposition to trusts. Gage had even opposed parts of McKinley's tariffs because they aided trusts. It might be argued that McKinley's behind-the-scenes approach was more effective than Roosevelt's headlines. There is also evidence that McKinley would have become more aggressive in his second term. In any case, Roosevelt clearly cut deals with J. P. Morgan during the Panic of 1907, allowing Morgan to create a steel monopoly and destroy Westinghouse Electric (the only competition for Morgan's General Electric).

Roosevelt's second term started with public relations problems. Scandals in the railroad and insurance industries had been making headlines, and the year 1905 was marked more by scandals in finance. Parties, corporate crimes, and overspending filled the nation's newspapers. On January 31, 1905, the greatest ball of the Gilded Age would occur—the infamous ball of James Hazen Hyde at New York's Sherry's Hotel. The young heir of the insurance fortune built by his father, 28-year-old Hyde had become the major stockholder and director of the Equitable Life Assurance Society. The Equitable Life Assurance Society, at the time, was one of America's largest insurance companies, with over 300,000 policyholders and over a billion dollars in force. During that period, insurance companies were the major investors in Wall Street, and Equitable was a major holder of railroad stocks. The Hyde Ball would soon change all of that. The event would attract over 600 guests, and it even encouraged full press coverage.[7]

The guests were predominantly from America's old money, including the Astors, Belmonts, Depews, and Vanderbilts. Many United States Steel executives were in attendance, and a young Franklin D. Roosevelt represented the old New York Roosevelt family. The Hyde Ball lasted from 6:00 p.m. to 7:00 a.m. Three meals were served during this time, and the menu was French, as was the entertainment. The total bill for the festivities was around $200,000. Several stories quickly started to circulate that Hyde had used Equitable Life Assurance Company money for the party. The scandal would drag down stocks. Policyholders lost millions as they read about the over-the-top opulence of the Hyde party. An internal report found Hyde to have used thousands from the company's funds, and a recommendation was made that he be fired, required to make some payback, and subjected to a New York state investigation. Outrage would move from the ballroom to Wall Street and finally to Main Street. The scandal would lead to the Panic of 1907.

The Panic of 1907 would mark a brief return of the Republican Party to Ohio republicanism as Americans looked for jobs. By early 1907, the great expansion and prosperity that had started with the McKinley administration had run its natural course. The stock market already had problems in specific industries, and a market downturn in the summer of 1907 spread quickly to the banking system, starting the panic. In addition, financial scandals had rocked a number of important insurance and financial companies. The stock market slumped again in October; the Dow Jones average would lose 25 percent by month's end. The situation had reached crisis stage with little hope of stabilization. While the New York exchanges struggled, regional markets such as Pittsburgh and Boston closed for lack of liquidity. Interest rates were spiraling out of control as stock prices plummeted day after day. The steel industry orders stopped, and only 75 percent of the mills were working.

This time the currency problem had international roots. Currency problems in Europe had already started a wave of gold hoarding. Even world markets such as Japan had a currency shortage. At the time, only a few Americans realized what was taking place in the world's financial centers. Soon insurance and trust companies found themselves unable to get credit. Without credit, financial operations froze, and insiders at the stock exchange drove stock prices down. The public began to panic and looked to take cash out of banks.

The Panic of 1907 was different because of its speed. Some creative individuals earned as much as ten dollars a day to wait in bank lines as depositors tried to salvage other parts of their life savings. The drawdown on bank reserves caused banks to call in loans from big and small companies. In Boston, retailers had "panic prices" to help generate cash. The world's biggest banker, J. P. Morgan, studied the course of the panic for opportunities. He held day-and-night meetings in his New York library as he moved to take control of the situation. He even forced the banks to issue scrip in lieu of cash to keep the banking system floating. Lacking any government regulation, the public and the government looked to Morgan as their savior. It was an image promoted by the *New York Times*, as Morgan controlled most of the paper's debt. The image of savior would work to Morgan's advantage as he stood to make millions and settle old scores.

The president of the United States at the time had no way to influence financial markets. Even Teddy Roosevelt had no choice but to ally himself with Morgan. Morgan's European connections promoted this image as well. Europe was also near collapse, and renowned banker Lord Rothschild called Morgan, the world's greatest financier. Morgan was informally in charge of the American money supply, lacking a Federal Reserve as we do today.[8] President Roosevelt and Congress could only watch as the nation spiraled into depression. Morgan controlled not only the nation's press and banks, but also most of its major corporations. J. P. Morgan and Company officers served as directors in 114 corporations with a capitalization of $22.5 billion compared to the total capitalization of $26.5 billion for all of the New York Stock Exchange. New York bankers were said to be hourly coming and going from Morgan's library. J. P. Morgan was clearly in control, and he was able to stall the panic in October by getting into a bank alliance to save the market. Still, many companies remained only days away from collapse, and Morgan was the only one who could save them.

President Roosevelt sent his secretary of the Treasury to ask for help to prevent a full financial collapse. Morgan would help, but not without concessions from Roosevelt. Additionally, Morgan's price was high. First, he settled an old score with George Westinghouse, a former huge supporter of McKinley. Years earlier, Westinghouse Electric had refused to join Morgan's General Electric Trust. Westinghouse's company was to be allowed to go bankrupt,

Political cartoon of the Panic of 1907 showing lava, "common honesty," erupting from a mountain in the background. In the foreground people are fleeing with "secret rate schedules," "rebates," "stocks," and "frenzied accounts." Cartoon from *Pluck Magazine*. Library of Congress.

and while George Westinghouse would personally be crushed, Morgan would not take over Westinghouse Electric directly. The bigger part of the deal was that Morgan would be allowed to expand the world's biggest trust, United States Steel.

Years later in his autobiography, Roosevelt used the following justification: "It was necessary for me to decide on the instant, before the Stock exchange opened, for the situation in New York was such that every hour might be vital.... From the best information at my disposal, I believe that the addition of the Tennessee Coal and Iron property would only increase the proportion of the Steel Company's holdings by about four percent.... It offered the only chance for arresting the panic, and it did arrest the panic."[9] Morgan had won. In addition, his saving of the brokerages was hailed as a miracle in the popular press, which he controlled. Once again, Morgan was a savior.

Conservative Republicans of the time suspected that Morgan had caused the Panic of 1907 to take over companies such as Westinghouse Electric. Wisconsin's populist senator Robert La Follette stated in 1907 that Morgan and his associates "deliberately brought on the late panic, to serve their own ends."[10] John Moody charged that Morgan and his connections stopped the panic by taking a few dollars out of one pocket and putting millions into another. Upton Sinclair used the panic as a basis for his novel *The Money Changers*. In the work, a Morgan-like character orchestrates a financial crisis for private gain while destroying ordinary people across the nation. The Senate committee, investigating the Panic of 1907 for years, concluded Morgan had taken advantage of the situation. Teddy Roosevelt testified in 1909, when he was no longer president, that he had given tacit approval to Morgan and Frick to proceed for the good of the country.[11] While Roosevelt saved the country, he personally gained nothing. Morgan supported William Taft in the primary.

Going into the coming presidential election, the Republican Party was divided between conservatives and the emerging progressives. Republicans were also divided on issues such as tariff levels, government versus individual rights, and the role of the executive. The days of McKinley's Ohio republicanism had passed. The decades of rapid corporate growth had brought with it many social ills. Conservatives wanted these problems addressed through legislation, while progressives wanted aggressive executive action. The big-business leaders were now open to reducing tariffs, as they needed to push their surplus through exports. Still, these business backers wanted a conservative in office. Big bankers like J. P. Morgan wanted no more of the progressives, fearing government regulation of banks after the Panic of 1907. Followers of Ohio republicanism were always, at heart, populists, and they realized some adjustment was needed. The Republican nominee fight was eased as Teddy Roosevelt decided not to run. The logical man to bring the party together was Ohio Republican William Taft, who was Roosevelt's secretary of war and one of the most likable people in politics. Taft was a business conservative with a heart; as a judge, he had consistently supported unions and worker strikes. This image would allow him to hold together the old McKinley voting coalition of labor and management against the social progressives in both parties.

Chapter Fifteen

Ohio Republicanism Reformed and Adapted for the Times

Ohio republicanism under Roosevelt was in the wilderness, but its roots with the American voters ran deep just below the surface. William Taft would, in effect, serve McKinley's second term. Taft would address much of what McKinley had stated in his second-term inauguration speech. The two men wanted to expand international trade, expand investment in the merchant marine, scale back tariffs, address the abuses of trusts, and promote better conditions for workers. Taft still questioned the return to the gold standard under Roosevelt. However, the Republican platform after the Panic of 1907 included gold to at least gain the support of America's bankers. This point was a political concession to J. P. Morgan. All of these plans reflected a trend toward economic moderation in trade tariffs, first identified by McKinley. The difference would be in the two men's approach. McKinley was a populist, while Taft was a legalist. McKinley rose through the political arena, while Taft rose through the legal and administrative avenues. Taft had been a Judge in an Ohio superior court (1887–1890), a U.S. solicitor general (1890–1892), a U.S. circuit court judge (1892–1900), governor of the Philippines (1901–1904), and secretary of war (1904–1908). Not surprisingly, he became chief justice of the U.S. Supreme Court after his presidency.

Taft's major problem was dealing with the conservative-progressive divide in the Republican Party and nation. The Panic of 1907 was over, but it left many fears. The public did not trust business and government, and the cries for reform came from all corners of the nation. Abuses in industry had sold newspapers for over a decade. America's government was divided, with conservative Republicans in the Senate and the House reflecting the progressive trend in the nation. From the perspective of the Ohio republicanism base, one shortcoming of Taft's was his following of the Roosevelt policy of ignoring social issues. Adherents to Ohio republicanism still demanded expanded civil rights for blacks, temperance, and Christian-based morality. As a Unitarian, Taft was seen by many as lacking in this last quality. Still, Ohio republicanism, while calling for social issues, tended to vote with its pocketbook first. While Taft was weak on religion, many Republicans were more concerned with his public morality. Ohio republicanism had always been a strange, almost undefinable mix of economics, moral values, and social issues.

William Howard Taft was born in 1857 in Cincinnati, Ohio. The Tafts and his mother, Louisa Torrey, traced their roots to New England stock of the 1700s. Additionally, the Tafts were distant relatives of Ralph Waldo Emerson. Like Emerson, the Tafts were Unitarians who did not believe in the divinity of Christ. Religion would thus be a problem throughout William Taft's political career. His father, Alphonso Taft (1810–1891), was an antislavery Whig and founding figure in the Ohio Republican Party. Alphonso Taft also served as U.S. attorney general and secretary of war under President Ulysses S. Grant. William Taft benefited from a strong education, graduating from Cincinnati Woodward High School, which had been founded by the College of Teachers as one of the nation's first high schools. His early schooling was based on the *McGuffey Readers*. In fact, like all of the Ohio presidents, he proclaimed the importance of the *McGuffey Readers* in his education. In a letter to Henry Ford (an avid admirer and collector of the William McGuffey texts) Taft stated: "I attended public schools in Cincinnati and began with the first of the McGuffey readers [small r] and continued clear through to the sixth. The McGuffey readers and Ray's arithmetic were the mental pabulum for my early youth, and while doubtless there have been improvements in them, I venture to think they were instruments by which primary education could be thoroughly given. I am glad to express my gratitude for McGuffey readers."[1]

Taft went on to graduate from Yale University and receive his law degree from the University of Cincinnati, another institution with deep ties to Ohio's famous College of Teachers. Clearly, this was an education rooted in the philosophical foundational institutions of Ohio republicanism. Taft was the perfect son of the movement with the exception of his Unitarianism. Still, as with Ohio republicanism and McGuffeyism, his beliefs were based on Christian morality without any denominational basis.

Taft's first political job came in 1878, when President Arthur appointed him as a tax collector. Interestingly, this job had been held by William Harrison in the late 1790s in the very heart of old Transylvania. Taft practiced law in Cincinnati from 1883 to 1887. He was appointed to an Ohio superior court vacancy in 1887. The next year he was elected to a term of his own, and this was the only elected office other than the presidency that he ever held.

Taft demonstrated a support for labor issues consistent with Ohio republicanism. Basically he was prolabor without necessarily supporting the spread of unions. In 1890, President Benjamin Harrison called Taft to Washington to the post of solicitor general. Two years later Harrison named him to the U.S. circuit court for the Sixth District. Taft's record as a state and a federal judge proved him extremely competent, and he was sympathetic to the growing problems of labor in the nation.

Taft began to gain a national reputation in 1900, when President McKinley appointed him head of a commission to terminate U.S. military rule in the Philippine Islands, which had become an American possession after the Spanish-American War. The appointment gave Taft his first opportunity to demonstrate ability as an administrator to the nation. In 1901, McKinley named Taft the first civil governor of the Philippines, but the position extended into the Roosevelt administration. Taft's governorship of the islands (1901–1904) became the gold standard in colonial administration for any nation. In marked contrast to the military occupation, Taft had shown no trace of racial prejudice. He was sympathetic to the problems of the Filipinos, and he asked for favorable trade terms for the Philippines. Roosevelt twice offered Governor Taft a place on the U.S. Supreme Court, but Taft declined, wanting to finish his work in the Philippines. Roosevelt had come to regard Taft as his eventual successor and convinced him to join his cabinet. Taft accepted the post of secretary of war in 1904 with the understanding that he could continue to oversee Philippine affairs from Washington.

Roosevelt continued to groom Taft for the presidency, using him as a general problem solver. Between 1904 and 1908, he had direct charge of the construction of the Panama Canal. The canal had been a dream of Ohio republicanism for decades. In 1906, when revolution threatened Cuba, Taft brought peace through negotiations. In Tokyo in 1907, he improved Japanese-American relations strained by the abuse of Japanese immigrants in California. Roosevelt was clearly grooming Taft to be president. The nation, as a whole, was shifting to the progressive view, but no Republican could win the nomination without Ohio. Midwestern conservativism and Taft appeared to bridge the gap.

In 1908, the only two Republican contenders running nationwide campaigns for the presidential nomination were Secretary of War William Howard Taft and Governor Joseph B. Foraker, both of Ohio. Foraker was not aligned fully with the Republican Party. He had served as governor of and U.S. senator from Ohio, but he was never accepted by mainstream Ohio Republicans such as McKinley, Hanna, and Sherman. He was also persona non grata at the Roosevelt White House.[2] Foraker had little hope of winning, but true to his rebel background, he ran anyhow. In the nomination contest, four states held primaries to select national convention delegates. Taft won most of the primaries and the caucuses, claiming a big victory in Ohio. Roosevelt brought in support from the party's progressive wing.

William Jennings Bryan quickly won the overwhelming support of the Democratic Party for the third time, reflecting the growing progressive mood of the nation. The election, however, was no contest. Businessmen continued to support the Republican Party, and Bryan failed to secure backing from labor in the old McKinley alliance strongholds. Bryan carried the South, where Republicans' civil rights stance was deeply hated and the black vote was fully suppressed. He ended up with the worst of his three defeats in the national popular vote, losing almost all the northern states to Taft and the popular vote by eight percentage points. As bad as the loss appeared, Bryan's progressivism gained votes in many Republican counties.[3]

The progressive wing of the Republican Party was soon disappointed. Taft kept only Agriculture Secretary James Wilson and Postmaster General George von Lengerke Meyer (who was shifted to the Navy Department). The new president could not be separated from his Ohio republicanism roots. Taft's administration was filled with conflict between the conservative and progressive wings of the Republican Party. He often sympathized with the progressive wing, but his actions were conservative. Roosevelt left for a yearlong African safari but quickly heard of Taft's cabinet picks. Taft agreed with Roosevelt on the need for conservation, but he felt it should be accomplished by legislation rather than executive order. This approach was consistent with traditional Ohio republicanism, but it went in the face of Roosevelt's approach. Taft did not retain James Garfield,[4] an Ohioan, as secretary of the interior, choosing instead a westerner, former Seattle mayor Richard A. Ballinger. Roosevelt was surprised at the replacement, believing that Taft had promised to keep Garfield; and this change was one of the events that caused Roosevelt to realize that Taft would choose different policies.[5]

Taft soon angered most progressives in his party, including Wisconsin's Robert M. La Follette (1855–1925). La Follette was a powerful Republican labeled an insurgent, as he was a bulldog for high protective tariffs. Others labeled him a progressive because he (like Taft) wanted to be tough on trusts. La Follette was not a full supporter of progressivism, wanting high tariffs when most progressive Republicans had been soured by the abuses of trusts and wanted lower tariffs. He opposed any reduction in duties, maintaining he was a true follower of William McKinley.[6] La Follette had served on McKinley's Ways and Means Committee that had passed the great protective Tariff of 1890.

La Follette actually had a better claim to being the champion of Ohio republicanism than Taft. He had been groomed by William McKinley, and like McKinley, he was a populist. As a populist, La Follette crossed the political lines of conservativism, progressivism, and socialism. He saw everything in

Clockwise from upper left: William Taft, Mrs. Taft, and their children Helen, Robert and Charley in 1910. Library of Congress.

terms of what was good for the American worker. If business supplied jobs, he supported business; if business abused workers, he opposed business. Thus La Follette was a true disciple of Ohio republicanism as it had evolved under McKinley. Historians see La Follette as running a 20th-century Tea Party movement: "In the early 1900s, he led a grassroots revolt against the GOP establishment and pioneered the ferocious tactics that the Tea Parties use today—long-shot primary challenges, sensational filibusters, uncompromising ideology, and populist rhetoric."[7] Taft was unable to rein in these insurgents, and that would hurt him with his Ohio republicanism base.

Joseph Gurney Cannon (1836–1926), who was a United States politician from Illinois and leader of the Republican Party, became another problem. Cannon served as Speaker of the United States House of Representatives from

1903 to 1911, and many consider him to be the most dominant Speaker in United States history, which was a problem for President Taft.[8] Joe Cannon was the one politician that even Teddy Roosevelt feared and warned Taft about.[9] The conservative Cannon had a tight hold on Congress, and he blocked any effort by Taft on tariff reform. However, Cannon was also caught in the battle between conservatives and progressives within the Republican Party. Progressive Democrats and Republicans united to down him.

In 1910, after two failed attempts to curb Cannon's absolute power in the House, a coalition of 42 progressive Republicans and the entire delegation of 149 Democrats led a revolt. The timing and plan was pure politics. With many of Cannon's most powerful allies absent from the House Chamber but enough members on hand for a quorum, Senator Norris introduced a resolution that would remove the Speaker from the Rules Committee and strip him of his power to assign committees. Cannon supporters proved difficult to find since many were Irish had spent the day at various St. Patrick's Day celebrations. The battle of filibusters and political maneuvering lasted two days. Eventually, the progressives prevailed and voted out Cannon. Cannon managed to save some face by promptly requesting a vote to remove him as Speaker, which he won handily since the Republican majority would not risk a Democratic speaker replacing him. While Taft's enemy was thus removed, the Republican Party was left with much bad blood and division. Supporters of Ohio republicanism were as confused as they were divided. Ohio industry, which had been the barometer of economic policy, was confused on tariff levels. Even big business seemed puzzled, as the nation's best-known capitalist, steel king, and Republican backer, Henry Clay Frick, felt the steel industry could tolerate higher tariffs.

Taft and Ohio republicanism were evolving economically in this confusion. The root of Ohio republicanism had been and would always be putting America first, but conservatives were split on the level at which to carry out this plan. The problem was that protecting American industry and helping it prosper was no longer as simplistic as imposing high tariffs. America's industries needed cheap imported raw materials, as well as an international market for their surplus products. Again, Ohio was where that realization and evolution was centered. In 1909, a new Ohio industry was on the rise—rubber. The world was in the midst of a rubber boom, as auto production surpassed 3 million cars worldwide, with Ford dominating. Akron, Ohio, had established itself as the world's center for rubber production. Firestone, Goodrich, and Goodyear were already headquartered in the city. America's million-dollar producing industry had passed from steel to rubber. With the booming future for autos, rubber was the world's most strategic material, and something for which the United States had no resources.

Taft knew firsthand that the auto and rubber industries would join steel as the heart of industrial and technological might. In 1909, President Taft entered the White House in a huge, chauffeured, steam-powered car (America's first White House car). The White Motor Company, a branch of the White Sewing Machine Company of Cleveland, provided its seven-passenger, 40-horsepower Model M as a touring car for the chief of state. Taft would leave the White House in 1912 in a Pierce-Arrow. The government purchased for First Lady Helen Herron Taft a gasoline-powered Pierce-Arrow, manufactured in Buffalo, New York. During his presidency, Taft's passion for cars extended to his Baker electric vehicle, a model that was especially popular with women in the era, as it did not require any cranking. Taft became a car enthusiast and close friend of Harvey Firestone. Both men realized that rubber was going to require a change in trade policy.

The closest rubber tree to Akron was 3,200 miles away, and the closest commodity market for semiprocessed rubber was over 3,000 miles away. In 1909, South America produced all the raw rubber, but England controlled its production and sale of a semifinished slab of rubber for industry. The auto tire industry was dominated by America, but France and others offered tough competition. Ohio needed cheap imports of raw and semiprocessed rubber, as well as some protection from cheap European tires. Ohio's fastest-growing industry would require trade treaties versus tariff management by Congress to achieve the balance for industry growth. Ohio republicanism was changing, but it would always be an America-first approach. Taft proved adept at leading this new Ohio-based trade policy for the nation. Ohio now realized the international nature of industry, whereas other parts of America still focused on simple protectionism. Taft would lead this new liberalization of tariffs to support international business growth.

The battle over tariff levels would split the Republican Party for decades and test the economic platform of Ohio republicanism. As president, Taft proposed the first change in tariff laws since the Dingley Act of 1897 under William McKinley. President William Howard Taft called Congress into a special session in 1909 shortly after his inauguration to discuss the issue. Thus, the House of Representatives immediately passed a tariff bill sponsored by Sereno E. Payne of New York that called for reduced tariffs. However, the United States Senate speedily substituted a bill written by Nelson Aldrich of Rhode Island that stipulated fewer reductions and more increases in tariffs. In addition, the measure called for free trade with the Philippines. At the time, the Philippines were seriously challenging the South American and British raw-rubber monopoly, and the islands would therefore be needed for the future growth of the American rubber industry. Better than anyone, Taft knew the importance of free trade with the Philippines. He realized that the simple tariff protection of the steel industry could not be applied to emerging industries such as rubber. The key was to give America the advantage. Still,

President William Howard Taft and Mrs. Taft seated in the back of a convertible automobile with the roof down, 1909. Library of Congress.

many conservative Republicans believed that stonewalling lower tariffs was necessary to protect their political position from the free-trading Democrats. Many Republicans also saw lower tariffs as a further step toward progressivism in general.

With Joe Cannon still the Speaker, a compromise would be needed. The legislative bargain did indeed lead to a political breach within the protectionist Republican Party. Taft signed the bill and took the firestorm of criticism. The Payne-Aldrich Tariff Act of 1909, which lowered 650 tariffs, raised 220 tariffs, and left 1,150 tariffs untouched, was signed with the president's full support in 1909. Taft took a firestorm of criticism for his actions, but he believed that the compromise would preserve party unity. Instead, the Payne-Aldrich Tariff Act further split the Republicans, eventually leading Theodore Roosevelt's "Bull Moose" Progressives to splinter from Taft's Republicans. But even inside Taft's camp and Ohio republicanism as a movement, there was a reopening of an old conservative fault line over tariffs.

As president, Taft returned to his political roots. He appointed conservatives to many key government posts, which put him in opposition with Roosevelt holdovers. Taft's secretary of the interior, Richard A. Ballinger, was accused of colluding with private business to release valuable Alaskan coalfields for development. Roosevelt saw this allegation as a way for Taft to dump

Ballinger, who was a perceived attack on Roosevelt's beloved conservation program. Taft's refusal to fire Ballinger and his firm position against Gifford Pinchot, Roosevelt's head of the Forest Service, forever alienated him from Roosevelt supporters. Pinchot alleged that Ballinger was in league with big timber interests. Roosevelt conservationists sided with Pinchot, and Taft alienated yet another vocal constituency. Taft also betrayed a platform pledge by going along with the Payne-Aldrich Act, which not only failed to substantially reduce tariff duties, but actually raised several of them. In effect, no one was happy with the Payne-Aldrich Act. The issue of taxing the wealthy became a means to pacify the progressives.

Progressive Democrats and Republicans saw a proposed income tax as a substitution for tariff revenues. Progressives saw tariffs as a tax on the poor, so an income tax seemed a better path. Even the Socialist and Populist Parties supported income tax. The progressive mood was against wealth of any kind. Roosevelt had ignored the push for income taxes, preferring trust-busting.

A divided Republican Party allowed the press to pressure Taft to be more progressive than his Ohio roots. Taft agreed to support income taxes for corporations and businesses to help assure the public. This type of government expansion went against the heart of Ohio republicanism, but its success with the voters was a reflection of the antibusiness mood of the time. Supporters of Ohio republicanism in a split Republican Party lacked the votes to prevent an income tax.

The new tax on corporate net income was 1 percent on net profits over $5,000. Of course, a tax on the rich was popular. Even the high priest of American capitalism supported an income tax. In 1911, the Supreme Court, in *Flint v. Stone Tracy Company*, upheld the measure. An income tax on individuals (unlike the tax on corporations) required a constitutional amendment. The personal income tax was to focus only on those making $500,000 or more, which at the time was less than 1 percent of the population. The rate was to be 1 to 7 percent. Personal income tax was passed with little controversy in July 1909, with a unanimous vote in the Senate and a 318–14 vote in the House. It quickly was ratified by the states; and in February 1913, it became a part of the Constitution as the 16th Amendment, as Taft was leaving office. It should be noted that once the government got the ability to tax, rates and income brackets quickly accelerated. Ten years later, the income tax was on *all* wage earners and ranged from 4 percent to 58 percent. Corporations were taxed at a 12 percent rate.

The split and divide on economic issues threatened the balance of conservative social issues in the Republican Party. Progressives tended to be liberal on both economic and social issues. Temperance was still a pillar of Ohio republicanism, the progressive trend of the nation, and a divided Republican Party had muted social issues. President Taft found himself at the forefront of the stress of Ohio republicanism as a political force. The movement had lost the force of abolition, slavery, and civil rights as motivating issues.

Ohio republicanism and presidents such as Theodore Roosevelt had avoided the issue of temperance and prohibition at the national level. But in old Transylvania and western states including Kansas, prohibition and temperance were still major issues. Methodists, in particular, had kept a ban on alcohol at the forefront in states like Indiana. Ohio presidents were often held to a standard of personal temperance, and Taft was a teetotaler. The movement and its link to grassroots Ohio republicanism remained strong and growing during the Taft administration. Like McKinley, Taft was aggressive on side issues such as saloons, illegal liquor, and transportation of liquor from wet counties to dry ones. Still, the Anti-Saloon League was disappointed in Taft and actively campaigned against him, often painting him as a big beer drinker (which he was not).[10]

Taft did remain aggressive, if not more aggressive on trust-busting, but he never attacked big business in public. He behaved like a true progressive early in his presidency. He filed twice as many antitrust suits as Roosevelt and expanded the former president's program of conserving public lands over the demands of raw material companies. Taft also supported the Mann-Elkins Act of 1910 that expanded the government's use of the Interstate Commerce Commission to cover regulation of telephone, telegraph, and cable companies. The act also enabled the commission to suspend rates set by railroads. Still, the national press had driven the issue of trusts, abuse, and the opulence of the wealthy to be the primary focus of the nation. Teddy Roosevelt had now become an open critic of Taft.

Chapter Sixteen

The Republican Party in Rebellion and the Election of 1912

The election of 1912 highlighted the decade-old split in the Republican Party. It would mark the beginning of the end for Ohio republicanism as a national policy. Political scientists see the election as a change election: "It was the climactic battle of the Progressive Era that arose at the dawn of the twentieth century, when the country first tried to come to terms with the profound challenges posed by the Industrial Revolution. It should be noted that the 1912 election was not a major realigning election. It did not determine the fortunes of parties as decisively—or lead to the emergence of a new political order—as did the election of 1800, the election of 1860, or the election of 1936. But it was a critical prelude to the New Deal and, more than this, a contest that initiated important changes that redefined the meaning and practice of self-government in the United States."[1] Furthermore, the contest marked a true shift in Ohio republicanism as the dominant political viewpoint and a return to progressive government philosophy.

The 1912 election also set certain historical markers. The Democrats returned to power for the first time since the Civil War. The party took control of not only the White House but both houses of Congress as well, a feat the Democrats had only achieved briefly from 1893 to 1895 under President Grover Cleveland. The 1912 election resulted in the first lowering of tariffs since the Civil War. Furthermore, it represented the political resurgence of the South and a setback for the civil rights movement of Ohio republicanism.

Ohio republicanism had brought a prosperity and industrial dominance to America, but as McKinley had feared, unregulated capitalism would be subverted by the greedy. It would be a mistake to look at America's great industrialists as the full problem. The real issue was not big business as much as big banking. However, the public did not appreciate this distinction. Bankers had manipulated and even destroyed industrialists for their own gain, and many of these industrialists had been the financial pillar of Ohio republicanism. Big banking also tended to be international versus nationalistic. Bankers made money on the flow of money, not the national direction of its movement. The United States from 1860 to 1912 had been banking's Wild West. Bankers faced little regulation as the concept of trusts grew faster than the necessary legislation to patch new problems. Without financial management such as that provided by the Federal Reserve, the government was often held ransom, as in the Panic of 1907. Bankers controlled industry and government. Of course, businesses behaved badly with their new wealth, making headlines easy for a yellow press. It was the perfect environment for progressivism in government and socialism in the streets.

Ohio republicanism also did not adapt to the changes in society. The influx of European workers to man the factories overtook the civil rights focus of the nation. The press became a new force capable of directing the country's attention. Poor factory wages and worker rights carried the headlines, as personal liberties declined and segregation created a new type of slavery in the South. The South's support became a given for the Democrats, and the Republicans were forced to battle for northern and midwestern votes. The industrialized North was rapidly changing as well. Statistics suggest that the real issue was more the distribution of wealth versus the low wages of factory workers. In fact, it was the factory salaries that were pulling European workers to America. Wages in American steel mills of the time were three to four times those in Europe. This is not to argue that the hugely profitable American industries could not have paid more. The class differences were still startling, as the wealthy had four-day parties, built mansions that rivaled the kings of Europe, owned 12 to 20 cars for a single family, and summered in the Alps. They were the Hollywood stars of their day, and they made it easy to sell newspapers.

The abuses and opulence of the wealthy, documented by a yellow press, had changed the American view of industrialism. McKinley's great alliance of populism and industrialism, capital and labor, managers and workers was being questioned by the electorate. The Republican Party was split by the change. This division had roots in Teddy Roosevelt's shift to progressivism to address trusts. Roosevelt had changed the major thrust of the Republican Party and its link with Ohio republicanism. President Taft was unable to heal the growing division, though he did try to align the progressive Republicans with conservative supporters of Ohio republicanism. The problem would become personal with the bigger-than-life personalities such as President Taft, former president Roosevelt, and Speaker of the House Joe Cannon.

In 1909, the tariff issue had put the two wings of the Republican Party in open rebellion. Joe Cannon's removal as Speaker in March 1910 laid the divide open to the public. Roosevelt and his surrogates were leaking their disappointment with Taft's first year. The clash accelerated in June 1910, when Taft elected not to greet Roosevelt upon his return from his safari in Africa. Two years later, Roosevelt declined Taft's invitation to the White House but praised the president's progress on a number of fronts, including railroad legislation and a postal savings bill. Roosevelt then entered the Republican primary as a contender against Taft.

Taft went into the 1912 primaries with a press problem. He had never courted journalists as had President Roosevelt. Furthermore, Taft believed the yellow press had set the agenda for the country, and that it graded his success on the degree to which he met their criteria on action, not on the good of the nation. Corporate greed and abuses sold the newspapers and created a "mass hysteria."[2] Taft felt reporters had attacked him unfairly based on their perceived agenda. Taft described the situation in this manner: "In which anything asserted with sufficient emphasis, without proof, will be believed about any man, no matter how disinterested or high his character."[3] In another letter, Taft discussed the mood of the country and the yellow press: "The people are restless, they have a yearning for something startling and radical that we are not likely to furnish them, and they have a degree of suspicion of public men, promoted by muckraking newspapers and magazines, that it will take some time for the country to recover from."[4] The public faced a bewildering choice of two progressives and a progressive-leaning conservative. In the primary, the choice was clearer. The Republican Party was also starting to use open-voting primaries versus state conventions.

Roosevelt took nine of the 13 electoral Republican primaries in the spring of 1912. Most national delegates at the time were chosen in state conventions. Taft prevailed at these with the backing of the old guard of the party and Ohio republicanism. Political convention battles produced endless credentials challenges by the voting delegates, with Roosevelt and Taft supporters claiming to have won the same state. The floor fight continued for days, but in the end, Taft won by two votes. The progressive leaders, however, rallied their supporters around Roosevelt, who vowed to run under a separate party. They returned to the convention and voted present as they worked to form the Progressive Party.[5] Roosevelt would be the nominee of this new Bull Moose Party.

Democrats tapped into the progressive movement with their own antitrust candidate. More importantly, a progressive Democrat could expand the movement into unionism and socialism. The Democrats selected Thomas Woodrow Wilson (1856–1924), a true big-government progressive. Wilson was from a southern family that had owned slaves and supported the Confederacy, but he was educated at Princeton University and would climb to be the university's president. In 1908, he ran for governor of New Jersey and won. Wilson beat the national Republican trend where Taft carried New Jersey, thus becoming the darling of the Democratic Party. Wilson was a strong progressive believing government should control business. He also leaned heavily to the socialist side on government-supported social programs. This socialist aspect would become evident in Wilson's presidency, but was difficult to see in his campaign speeches.

Wilson's progressive socialism was not the will of the people. Most in America associated progressivism with the way Roosevelt had used it against the banking trusts. Roosevelt retained the Republican base by a policy of identifying good versus bad trusts. Wilson, however, was opposed to any form of trust. He represented the hard left of the Democratic Party, and he was not the favorite going into the convention. The convention deadlocked for over 40 ballots—no candidate could reach the two-thirds vote required. The leading contender was House Speaker Champ Clark, a prominent progressive who was strongest in the Border States, while the dark horse Wilson had the southern states because he supported the suppression of civil rights for blacks. Wilson also gained votes by being the anti-boss candidate of the party.

Wilson consulted Louis D. Brandeis (1856–1941), who promoted government regulation, if not elimination, of corporate trusts, for advice on economic policy. Brandeis became a legal leader of the progressive movement and used the law as the instrument for social change. In particular, he attacked trusts of all types, becoming the people's advocate of his day. Wilson's campaign had an aggressive focus on the elimination of monopoly in all forms. He also concluded that major reforms in banking and a lower tariff were needed to assure free market principle.[6] Wilson positioned himself to be a bigger progressive than Roosevelt.

Wilson was a populist. But unlike the right-wing populism of William McKinley and the center populism of William Jennings Bryan, Wilson's philosophy embraced the Left. He aimed to end the era of big business. He refused any campaign money from trusts or corporations. Wilson brought in labor unions as well as their members, fracturing Ohio republicanism's alliance with the worker. The nation's labor force had shifted from the 1890s from a native workforce to an immigrant workforce. That shift and the related labor unrest had caused a rise in the Socialist Party, which was running Eugene Debs as its candidate. But Wilson was well positioned to take the labor vote.

Wilson changed politics by campaigning and receiving the endorsement of the American Federation of Labor. With its approval, the union made a major break with its stand not to endorse political candidates. Wilson supported the spread and protection of unions, taking more votes from the high-tariff workers of the old Republican worker alliance. As McKinley had built the worker alliance for Republican voters for decades, Wilson now did the same with union workers for the Democratic Party. The Democrats' relationship with labor unions would be a major blow to Ohio republicanism and the dominance of the Republican Party since the Civil War.

Wilson stood in stark contrast to Ohio republicanism on economic and social issues. Wilson adroitly avoided social questions in his campaign, but he was clearly, at minimum, a segregationist. He believed that slavery was wrong on economic labor grounds, rather than for moral reasons.[7] Wilson held the southern view that the South had been demoralized by northern carpetbaggers, and the Radical Republicans had imposed extreme measures. Wilson believed in leaving the South alone to maintain Jim Crow laws. His early career showed little of these beliefs, though he was known to discourage black admissions at Princeton.[8] Wilson's positions, however, would assure him the solid South. In fact, many southern states didn't even have Taft on the ballot.[9] The divided Republicans were the opening for the first southern-leaning candidate to win the presidency since the pre–Civil War decades.

Wilson won the election, gaining a large majority in the Electoral College and winning 42 percent of the popular vote, while Theodore Roosevelt won 27 percent, William Taft 23 percent, and Eugene Debs 6 percent. In the Electoral College a huge amount of votes was needed to win. Wilson had well above the required amount with 435 votes, while Roosevelt had 88, Taft only 8, and Socialist Eugene Debs none at all.

Chapter Seventeen

Twilight of Ohio Republicanism

Woodrow Wilson would turn the nation on a new path after 60 years of Ohio republicanism. The progressives of the Wilson era were much different than progressives of today. In any case, Wilson's progressivism was a radical change for the nation; it was based economically on reduced tariffs and big-government solutions. Woodrow Wilson also expanded the application of progressivism to labor socialism. He proved a strong supporter of unions and formed a strong alliance that would erode the McKinley labor alliance. Interestingly, Wilson's support of labor rights did not translate into support for other social movements. He opposed civil rights and women's rights, which had been promoted under the Ohio republicanism movement. In this respect, early progressivism was far different from the modern ideology. Early 20th-century progressivism, like Ohio republicanism, must be looked at as a unique movement based on the environment of the times. It doesn't match any single political philosophy of today. Wilson's progressivism was rooted in big government, which is one of the few links to today's progressivism.

The fall of Ohio republicanism at its very root was the abuses of the industries that had been built by protectionism. These abuses arose from the rise of big banking, which had injected a greedy quest for maximum profits not shown by early industrialists such as George Westinghouse, Harvey Firestone, H. J. Heinz, and others. Bank-built industrial trusts had moved the heart and soul of these companies to faceless managers in New York. Manufacturing operational executives no longer arose from the factory floor, but were appointed by far-off New York bankers. The public no longer saw industry as a job creator, but as a type of economic plantation. These abuses had created a strong union movement that replaced the paternalism of Ohio republicanism. It had also divided the Republican Party between progressives and conservatives. Conservative Republicans found themselves on the wrong side of the American laborer.

In 1912, the issue of tariffs remained dominant, even though the views had shifted. The hatred of corporations had transformed the public in support of lower tariffs. Jobs were plentiful, as immigrants were needed to maintain the growth of factories. Immigration also put downward pressure on wages, as unions struggled with corporations for representation and pay increases. Still, the overall prosperity of the nation took the focus away from job creation and put it on wages. The old McKinley alliance was based on employment versus salary.

Wilson pushed through Underwood-Simmons Tariff of 1913 with control of both bodies of Congress. It was the first law to substantially lower rates in 50 years, and the free list of goods on which no import duties were charged was expanded to include iron, steel, raw wool, and sugar. Iron and steel had been the most protected of all industries since the Civil War. The attack on steel went to the very geographic heart of Ohio republicanism. To make up for the revenue shortfall that lower rates caused, the law included a provision for implementing the federal income tax established in the just-ratified 16th Amendment. A tax of 1 percent was levied on all incomes over $4,000, with the tax rate going up to 7 percent for the highest earners. Wilson would begin the growth of taxes and government that Ohio republicanism had held down for decades.

Wilson's most important domestic program, however, was the reorganization of the nation's banking system. The momentum for banking reform had been rooted in the Panic of 1907 and the actions of J. P. Morgan. In 1912–1913, the Pujo Committee, a joint United States congressional subcommittee, was formed to investigate the so-called money trust of Wall Street bankers and financiers that exerted control over the nation's finances. After a resolution introduced by Republican congressman Charles Lindbergh, Sr., for a probe on Wall Street power, Democratic congressman Arsène Pujo of Louisiana was authorized to form a subcommittee of the House Committee on Banking and Currency.

The Pujo Committee showed how Morgan had saved the country in the Panic of 1907, but at a cost. Teddy Roosevelt had argued he had no choice but to deal Morgan for the good of the country. It was this type of power that caused a political outcry for reform. After months of hearings, amendments, and debates, the Federal Reserve Act passed Congress in December 1913. The bill passed the House by an overwhelming majority of 298–60 on December 22, 1913. Wilson and the Democrats hoped the measure would break the reliance of the federal government on the banking trust. While it was a Democratic bill, progressive Republicans supported the idea of a central bank, having seen the pressure put on Roosevelt in the Panic of 1907.

Labor reform was a big item on Wilson's agenda, as he wanted to break once and for all from the McKinley labor alliance. Wilson and the Democrats supported the decade-long initiatives of the American Federation of Labor and United Mine Workers to have a Department of Labor. Taft and conservative Republicans opposed such a department based on the fact that it would create more government regulation. A Federal Department of Labor was the direct product of a half-century campaign by organized labor growing out of the progressive movement. The department's purpose was to foster, promote, and develop the welfare of working people to improve their working conditions and to enhance their opportunities for profitable employment. The act establishing the Department of Labor passed Congress on March 4, 1913, and was signed by a reluctant President William Howard Taft, just hours before Woodrow Wilson took office.

A bloody strike in Colorado also played into Wilson's plans. The Ludlow Massacre was an attack by the Colorado National Guard and Colorado Fuel and Iron Company camp guards on a tent colony of 1,200 striking coal miners and their families at Ludlow, Colorado, in 1914. About two dozen people, including miners' wives and children, were killed. Capitalist John D. Rockefeller, Jr., was the mineowner, and he was widely criticized for his refusal to fully negotiate. Woodrow Wilson had personally asked for a dialogue, but after the violence, he was forced to send in federal troops. The union lost its demands, but the strike created a commission in Washington. A United States Commission on Industrial Relations conducted hearings in Washington, collecting information and taking testimony from all involved, including John D. Rockefeller, Sr.. Rockefeller testified that, even after knowing guards in his pay had committed atrocities against the strikers, he "would have taken no action" to prevent the attacks.[1] The commission's report suggested many reforms sought by the unions, and it provided support for bills establishing a national eight-hour workday and a ban on child labor.

After the Ludlow Strike, Wilson and the Democrats took on an aggressive drive to support labor unionization and national organizations. One historian noted: "Here was an indication of how things had changed in Woodrow Wilson's Washington, where the AFL made an alliance with the Democratic Party in return for relief from debilitating court battles for a place in the halls of political power."[2] This new alignment would change once-solid industrial cities, such as Pittsburgh, from Republican to Democratic. In the 1930s, this alliance would lead to a reign of Democrats for many decades.

On other social issues, Wilson opposed Ohio republicanism and the future of progressivism. Wilson's progressivism would not be recognizable to many progressives today. He did not openly support a constitutional amendment to give women the right to vote, but he backed action by the individual states, as called for in the Democratic Party platform. Wilson fully supported segregation and Jim Crow laws in the South, albeit in a low-key way. In doing so, he helped solidify the South for the Democrats in the future. Interestingly, at the time, labor unions supported segregation and lined up with Wilson.

The Democrats controlled government in Wilson's first term and successfully passed a great deal of legislation, overturning decades of Ohio republicanism. The major division in the Republican Party was far from over. This time, however, Republican progressives switched over to Wilson. The 1916 election was focused on foreign affairs versus domestic issues. The growing war in Europe had both progressives and conservatives concerned. America was more divided this time between war hawks and isolationists. President Wilson had firmly stood to keep America out of the war, and this stand even played extremely well with Ohio voters and old followers of Ohio republicanism. Wilson would solidly win in the state. Had Wilson lost there, the Republicans would have won the White House. Ohio republicanism was not dead, but it had been muted again by the times.

Ohio had a large pro–German population in the old strongholds of Ohio republicanism around Cincinnati and the Western Reserve, as well as in other centers such as western Pennsylvania and the Upper Midwest. Ohio senator (and future president) Warren Harding, as party chairman, was forced to go easy on this key topic. "There were too many pacifists and pro–German Americans in Ohio and elsewhere in the United States for Harding to indulge in overly belligerent talk about German atrocities, at least before the presidential election of 1916. If he was going to be party keynoter at the Chicago nominating convention in June, 1916—and party officials expected that he was—it would be wise for him to curb his tongue and his feelings."[3] Still, the Republicans were linked with the war hawks of the time.

The Republicans wanted someone to bring the party together. A number of candidates were openly competing for the 1916 nomination, but they represented the two sides of the 1912 split. These were conservative senator Elihu Root from New York (McKinley/Roosevelt cabinet member) and liberal senator John W. Weeks from Massachusetts. Neither seemed capable of ending the divide. There was a movement for a dark horse Ohio senator (and future president) Warren Harding that was stopped by the Roosevelt progressives.[4] Instead they turned to Supreme Court justice Charles Evans Hughes, who had been serving on the court since 1910, and who had the advantage of not having publicly spoken about political issues in six years. He had been put on the court by President Taft and had his support. Although he had not actively sought the nomination, Hughes made it known that he would not turn it down; he won the nomination on the third ballot. Charles W. Fairbanks, formerly Teddy Roosevelt's vice president, was nominated as Hughes's running mate. Hughes was the only Supreme Court justice to be nominated for president by a major political party. On surface, it was a balanced ticket; but once again a large group of progressive Republicans bolted to support Wilson. As a concession to supporters of Ohio republicanism, Ohio senator Warren Harding would be the convention's keynote speaker.

Warren Harding's keynote speech branded the Ohio republicanism of former presidents as "Americanism." He argued for a return to the industrial-labor alliance of McKinley:

> We believe in American markets for American products, American wages for American workmen, American opportunity for American genius and industry, and American defense for American soil. American citizenship is the reflex of American conditions, and we believe our policies make for a fortunate people for whom moral, material, and educational advancement is the open way. The glory of our progress confirms. The answered aspirations of a new world acclaim. We have taken the ideal form of popular government and applied the policies which had led a continent to the altars of liberty and glorified the preserve and defend and go unfalteringly on. Power is the guarantor of peace and conscience the buckler of everlasting right. Verily, it is good to be an American.[5]

Harding's Americanism would serve as the foundation for the renaissance of Ohio republicanism in 1920; but for Americans wanting to be isolated from world war, the idea was too nationalistic for the times. Interestingly, Wilson used the campaign slogan "America First" to mean he would keep America out of foreign wars. Harding used the motto in economic terms.

The race was close, but the remaining scars of the Republican split seemed to have made the difference. Wilson's victory marked the first time that a Democratic Party candidate had won two consecutive presidential elections since Andrew Jackson's reelection in 1832. The result was exceptionally close, and the outcome remained in doubt for several days, partially because of the wait for returns from California in the West. The state proved to be key, as Wilson won it by only 3,800 votes. The electoral vote was one of the closest in U.S. history—with 266 votes needed to win, Wilson took 30 states for 277 electoral votes, while Hughes won 18 states and 254 electoral votes. Wilson was the second of just four presidents in U.S. history to win reelection with a lower percentage of the electoral vote than in their prior elections. This was the last presidential contest before the ratification of the 19th Amendment to the United States Constitution, which granted women the right to vote. The election took place during the time of the Mexican Revolution and Europe's involvement in World War I.

Wilson's second term was all about America's entry into World War I. In March 1917, several American ships were sunk by Germany, leaving Wilson no choice; the cabinet was unanimously in favor of war. The declaration of war by the United States against Germany passed Congress by strong bipartisan majorities on April 4, 1917. Wilson had a unique approach to war and government. He saw the war as the force to take over private industry and even make certain reforms in the operation of industry. In particular, he believed it was an opportunity to expand unionization.[6] More favorable treatment was extended to those unions that supported the U.S. war effort, such as the American Federation of Labor (AFL). Wilson worked closely with Samuel Gompers and the AFL, the railroad brotherhoods, and other unions, which saw enormous growth in membership and wages during Wilson's administration. Wilson challenged the idea of a private war industry that was a principle of Ohio republicanism born out of the Civil War.

Ohio republicanism was saved not by an election this time, but the failure of government control over private industry to perform. Initially, the Wilson administration was overwhelmed by the need to wage war. Wilson had spent years avoiding a buildup. Initially, he hoped to control wartime production through government agencies, but the demands were overwhelming. President Wilson had resisted war preparation until the United States entered the conflict in 1917. He then considered the nationalization of large industries such as railroads, steel, rubber, and shipbuilding. Private industry resisted, and Wilson looked to control things through new bureaucracies such as the National War Labor Board and government corporations.

The United States, at the beginning, lacked even the basic ships to transport an army to Europe. Wilson put the Emergency Fleet Corporation in place to spearhead America's shipbuilding. By April 1918, the Fleet Corporation had failed to meet the country's needs; the company had failed to pull together private business in a coordinated effort. America needed to ship 350,000 men and supplies a month, and the Fleet Corporation was sending less than 100,000. Within a few months, the Emergency Fleet Corporation had become a hopeless bureaucracy with a demoralized workforce. Wilson looked to Henry Ford to head up the Fleet Corporation, but Ford, like Carnegie, wanted little direct involvement in a war against Germany. Wilson was forced to turn to capitalist Charles Schwab, the president of Bethlehem Steel, a major supporter of Ohio republicanism, and a national industrialist. Wilson was also pressured by England's secretary of the navy Winston Churchill to name Schwab.[7] Schwab had been a major supporter of Ohio republicanism throughout his career as president of United States Steel and then Bethlehem.

Schwab quickly addressed the bureaucratic organization of the Emergency Fleet Corporation. He moved headquarters from Washington to the shipyards of Philadelphia, and he broke up the bureaucracy, simplifying the infrastructure and hierarchy. Schwab also limited the government's control by cutting its red tape. He removed political appointments and replaced them with businessmen. Schwab found the government cost-plus system the worst of any approach of management. The cost-plus system meant that the contractor was paid for all materials and labor to build a ship, and that a percentage of the costs was given to the contractor as a "profit." Schwab was appalled at a movement system where higher costs meant higher profits. It was to the advantage of the contractor to use more materials and labor hours in the building of a ship. The arrangement was pure inefficiency, rewarding ineffectiveness with higher profits. Schwab saw it as industrial socialism or industrial welfare. In addition, the cost-plus system required the use of government supervision and inspection to keep things honest and moving forward. Schwab applied the basics of capitalism to motivate the workers with production bonuses and awards.

The results made headlines as American ships were launched in record speed. Schwab resigned from the Emergency Fleet Corporation in late 1918. Endless industry dinners honored him, and national editorials applauded him across the nation. The record seems clear, but Wilson never fully recognized Schwab's contribution to winning the war. The men's relationship grew cold, and Wilson feared Schwab's political and financial power to oppose him. Schwab would use his new popularity to seek out a Republican candidate to return the nation to capitalism. Politics continued in 1921 as a Special House Committee investigated Schwab's and Bethlehem's profits while heading the Fleet Corporation.

Wilson, however, was more successful in forcing government contractors to unionize. Wilson's agency was known as the National War Labor Board (NWLB), and it had limited authority, requiring the president to force compliance. The makeup of the board was progressive, but Wilson adroitly appointed former president Taft as the co-chair. The change was more in the NWLB's mission as stated. Priority one was to prevent production disruption caused by strikes and lockouts, which could be used to force unionization. The NWLB stated its principles as: the right of labor to organize, the lack of action against organizing efforts by the companies, the right of union shops to exist, the right of the worker to a "living wage," and the use of regional "prevailing wages" to apply.[8] The Wilson administration often used these broad philosophies to award contracts to unionized workers. Even more disturbing was the government's propensity to support union activity and collective bargaining where none had previously existed. The NWLB strong-armed factories and company officers whenever possible. Collective bargaining became an unofficial requirement for government orders, and while the Republican Party would oppose this measure, it was in the minority.

The end of the war in 1919 brought new economic problems for America. Unions prepared to increase wages, and soldiers tried to enter the contracting postwar labor market. Union organizers had been encouraged under the Wilson administration; in particular, the American Federation of Labor hoped to organize in the steel, rubber, and meat-packing industries. There were real issues in the public mind concerning improved workplace environments. Ohio republicanism and progressivism both recognized the problem but approached it differently. Progressivism believed the answer was in unionization, collective bargaining, and government regulation. Ohio republicanism believed in private industry solutions, such as the management-employee organization models used at Goodyear Rubber and Millvale Steel with limited government regulation. Ohio presidents such as William Taft saw the labor issues as legal issues in which the courts could act as regulators. The massive national steel strike of 1919 involved 350,000 steelworkers. At the heart of the strike was the elimination of a 12-hour day and union representation, issues that had gone back to the Great Railroad Strike of 1877. More than anything, Wilson had hoped for the elimination of the 12-hour day to be a legacy item of his presidency. He had suffered a stroke, and his cabinet refused to intervene. The result was a defeat of union strikes in major industries. Still, the issue remained with the voters.

As the election of 1920 approached, the issues were similar to those in the post–Civil War decades of Ohio republicanism's dominance. Economic concerns, unemployed veterans, labor unrest, and the role of government were the important matters. Big-business monopolies had moved to the back pages of the news as a recession loomed. Businessmen were concerned about the rise of socialism in the progressive movement. Government was challenging the type of capitalism that had built the nation's great industries. Ohio senator Warren Harding, the 1916 Republican keynote speaker, was popular with the public and business and offered a return to Ohio republicanism and conservativism.

Chapter Eighteen

A Renaissance of Ohio Republicanism

It is truly unfortunate that scandals destroyed the legacy of President Harding and hurt the legacy of Ohio republicanism. Only recently have historians started rethinking his presidency and its legacy.[1] Warren Gamaliel Harding (1865–1923) was the 29th president of the United States, serving from March 4, 1921, until his death in 1923. Harding was born on November 2, 1865, in Corsica, Ohio (now known as Blooming Grove). His parents, George and Phoebe Dickerson Harding, were both doctors, and his family had roots back to the 1670s in New England. Harding's parents were also strong abolitionists, and they had moved to Blooming Grove, Ohio (near the city of Marion), prior to the Civil War. True to his abolitionist roots of Ohio republicanism, Harding was educated with *McGuffey Readers* while he attended a one-room schoolhouse. He also used the *McGuffey Readers* in his brief career as a teacher. Moreover, Harding was known to use stories from the *Readers* in his dealings. He had been a member of several Protestant sects, including the Methodists and Baptists. In many ways, Harding was the perfect son of Ohio republicanism.

As a senator, Harding actively supported business interests by returning to a McKinley-type policy for high protective tariffs. On social issues Harding would return the Republican Party to the roots of Ohio republicanism. Like many other Republicans, he also endorsed the 18th Amendment to the United States Constitution and the Volstead Act on the prohibition of alcohol, even though he thought Prohibition was a moral issue that could not be policed. The 18th Amendment effectively prohibited alcoholic beverages in the United States by declaring the production, transport, and sale of alcohol illegal. The consumption or private possession of alcohol was legal. The separate Volstead Act set down methods for enforcing the 18th Amendment, and it defined which intoxicating liquors were prohibited, and which were excluded from

President Harding (hatless, being saluted), 1922. Library of Congress.

prohibition, such as those used for medical and religious purposes. The amendment's ratification by the states was certified on January 16, 1919, and it took effect on January 16, 1920.

As president, Harding would come to office with the 18th Amendment in place. Prohibition had long been embedded in Ohio republicanism, but often the Republican elected officials gave it only tacit support over the years. In the 1916 election, Woodrow Wilson and Republican candidate Charles Evans Hughes ignored the Prohibition issue, as did both parties' political platforms. Prohibition had always been a grassroots movement that national and high-level state politicians often tried to avoid. Still, Republican officeholders were expected to be supportive, especially in old Transylvania. In the amendment's passage, however, they were bipartisan. In 1917, the Senate passed a resolution of the amendment to be presented to the states for ratification. The vote was 65 to 20, with the Democrats voting 36 in favor and 12 in opposition, and the Republicans voting 29 in favor and eight in opposition. In the House, the vote was 282 to 128, with the Democrats voting 141 in favor and 64 in opposition, and the Republicans voting 137 in favor and 62 in opposition. Four independents in the House voted in favor, and two independents cast votes against the amendment. Politicians from both parties were probably happy to see the issue settled so that they could peacefully return to drinking in private.

Warren Harding was a rising star in the party as the 1920 presidential race approached. One presidential historian said, "No darker 'dark horse' ever ran for president than Harding."[2] The 1920 nomination was considered wide open, but America's industrialists wanted a return to the favorable planks of old Ohio republicanism. Harding's 1916 keynote address had praised putting American industry first and had caught the attention of the nation's greatest capitalists, such as Henry Clay Frick and Charles Schwab. There are many legends about how a small group of American businessmen helped in the election of Warren Harding. Many of these stories color Harding as a puppet of big business. But like William McKinley, Harding would be his own man standing against his big-business supporters on matters like collective bargaining for workers.

One of Harding's major strengths (which would become his weakness) was his close ties to steel executives, financiers, and industrialists, such as Charles Schwab and Andrew Mellon. Harding had worked with Schwab on the shipbuilding committee during World War I. They had become good friends and part of a Washington-Pittsburgh-New York poker club. These informal poker games included some of America's most powerful men: President Taft; future president Herbert Hoover; Henry Clay Frick; Charles Schwab; financier and future secretary of the Treasury Andrew Mellon; Philander Knox, who served as United States attorney general (1901-1904), senator from Pennsylvania (1904-1909, 1917-1921) and secretary of state (1909-1913); Henry Sinclair of Sinclair Oil; and many other senators and industrialists. It is possible that at some games more than 60 percent of America's industrial assets were represented at the table.[3]

Henry Clay Frick wanted his friend Andrew Mellon to run, but Charles Schwab and many steel executives were behind Harding. Frick held a private dinner in 1919 that included George Perkins (United States Steel and J. P. Morgan Company), Dan Hanna (son of Senator Mark Hanna), Ambrose Monell (International Nickel), George Whelan (head of United Cigar), Henry Sinclair (Sinclair Oil), A. A. Sprague (Chicago Wholesaler), George Harvey (New York journalist and Republican super delegate), and others.[4] Retired Andrew Carnegie opposed the Republicans, wanting to see Wilson's League of Nations adopted. Ambrose Monell was the link for the steel executives loyal to their old boss Carnegie, who publicly avoided any connection with Frick. The dinner was the source of a major fund to defeat the League of Nations and the progressive Democrats. Those in attendance choose Warren Harding as the Republican candidate—Harding had made several trips to Pittsburgh and had played poker with a number of these business leaders. He had also been a close associate of their favorite son, William Taft. Dinner attendee

William Boyce Thompson (1869–1930) was an American mining engineer, financier, prominent figure in the Republican Party, and founder of Newmont Mining. Thompson and George Harvey would assure Harding's nomination at the convention.

The Republican Convention was deadlocked in the early balloting, but George Harvey and William Thompson famously turned the vote. Recently the convention was remembered as follows: "George Harvey checked into Chicago's renowned Blackstone Hotel. He was in the Windy City to attend the Republican National Convention. A bellhop took Harvey up to the fourth floor and showed him into his spacious two-room suite. Harvey's name has faded from public memory, but the reception room of suite 404 was destined to become the most famous hotel room in American political history. It was the original 'smoke-filled room'. ... Reporter Kirke Simpson filed a story in 1920 that read, 'Harding of Ohio was chosen by a group of men in a smoke-filled room early today.'"[5] This is believed to be the original use of the term *smoke-filled room*.[6] Harvey was rewarded after the election with an appointment as ambassador to Britain.

Oilman Henry Sinclair had been assigned at the 1919 dinner to the job of building a campaign chest to defeat the League of Nations and elect Harding. The fund was believed to be over $3 million and the largest war chest of any previous presidential candidate. Schwab was considered one of the largest contributors, but the list was long, including Henry Clay Frick, George Westinghouse, H. H. Westinghouse, John Rockefeller, Andrew Mellon, Walter Chrysler, Harry Sinclair, and most of the Pittsburgh executives. Of course, the original dinner in 1919 and the Chicago smoke-filled room kept all secret so as not to offend progressive Andrew Carnegie. Many owed their careers to him.

Democrats nominated Governor James M. Cox, a newspaper editor from Ohio, as their presidential candidate. Thirty-eight-year-old Assistant Secretary of the Navy (and future president) Franklin D. Roosevelt, a fifth cousin of the late president Theodore Roosevelt, was the nominee for vice president. Governor Cox launched a whirlwind campaign that took him to rallies, train station speeches, and dinner addresses, whereas Senator Harding relied on a front porch campaign similar to those of Garfield and McKinley. The economy was once again the issue, as war production was over and veterans returned to the United States looking for work. Nationalism was on the rise, and the fall of Russia to the socialists brought fears of labor and social unrest. Ohio republicanism offered the solution to these problems.

Wilson's progressive international policies had broken support in traditional Democrat ethnic strongholds. The Irish Catholic and German communities were outraged at Wilson's perceived favoritism of their traditional enemy Great Britain. He opposed the Irish Republican Army in its fight for freedom. Furthermore, Wilson had outraged German Americans with this statement: "Any man who carries a hyphen about with him [a reference to "hyphenated Americans" who claimed dual ancestry, such as an Irish American], carries a dagger that he is ready to plunge into the vitals of this Republic when he gets ready."[7] The German farmers that had supported the Democrats' antiwar and low-tariff laws returned to the Republican Party in large numbers.

The League of Nations was also unpopular with both the Germans and the Irish, who saw it as a reversal of Wilson's "America First" pledge prior to the war. After the war, the electorate still harbored noninterventionist and nationalist sentiment.[8] A first-term U.S. senator from Ohio named Warren G. Harding exploited this message of "America First" and won the presidency in 1920. Harding's landslide victory in 1920 earned him 60 percent of the popular vote, which was one of the highest percentages ever. Even Franklin D. Roosevelt, at the height of his popularity, did not receive a greater portion of the popular vote. Harding's victory margin of 26.2 percent in the popular vote (60.3 percent to 34.1 percent) remains the largest popular-vote percentage margin in presidential elections.

Warren G. Harding's administration was determined to roll back the twenty-year momentum of progressive legislation. Congress readily and easily got the president to support an end to progressivism. Wartime controls were eliminated, and taxes were slashed. Harding established a federal budget system, restored the high protective tariff, and imposed tight limitations on immigration. Unfortunately, he allowed many of his political supporters too much of a role in lesser decisions, which became major scandals. Harding's poker games made headlines during his presidency, and the players were known as the "Ohio Gang."

Harding's poker games were the stuff of legends. "He was a keen poker player, who once gambled away on a single hand an entire set of White House china dating back to the presidency of Benjamin Harrison."[9] Many of his poker buddies were business friends from Ohio. The Ohio Gang, also known as the "poker cabinet," was responsible for the Teapot Dome Scandal, America's biggest political indignity up until Watergate. This bribery incident that took place in 1921–1922, involved Secretary of the Interior Albert Bacon Fall. Fall had leased navy petroleum reserves in Teapot Dome in Wyoming, and in two other locations in California, to private oil companies at low rates without competitive bidding. The lease was given to another former poker buddy of Harding's, Henry Sinclair.

The Ohio Gang met regularly at the infamous Little Green House on K Street. Harding, much like Grant, allowed this group of friends too much power in his administration. Many of these politicians and industry leaders became associated with Harding during his tenure as a state politician. Attorney

Left to right, Henry Ford, Thomas Edison, Warren Harding and Harvey Firestone on a famous road camping trip in 1921. Library of Congress.

General Harry M. Daugherty, Interior Secretary Albert B. Fall, and Navy Secretary Edwin C. Denby were considered responsible for acts of corruption and crony capitalism. One of the darker members of the Ohio Gang was Jesse Smith, who worked for Attorney General Daugherty. These individuals were the main operatives in the Teapot Dome Scandal.

Harding's role in the scandal was never fully defined, but Secretary of Commerce Herbert Hoover believed Harding was not directly involved and did take steps to resolve it. Hoover noted in his memoirs:

> One day after lunch when we were a few days out, Harding asked me to come to his cabin. He plumped at me the question: "If you knew of a great scandal in our administration, would you for the good of the country and the party expose it publicly or would you bury it?" My natural reply was "Publish it, and at least get credit for integrity on your side." He remarked that this method might be politically dangerous. I asked for more particulars. He said that he had received some rumors of irregularities, centering around Smith, in connection with cases in the Department of Justice. He had followed the matter up and finally sent for Smith. After a painful session, he told Smith that he would be arrested in the morning. Smith went home, burned all his papers, and committed suicide. Harding gave me no information about what Smith had been up to. I asked what Daugherty's relations to the affair were. He abruptly dried up and never raised the question again.[10]

Republican Senator Robert M. La Follette, Sr., of Wisconsin led an investigation by the Senate Committee on Public Lands. The scandal grew as Follette's Senate office was broken into. The press found evidence of bribery and even sex scandals that captured the imagination of the public. Eventually Secretary Fall was found guilty and imprisoned. Oilman Henry Sinclair was found not guilty but spent six months in jail for contempt of court. Most historians agree that Harding was not directly involved in these misdeeds, but his poor management of the office was notable.[11] In June, President Harding set out on an intended 15,000-mile cross-country speaking tour labeled the "Voyage of Understanding," which included the first-ever presidential visit to Alaska. On August 2, 1923, Harding died of a heart attack in San Francisco.

Harding's untimely death during hearings on his administration's misconduct did help his popularity, but sexual scandals appeared after his death. Harding had been involved in an extramarital affair during his tenure as lieutenant governor of Ohio and as U.S. senator for Ohio. This scandal continues today, as the Library of Congress opened his love letters to the public in 2014. In 2015, DNA tests confirmed another affair and a child.[12] In the end, the scandals had little effect on the election of Harding's vice president, Calvin Coolidge, but they destroyed Harding's own legacy and forever tarnished his reputation. Still, Harding would extend the legacy of Ohio republicanism for another decade. Over the next ten years, the presidency would be controlled by two of his cabinet members—Vice President Calvin Coolidge and Secretary of Commerce Herbert Hoover. Most of those who followed Harding cleaned up his scandals and returned to the core principles of Ohio republicanism.

Charles M. Schwab at the White House to discuss progress on the Harding Memorial in 1924. Schwab was the New York City chairman of the memorial. Library of Congress.

The most overlooked part of Harding's legacy of Ohio republicanism was his bold stand on civil rights, including women's rights. In October 1921, President Harding delivered a forthright speech in Birmingham, Alabama,[13] refuting Jim Crow laws and attacking the heart of racism in America. It was a flashback to the spirit that had brought about the birth of Ohio republicanism and the Republican Party. Harding's remarks had the boldness of the early Ohio republicanism. He condemned lynchings, committed primarily by white supremacists against African Americans in the Deep South during the Wilson years. Harding brought civil rights back as a necessary component of Ohio republicanism. He equated civil rights, women's rights, and workers' rights with social justice given to Americans from the Founders. Harding's Americanism was a total vision of a united philosophy supporting Ohio republicanism. Social, economic, and labor rights were at the heart of America, creating a true America-first philosophy. Government was to provide the same protection for blacks as tariffs did for workers. It was the McKinley message applied with more force and consistency.

Similarly, Harding would leave his mark on collective bargaining and the rights of union organization without the support of his poker gang. He would achieve what Woodrow Wilson, the unions, the Great Steel Strike of 1919, and the socialists never could. William McKinley had tried to bring the parties together for years and had failed. Republican supporters, to a large degree, had opposed such efforts on behalf of labor for decades. Working with Judge Gary of United States Steel, Harding brought an end to the 12-hour day, which the union strike of 1919 had failed to establish. Harding had worked relentlessly by holding labor management conferences at the White House. His initial White House meeting with 40 steel executives (including some poker buddies) ended in bitterness on both sides, but Harding took the matter to the public to apply pressure.[14] Ending the 12-hour day would be an achievement that had been the core of many bloody strikes in America and had eluded at least ten presidents, both Democratic and Republican. However, that achievement's timing would ensure that it would be lost to mainstream history.

A labor historian in 1977 summarized it best: "On the inside page, almost hidden behind the banner headlines announcing the death of Warren G. Harding, *The New York Times* of August 3, 1923 carried a notice of historical importance to American labor: the Directors of the Iron and Steel Institute had announced the total elimination of the twelve hour day."[15] In the end, Harding's legacy will always be one of what might have been, but he did bridge the transition back to Ohio republicanism in national politics. That legacy would continue as the Republicans and Ohio republicanism politics controlled the nation until the election of Franklin Delano Roosevelt in 1932.

Chapter Nineteen

Is There a Ghost of Ohio Republicanism?

Recent successes of Donald Trump and Bernie Sanders have shown resurgence in populism and nationalism. The old tenets of Ohio republicanism—high tariffs, American jobs, veteran affairs, national pride, religious liberty, and moralistic government—have become popular again. Over the past few decades, there has been a surge of the use of *McGuffey Readers* in homeschooling. Ohio republicanism is far from dead, but it does not reside in the established modern-day Republican Party (or the Democratic Party). While the Republican Party had owned Ohio republicanism until 1932, it has had no party home since then.

The 1930s, the Depression and World War II had created a new fault line inside Ohio republicanism, with each party taking an opposing stance. Democrats became the defenders of free trade (at least till the 1990s), and by 2000, the voter had no place to support protectionism. The Republican Party held on to a limited nationalism, but it also took on the role of America as the world's policeman and defender of democracy. Both parties embraced bigger government, but the Republicans offered a little less. The Democrats wrested civil rights from the Republican Party in the 1960s. Both parties embraced globalization and a move to world governance, concepts deeply hated by followers of Ohio republicanism. No party had any moral values, but Republicans took on religious liberty. Both parties decried the simplicity of populism as inconsistent with enlightened democracy (the establishment). Populism had been the heart of democracy of Ohio republicanism. These divisions muted and eliminated the Ohio republicanism voter.

The Reagan election of 1980 showed a resurgence of populism and nationalism as the core states of Republican dominance from 1868 to 1932. Still, the two-party system itself was the best defense against a rise of Ohio republicanism. The ideas of Ohio republicanism were not dead, only restrained by the two-party system, which gave the voter no option to support the philosophy. Like the old ghost of the Whig Party often haunted the Republican Party, a ghost of Ohio republicanism haunted the Republican Party and the Democratic Party in the election of 2016. Trump won big in old Transylvania and carried the old strongholds of Ohio republicanism—Ohio, Indiana, Michigan, Pennsylvania, Iowa, Wisconsin, West Virginia, and Kentucky. Workers crossed party lines to vote for America, first rejecting the internationalism of both parties. West Virginia, western Pennsylvania, eastern Ohio, and Kentucky of old Whig territory and Transylvania returned to voting for protectionism, tariffs, nationalism, social issues, and veteran issues, and rejected globalization. Trump offered a way to cross party lines and vote for the Ohio republicanism of old. Ohio's heartland would lead the nation in a new shift back to the philosophy's principles. Areas like Youngstown, Warren, and Niles, Ohio, returned to the previous Republican strongholds, which were dominated by Ohio republicanism. This was the birthplace of William McKinley, and the birthplace of James Garfield was also nearby. Trumbull and Mahoning Counties of the Youngstown area were solidly Republican before going Democratic in the 1936 election; and before supporting the Republican Party, the area was a bastion of Whig votes.

President Trump became the first nonincumbent Republican to win Trumbull County since Herbert Hoover in 1928. Trump's margin of victory in Trumbull County was 6.4 percentage points. Even before the presidential election, the Ohio primary augured a voter shift. The Mahoning County Republican chairman was even more surprised than the Democrats in the Ohio primary: "I looked at Republican turnout on election night and I saw 34,000 Republicans had voted. I nearly fell off my chair because there were only 14- or 15,000 Republicans in Mahoning County."[1] CNN noted in the same interview, "Most shocking of all, is that 18 Democratic precinct captains—local party officials in the county—were among the switchers. Dave Betras, the county Democratic chair, summarily fired them." These were not people aligning with Republicans, but voters who believed in tariffs, the "America First" concept, nationalism, and populism—they were the descendants of Ohio republicanism. These voters were loyal to a political view, not to the Republican Party or even to Donald Trump.

The nearby Republican stronghold of Columbiana County had the largest landslide victory for a Republican since 1928, when Hoover got 77.3 percent of the vote. Columbiana County Republicans are not blue-blood Republicans; they are the true heirs of Ohio republicanism and have Whig roots. They, too, were rejecting the internationalism and free trade of the Republican Party. These were the voters who had been most affected by the death of Ohio republicanism as a political philosophy. The Mahoning Valley

Presidents Wilson (left) and Taft at the White House after Wilson's inauguration in 1913. Library of Congress.

had once included the great steel mills of Youngstown, Niles, and Warren along a 25-mile stretch. The closings of Youngstown Sheet and Tube, United States Steel, Sharon Steel, Copperweld, and Republic Steel from 1977 to the mid–1990s resulted in the loss of an estimated 50,000 jobs. Small businesses collapsed throughout the valley, and tax losses destroyed the city school system. Shopping malls were converted into Halloween haunted houses. By 1995, Youngstown looked like Germany at the end of World War II. The social and community infrastructure collapsed as crime took over the valley.

Youngstown reflects another part of deindustrialization, the loss of community identity and national pride. Local historians Sherry Lee Linkon and John Russo describe this phenomenon: "When mills began to close in the late 1970s, the core of community and individual identity shifted, and the meaning of Youngstown and the meaning of work in Youngstown would first be transformed and then deformed. Once a site of productive labor and class struggle, Youngstown would become a place known for economic loss and resistance. The struggle in Youngstown would not end in the closing of the mill."[2] Until 2016, neither party offered hope for these voters.

These ghost voters of Ohio republicanism managed the heavy job losses of the 1980s and 1990s by changing lifestyles—becoming two-income families and taking early retirement and social security. Politicians successfully refocused their attention during elections. Community efforts tried to bring in new industries. The new century, however, brought an attack on these voters' American dream. They were tired of being told that the jobs were never coming back. They were sick of hearing that the future was in informational jobs that never materialized. The ghost voters of Ohio republicanism were tired of endless federal retraining that only created jobs for teachers and government consultants. These voters were angered by the talk of a postindustrial age that offered nothing for them. They were enraged by national leaders of both parties telling them that they needed to move to where the jobs were. While steel mills rusted and collapsed, their workers were sick of the billions of dollars going to rebuild the Middle East because the United States had leveled it. To former factory workers, the American government was the same government that had destroyed Youngstown. The inheritors of Ohio republicanism resented the fact that their home prices had fallen to junk-bond levels while the housing market boomed in Washington D.C., New York, and Hollywood. They didn't want government to tell them what the future had to be; they wanted government to change the future. These beliefs were the populism of Ohio republicanism.

Ohio republicanism remains the spirit of hope for America. It represents the expectation that globalization and internationalism are not settled political policy. It embodies a raw nationalism and populism that most countries have tried to resist since World War II. For good or for bad, Ohio republicanism represents the voice of the people versus the wisdom of professional politicians. It rejects the trading of jobs to create political objectives. This philosophy is a type of realism that questions the record of peace and free trade. It questions America's recruitment of its sons and daughters to fight in endless wars, while the same government does nothing to employ these veterans when they return. Ohio republicanism sees a role for capitalism in democracy, while retaining government's role to regulate free enterprise. More and more, this viewpoint questions whether the enemy is big business or big government. It sees morality as a family, community and local-school issue, not one for the federal government. It questions whether the Constitution is just too complex for the average person to understand, requiring the government to tell citizens what it says (effectively eliminating its use). Ohio republicanism questions courts that have become Oracles of Delphi versus arbitrators of the law, which William Taft had left as his greatest legacy.

The Ohio republicanism of the Ohio presidents retains the spirit of the early American frontier. Ohio republicanism remains a political foundation if it can be tapped. In general, the concepts at its root are the voice of the people, limited government, American jobs ahead of economic philosophy, local school control, states' rights, nationalism, protectionism, and a rejection of internationalism. Ohio republicanism encompasses William Harrison's expansion of frontiers; Grant's love of the republic; Hayes's civil rights for all; Garfield's thoughtful common sense and religious liberty; McKinley's view of national capitalism and protecting American jobs; Taft's respect for a nation of laws; and, finally, Harding's (and Grant's) human failings. All of these things are part of the path forward in this fallen world. As the Ohio presidents showed, the American government is bigger than one man, always subject to the will of the people, and never owned by any political party.

Chapter Notes

Preface

1. George W. Knepper, *Ohio and Its People* (Kent, OH: Kent State University Press, 1989), 263.
2. James Perry, *Touched with Fire: Five Presidents and the Civil War Battles That Made Them* (New York: Public Affairs, 2003), xvi.
3. Kyle Kondik, "Why Ohio Picks the President," Sabato's Crystal Ball, July 13, 2016, The University of Virginia Center for Politics, http://www.centerforpolitics.org/crystalball/articles/why-ohio-picks-the-president/.
4. For a full discussion of the Ohio presidents and *McGuffey Readers*, see Quentin Skrabec, *William McGuffey: Industry's Mentor* (New York: Algora, 2009).
5. Kondik, "Why Ohio Picks the President."

Chapter One

1. Alexander McClure and Charles Morris, *The Authentic Life of William McKinley: Our Third Martyr President* (U.S. Congress, 1901), 321. (Copy at McKinley Memorial in Canton, Ohio, and Library of Congress.)
2. Murat Halstead, *The Life and Distinguished Services of William McKinley* (McKinley Memorial Association, 1901), 506.
3. Ibid.
4. McClure and Morris, *Authentic Life of William McKinley*, 307.
5. "American Economy," *Manufacturer and Builder* 20, no. 2 (November 1888).
6. Hayes to McKinley, November 6, 1866, Hayes Memorial Library, Rutherford B. Hayes Presidential Center, Fremont, Ohio.
7. William McKinley, "The Value of Protection," *North American Review* 150, no. 403 (June 1890): 747–748.
8. *Canton (Ohio) Repository*, September 24, 1900.
9. John Kasson, *Civilizing the Machine* (New York, Hill & Wang, 1977), 54.
10. Marshall Everett, *Complete Life of William McKinley* (Marshall Everett, 1901), 78.
11. McClure and Morris, *Authentic Life of William McKinley*, 350.
12. Quentin R. Skrabec, *The Pig Iron Aristocracy: The Triumph of American Protectionism* (Westminster, Md.: Heritage Books, 2008), 90–101.
13. Margaret Leech, *In the Days of McKinley* (New York: Harper & Brothers, 1959), 28.
14. Ibid., 22.
15. Chauncey Depew, *My Memories of 80 Years* (New York: Charles Scribner & Sons, 1924), 35.
16. Samuel Fallows, *Life of William McKinley—Our Martyred President* (Chicago: Regan, 1901), 23.

Chapter Two

1. Elisha Whittlesey to Joshua Giddings, May 13, 1824, MSS Whittlesey, Western Reserve Historical Society, Cleveland, Ohio.

2. Lee Benson, *The Concept of Jacksonian Democracy* (Princeton: Princeton University Press, 1961), 21–46.

3. James Stewart, *Joshua R. Giddings and the Tactics of Radical Politics* (Cleveland: Press of Case Western Reserve, 1970), 66.

4. David Heidler and Jeanne Heidler, *Henry Clay: Essential American* (New York: Random Press, 2010), 418.

5. "Speech, April 14, 1834," in *Papers of Henry Clay*, ed. James Hopkins and Mary Hargreaves (Lexington: University of Kentucky Press, 1959), 12.

6. Heidler and Heidler, *Henry Clay: Essential American*, 419.

7. Robert V. Remini, *Henry Clay: Statesman of the Union* (New York: W. W. Norton, 1991), 576.

8. Dolores Sullivan, *William Holmes McGuffey* (Rutherford, N.J.: Fairleigh Dickinson University Press, 1994), 151.

9. David Von Drehle, "The Demon Drink," *Time Magazine*, May 24, 2010, 56.

10. William Jennings, *Transylvania: Pioneer University of the West* (New York: Pageant, 1955), 123.

11. Pope John Paul II, Encyclical—*Contesimus Annus*, May 1, 1991, 46.

12. Alexander Hamilton, *Report on Manufactures*, January 15, 1790 (New York: Kessinger, 2010).

Chapter Three

1. Zachary Taylor died in 1850 in office, and his vice president, Whig Millard Fillmore, became president.

2. Francis Weisenburger, *The Passing of the Frontier: 1825-1850* (Columbus: Ohio Historical Society, 1941), 3: 548–550.

3. Knepper, *Ohio and Its People*, 211.

4. Michael F. Holt, *The Rise and Fall of the American Whig Party: Jacksonian Politics and the Onset of the Civil War* (Oxford: Oxford University Press, 1999), 272–274.

5. Jack Bauer, *Zachary Taylor: Soldier, Planter, Statesman of the Old Southwest* (Baton Rouge: Louisiana State University Press, 1985), 240–257.

6. *Cleveland Herald*, November 15, 1848.

7. Stewart, *Joshua R. Giddings*, 142–156.

8. Stanley Coben, "Northeastern Business and Radical Reconstruction: A Re-examination," *Mississippi Valley Historical Review* 46, no. 1 (June 1959): 67–90.

9. Henry Gannett, *The Origin of Certain Place Names in the United States* (Washington, D.C.: Government Printing Office, 1904), 132.

10. John Niven, *Salmon P. Chase: A Biography* (Oxford: Oxford University Press, 1995), 30–46.

11. Eugene Roseboom, *The Civil War Era: 1850-1873* (Columbus: Ohio Historical Society, 1944), 430–431.

Chapter Four

1. "American System" was the term used by Henry Clay in the 1820s, and it was adopted by the Whig Party and later the Republican Party.

2. Remini, *Henry Clay*, 230.

3. For a full discussion of the politics of the Iron Whigs, see Skrabec, *Pig Iron Aristocracy*.

4. James Madison, *Federalist Papers*, No. 41 (New York: Dover Thrift, 2014), 68.

5. James Madison, *Federalist Papers*, No. 42 (New York: Dover Thrift, 2014), 54.

6. William Armstrong, *Major McKinley: McKinley and the Civil War* (Kent, OH: Kent University Press, 2000), 90–93.

7. *Ibid.*, 56.

8. *Ibid.*, 55.

9. McKinley to Hayes, July 2, 1888, Rutherford Hayes Papers, Hayes Memorial Library.

10. Stefan Lorant, *Pittsburgh: The Story of an American City* (Lenox, MA: Donnelley & Sons, 1964), 123.

11. Peter Cain, *Free Trade and Protectionism: Key Nineteenth Century Journal Summaries* (London: Routledge, 1996), 25–39.

12. Benjamin Harrison, *Speeches of Benjamin Harrison, Twenty-Third President of the United States* (New York: Leopold Classic Library, 2015), 69–76.

Chapter Five

1. *New York Herald*, September 18, 1863, quote from page 6; and "Blair's Bitters," *New York Times*, October 30, 1863, quote from page 4.

2. Josiah Bunting III, *Ulysses S. Grant* (New York: Henry Holt, 2004), 2.

3. William Hesselshine, *U. S. Grant, Politician* (New York: Dodd, Mead, 1935), 69–120.
4. James Cash, *Unsung Heroes* (Wilmington, Ohio: Orange Frazer, 1998), 20.
5. U. S. Grant, "Reasons for Being a Republican," speech delivered on September 28, 1880, in Warren, Ohio, National Center for Public Policy Research website, https://nationalcenter.org/USGrant.html (link no longer works).
6. A. G. Frank, *Capitalism and Underdevelopment in Latin America* (New York: Monthly Review Press, 1967), 164.
7. *American Economist*, March 5, 1915, 117–120.
8. Morgan Wayne, *From Hayes to McKinley: National Party Politics, 1872–1896* (Syracuse: Syracuse University Press, 1969), 170, 303–319.
9. Bruce A. Campbell and Richard J. Trilling, *Realignment in American Politics: Toward a Theory* (Austin: University of Texas Press, 2014), 100–120.
10. Ulysses S. Grant, "Sixth Annual Message," December 7, 1874, The American Presidency Project, by Gerhard Peters and John T. Woolley, http://www.presidency.ucsb.edu/ws/?pid=29515. Also available via the Library of Congress.
11. "Panama Canal Proposal," 1881, The Gilder Lehrman Collection, The Gilder Lehrman Institute of American History, New York, accessed January 18, 2017, https://www.gilderlehrman.org/content/panama-canal-proposal-1881.
12. Geoffrey Perret, *Ulysses S. Grant: Soldier & President* (New York: Random House, 1997), 7.
13. William S. McFeely, *Grant: A Biography* (New York: W. W. Norton, 1981), 55.
14. W. H. Brands, *The Man Who Saved the Union: Ulysses S. Grant in War and Peace* (New York: Doubleday, 2012), 553.
15. Rutherford B. Hayes, *Diary and Letters of Hayes, Book III*, 80–83, Hayes Presidential Library, Fremont, Ohio.
16. Roseboom, *Civil War Era: 1850–1873*, 270–274.
17. Richard O. Curry, "The Union As It Was: a Critique of Recent Interpretations of the 'Copperheads,'" *Civil War History* 13, no. 1 (1967): 25–39.
18. Roseboom, *Civil War Era: 1850–1873*, 482.
19. Eric Ebinger, *100 Days in the Life of Rutherford Hayes* (Wilmington: Orange Frazer, 2016), 109–112.
20. *Annual Report of the Bureau of Labor Statistics* (Columbus, 1878).

Chapter Six

1. Philip Jordan, *Ohio Comes of Age: 1873–1900* (Columbus: Ohio Historical Society, 1943), 51.
2. Cash, *Unsung Heroes*, 47.
3. The Free Soil Democrats supported the prevention of slavery's spread to the western states. The Free Soilers and the Whigs formed the foundation of the Union Party (Republican Party).
4. Allan Peskin, "Who Were the Stalwarts? Who Were Their Rivals? Republican Factions in the Gilded Age" *Political Science Quarterly* 99, no. 4 (1984): 703–716.
5. "The Compromise of 1877," November 20, 2016, Boundless U.S. History, retrieved January 29, 2017, https://www.boundless.com/u-s-history/textbooks/boundless-u-s-history-textbook/reconstruction-1865-1877-19/the-grant-administration-142/the-compromise-of-1877-757-2343/.
6. This point is often debated and attributed directly to President Hayes.
7. William Henry Smith and Charles Richard Williams, *The Life of Rutherford Birchard Hayes: Nineteenth President of the United States* (University of Michigan Library, January 1, 1914), 1: 73–74. Digital copy via Amazon.
8. Hayes, diary entry for January 16, 1881, in *Diary and Letters of Hayes, Book III*.
9. Cash, *Unsung Heroes*, 60–61.
10. Winfield Scott Kerr, *John Sherman: His Life and Public Services* (Boston: Sherman, French, 1908), 2: 101–103.

Chapter Seven

1. "For the Briefest Time, President Garfield Was an Inspiration," editorial, *Washington Post*, February 17, 2013.
2. Eliza Garfield to James Garfield, December 27, 1868, in *The Life and Letters of James Abram Garfield*, by Theodore Clarke Smith (Hamden, CT: Archon Books, 1968), 6.
3. Allen Peskin, *Garfield* (Kent, OH:

Kent State University Press, 1978), digital location 102.

4. Janet Podolak, "President James A. Garfield: Civil Rights Activist Ahead of His Time," *News-Herald* (Cleveland, Ohio), August 12, 2012.

5. *Ibid.*

6. Alan Gephardt, "'The Most Important Political Change We Have Known': James A. Garfield, Slavery, and Justice in the Civil War Era, Part II," February 15, 2013, The Garfield Observer (website of the Garfield Historical Center), https://garfieldnps.wordpress.com/2013/02/15/the-most-important-political-change-we-have-known-james-a-garfield-slavery-and-justice-in-the-civil-war-era-part-ii/.

7. James A. Garfield, "Inaugural Address," March 4, 1881, The American Presidency Project, by Gerhard Peters and John T. Woolley, http://www.presidency.ucsb.edu/ws/?pid=25823.

8. Peskin, *Garfield*, digital location 4674.

9. Cash, *Unsung Heroes*, 71.

10. Biographical Notes, James Garfield Papers, Presidential Manuscripts, Library of Congress.

11. Candice Millard, *Destiny of the Republic: A Tale of Madness, Medicine, and the Murder of a President* (New York: Anchor Books, 2011), 69–70.

12. *Cincinnati Enquirer*, June 7, 22, 23, and October 9, 12, 1883.

13. William T. Horner, *Ohio's Kingmaker: Mark Hanna, Man, and Myth* (Athens: Ohio University Press, 2010). For a full discussion of Hanna's mixed image, see pages 1–35.

14. *Ibid.* 2–15.

15. Thomas Beer, *Hanna* (New York: Knopf, 1929), 5.

16. Herbert Croly, *Marcus Alonzo Hanna* (New York: Macmillan, 1912), 66–68.

Chapter Eight

1. *New York Herald*, July 3, 1881.

2. Kenneth Ackerman, *Dark Horse: The Surprise Election and Political Murder of President James Garfield* (New York: Carroll & Graf, 2003), 379.

3. Peskin, *Garfield*, 602.

4. John Stuart Ogilvie, ed., *Life and Speeches of William McKinley* (1896; repr., New York: Kessinger, 2010), pp. 16–20.

5. John Pafford, *The Forgotten Conservative: Rediscovering Grover Cleveland* (New York: Regnery History, 2013), i–ii.

6. Henry F. Graff, *Grover Cleveland: The American Presidents Series: The 22nd and 24th President, 1885–1889 and 1893–1897* (New York: Henry Holt, 2002), 30–62.

7. Horace Samuel Merrill, *Bourbon Leader: Grover Cleveland and the Democratic Party* (Boston: Little, Brown, 1957), 5–39.

8. McClure and Morris, *Authentic Life of William McKinley*, 142.

9. *Ibid.*, 160.

10. Graff, *Grover Cleveland*, 84–89.

11. James R. Green, *Death in the Haymarket: A Story of Chicago, the First Labor Movement and the Bombing That Divided Gilded Age America* (New York: Pantheon Books, 2006), 162.

Chapter Nine

1. "Letter of Harrison Accepting the Presidential Nomination," September 3, 1892, The American Presidency Project (APP), http://www.presidency.ucsb.edu/ws/index.php?pid=76068. The APP is nonprofit and nonpartisan, and it is the leading source of presidential documents on the internet.

2. Beer, *Hanna*, 110.

3. Mark Summers, *Party Games* (Chapel Hill: University of North Carolina Press, 2004), 217.

4. John Bull was a cartoon reference to England, whose free trading had badly hurt the Irish. The Irish hatred of the British continued to run deep in America, and that hatred could be used to win Irish votes.

5. Richard Sheppard, "Homestead Steel Strike of 1892," *Susquehanna*, February 1988.

6. Paul Krause, *The Battle for Homestead 1880–1892* (Pittsburgh: University of Pittsburgh Press, 1992), 103.

Chapter Ten

1. *McKinley Memorial Addresses* (Cleveland: Tippecanoe Club, 1913), 91.

2. Full discussion of Pig Iron Kelly and the Ways and Means Committee can be found in Quentin R. Skrabec, *Pig Iron Aristocracy*.

3. *Canton Repository*, June 15, 1877.

4. *Congressional Record*, 1887, Library of Congress.
5. Wayne, *William McKinley and His America*, 67-71.
6. Trade reciprocity required a goal of balanced imports and exports between countries. It was a core principle for McKinley's trade approach.
7. Remini, *Henry Clay*, 221-226.
8. Jean Strouse, *Morgan: American Financier* (New York: HarperPerennial, 2000), 73.
9. Ogilvie, *Life and Speeches of William McKinley* (1896), 20-22.
10. *McKinley Memorial Addresses*, 120.
11. Joanne Reitano, *The Tariff Question in the Gilded Age: The Great Debate of 1888* (University Park: Pennsylvania State University Press, 1994), 129.

Chapter Eleven

1. J. H. Brigham to A. J. Rose, September 4, 1891, Rose Papers, Texas History Collection, Library of Congress.
2. Albert Rees, *Real Wages in Manufacturing 1890-1914* (Princeton: Princeton University Press, 1961), 74-77.
3. Benjamin F. Alexander, *Coxey's Army: Popular Protest in the Gilded Age* (Baltimore: Johns Hopkins University Press, 2015), 25-68.
4. Lorant, *Pittsburgh*, 551.
5. John K. Winkler, *Morgan the Magnificent* (Babson Park, MA: Spear & Staff, 1950), 123.
6. George Wheeler, *Pierpont Morgan and Friends: The Anatomy of a Myth* (Englewood Cliffs, N.J.: Prentice-Hall, 1973), 17.
7. Almont Lindsay, *The Pullman Strike: The Story of a Unique Experiment and of a Great Labor Upheaval* (Chicago: University of Chicago Press, 1943), 34-70.
8. Page Smith, *The Rise of Industrial America* (New York: Penguin Books, 1984), 200-234.
9. Ray Papke, *The Pullman Case: The Clash of Labor and Capital in Industrial America* (Lawrence: University of Kansas, 1999), 123.
10. Susan Hirsch, *After the Strike: A Century of Labor Struggle at Pullman* (Urbana: University of Illinois, 2003), 35-56.

11. *New York Tribune*, January 5, 1894.
12. The income tax provision was struck down in 1895 by the U.S. Supreme Court case *Pollock v. Farmers' Loan & Trust Co.*, 157 U.S. 429 (1895). In 1913, the 16th Amendment permitted a federal income tax.
13. Allan Nevins, *Grover Cleveland—A Study in Courage*, 5th ed. (New York: Dodd, Mead, 1933), 277.

Chapter Twelve

1. John E. Hill, *Democracy, Equality, and Justice: John Adams, Adam Smith, and Political Economy* (New York: Lexington Books, 2007), 174.
2. Strouse, *Morgan: American Financier*, 360.
3. *Ibid.*, 355.
4. Stanley Jones, *The Presidential Election of 1896* (Madison: University of Wisconsin Press, 1964), 167.
5. *Ibid.*, 170.
6. *Ibid.*, 167.
7. *Ibid.*, 167-212.
8. Halstead, *Life and Distinguished Services of William McKinley*, 137.
9. Charles Dawes, *Journal of the McKinley Years* (Chicago: Lakeside, 1950), 30-200.
10. Lawrence Goodwin, *The Populist Moment* (Oxford: Oxford University Press, 1978), 282.
11. Dawes, *Journal of the McKinley Years*, 45-67.
12. Armstrong, *Major McKinley*, 55.
13. H. H. Kohlsaat, *From McKinley to Harding: Personal Recollections of Our Presidents* (New York: Charles Scribner's Sons, 1923); and Judy Crichton, *1900* (New York: Henry Holt, 1965), 18-21.

Chapter Thirteen

1. Crichton, *1900*, 30.
2. Halstead, *Life and Distinguished Services of William McKinley*, 400-411.
3. Dawes, *Journal of the McKinley Years*, 108-123.
4. *Ibid.*, 100-102.
5. Halstead, *Life and Distinguished Services of William McKinley*, 489-493.
6. *Ibid.*
7. *Ibid.*, 476-478.

Chapter Fourteen

1. Donald Anderson, *William Howard Taft: A Conservative's Conception of the Presidency* (Ithaca: Cornell University Press, 1968), 2.
2. Doris Kearns Goodwin, *The Bully Pulpit: Theodore Roosevelt, William Taft, and the Golden Age of Journalism* (New York: Simon & Schuster, 2013), 258–259.
3. Dawes, *Journal of the McKinley Years*, 185.
4. David S. Barry, *Forty Years in Washington* (Boston: Little & Brown, 1924), 268–271.
5. Richard D. Heffner and Alexander Heffner, *A Documentary History of the United States* (*Updated & Expanded*) (New York: Penguin, 2013), 146.
6. John A. Fitch, *The Steel Workers* (1910; repr., Pittsburgh: University of Pittsburgh Press, 1989), 235.
7. Patricia Beard, *After the Ball* (New York: HarperCollins, 2003), 178–200.
8. In 1911 the Federal Reserve Act was signed by Democratic president Woodrow Wilson in an effort to free the government from the House of Morgan in financial emergencies.
9. Theodore Roosevelt, *The Autobiography of Theodore Roosevelt* (1913; repr., New York: Charles Scribner's Sons, 1958), 245.
10. Strouse, *Morgan: American Financier*, 589.
11. George Harvey, *Henry Clay Frick* (Privately printed, 1936), 309.

Chapter Fifteen

1. William Taft to Henry Ford, October 31, 1924, Ford Motor Company Records 1924, Benson Ford Research Center (The Henry Ford), Dearborn, Mich.
2. Everett Walters, *Joseph Benson Foraker: An Uncompromising Republican* (Columbus: Ohio History Press, 1948), 239–240.
3. Edgar Eugene Robinson, *Presidential Vote, 1896–1932* (Stanford: Stanford University Press, 1934), 11–16.
4. Son of President James Garfield.
5. Paolo Enrico Coletta, *The Presidency of William Howard Taft* (Lawrence: University Press of Kansas, 1973), 77–78.
6. David P. Thelen, *Robert M. La Follette and the Insurgent Spirit* (Madison: University of Wisconsin Press, 1986), 136–156.
7. Michael Wolraich, "The Original Tea Partiers: How GOP Insurgents Invented Progressivism," *Atlantic's Politics & Policy Daily*, July 22, 2014, https://www.theatlantic.com/politics/archive/2014/07/the-original-tea-partiers-how-gop-insurgents-invented-progressivism/374557/.
8. L. White Busbey, *Uncle Joe Cannon: The Story of a Pioneer American* (New York: Henry Holt, 1927), 109–200.
9. David M. Shribman, "Getting Rid of Uncle Joe," *Pittsburgh Post-Gazette*, March 14, 2010.
10. Daniel Okrent, *Last Call: Rise and Fall of Prohibition* (New York: Scribner's, 2010), 282.

Chapter Sixteen

1. Sidney M. Milkis, "The Transformation of American Democracy: Teddy Roosevelt, the 1912 Election, and the Progressive Party," the Heritage Foundation website, https://www.heritage.org/political-process/report/the-transformation-american-democracy-teddy-roosevelt-the-1912-election.
2. Anderson, *William Howard Taft*, 213.
3. Taft to Guild A. Copeland, February 9, 1910, William H. Taft Papers, Presidential Series 2, Library of Congress.
4. Taft to Speaker Reid, April 7, 1910, Taft Papers.
5. Karl Rove, "This Day in Convention History: Teddy and Taft," July 23, 2016, Fox News Opinion website, http://www.foxnews.com/opinion/2016/07/21/karl-rove-this-day-in-convention-history-teddy-and-taft-once-friends-now-bitter-rivals.html.
6. August Heckscher, *Woodrow Wilson* (New York: Easton, 1991), 255–270.
7. Gary Gerstle and John Milton Cooper, Jr., eds., *Reconsidering Woodrow Wilson: Progressivism, Internationalism, War, and Peace* (Washington, D.C.: Woodrow Wilson International Center for Scholars, 2008), 103.
8. Arthur Link, *Wilson: The Road to the White House* (Princeton: Princeton University Press, 1947), 502.
9. Richard M. Valelly, *The Two Recon-

Chapter Seventeen

1. Beverly Gage, *The Day Wall Street Exploded* (Oxford: Oxford University Press, 2009), 94.
2. Aaron Brenner and Benjamin Day, *The Encyclopedia of Strikes in American History* (New York: Routledge, 2009), 449.
3. Randolph C. Downes, *The Rise of Warren Gamaliel Harding 1865-1920* (Columbus: Ohio State University Press, 1964), 237.
4. "Hughes Movement Gains Strength with No Dark Horse Yet In Sight; Dickering With Moose Fruitless," *New York Times*, June 7, 1916.
5. Downes, *Rise of Warren Gamaliel Harding*, 245.
6. Spencer C. Tucker, ed., *World War I: The Definitive Encyclopedia and Document Collection*, 2nd ed. (Santa Barbara, CA: ABC-CLIO, 2014), 85.
7. Robert Hessen, "Charles Schwab and the Shipbuilding Crisis of 1918," *Pennsylvania History: A Journal of Mid-Atlantic Studies* 38, no. 4 (October 1971): 389–399.
8. Richard B. Gregg, "The National War Labor Board," *Harvard Law Review* 33, no. 1 (November 1919): 39–63.

Chapter Eighteen

1. John Dean, *Warren Harding* (New York: Times Books, 2007), 4–23.
2. Maxim Ethan Armbruster, *The Presidents of the United States: A New Appraisal* (New York: Horizon, 1960), 277.
3. For full discussion of the wealth of these poker buddies see Quentin Skrabec's *The World's Richest Neighborhood* (New York: Algora, 2010) and *The Carnegie Boys* (Jefferson, N.C.: McFarland, 2012).
4. Ferdinand Lundberg, *America's Sixty Families* (New York: Citadel Press, 1938), 62.
5. Rich Beyer, "Where There's Smoke, There's ... Political Intrigue?," *Politico*, March 3, 2008, https://www.politico.com/story/2008/03/where-theres-smoke-theres-political-intrigue-008803.
6. William Safire, *Safire's New Political Dictionary* (Oxford: Oxford University Press, 1993), 721–722.
7. Robert Siegel and Art Silverman, "During World War I, U.S. Government Propaganda Erased German Culture," on *All Things Considered*, National Public Radio, April 7, 2017.
8. Rich Rubino, "Trump Was Not The First to Use 'America First,'" *Huffington Post*, April 17, 2017, https://www.huffingtonpost.com/entry/the-etymology-of-america-first_us_5889767de4b0628ad613de3f.
9. "Warren G. Harding," *Independent* (London), January 19, 2009, https://www.independent.co.uk/news/presidents/warren-g-harding-1417416.html.
10. Herbert Hoover, *The Memoirs of Herbert Hoover: The Cabinet and the Presidency, 1920-1933* (New York: Macmillan, 1952), 48–55.
11. Leton McCartney, *The Teapot Dome Scandal: How Big Oil Bought the Harding White House and Tried to Steal the Country* (New York: Random House, 2006).
12. Russell Berman, "Harding's Terrible Tenure," *Atlantic* website, August 14, 2015., https://www.theatlantic.com/politics/archive/2015/08/warren-g-harding-nan-britton-affair/401288/.
13. Ronald Rodash and Allis Rodash, "Rethinking Warren G. Harding," *New York Times*, August 27, 2015, https://www.nytimes.com/2015/08/27/opinion/rethinking-warren-g-harding.html.
14. Hoover, *Memoirs*, 100–103.
15. William Moye, "End of the Twelve Hour Day in the Steel Industry," *Monthly Labor Review* 100, no. 9 (September 1977): 21.

Chapter Nineteen

1. Jeff Simon, Vanessa Yurkevich and Contessa Gayle, "Outside Cleveland, Thousands of Democrats Are Becoming Republicans," CNN Politics website, July 18, 2016, https://www.cnn.com/2016/07/18/politics/cleveland-youngstown-ohio-democrats-republicans-political-anthropology/index.html.
2. Sherry Lee Linkon and John Russo, *Steel-Town U.S.A.* (Lawrence: University of Kansas Press, 2002), 130.

Bibliography

Archival Sources

Arthur, Chester Alan. Papers. Presidential Papers. Library of Congress.
Garfield, James. Papers. Library of Congress.
Grant, Ulysses S. Papers. Library of Congress.
Hanna-McCormack Papers. Library of Congress.
Hayes, Rutherford. Papers. Hayes Memorial Library. Rutherford B. Hayes Presidential Center, Fremont, Ohio.
Letters, records pertaining to William McKinley, Howard Taft, and Warren Harding. Benson Ford Research Center, Dearborn, Michigan.
McKinley, William. Papers. McKinley Birthplace Home and Research Center, Niles, Ohio.
McKinley, William Papers. McKinley Presidential Library and Museum, Canton, Ohio.
Rose Papers. Texas History Collection. Library of Congress.
Sherman, John. Papers. Library of Congress.
Taft, William H. Papers. Library of Congress.
Whittlesey, Elisha. Papers. Western Reserve Historical Society, Cleveland, Ohio

Books and Articles

Ackerman, Kenneth. *Dark Horse: The Surprise Election and Political Murder of President James Garfield*. New York: Carroll & Graf, 2003.
Alexander, Benjamin F. *Coxey's Army: Popular Protest in the Gilded Age*. Baltimore: Johns Hopkins University Press, 2015.
"American Economy." *Manufacturer and Builder* 20, no. 2 (November 1888).
Anderson, Donald. *William Howard Taft: A Conservative's Conception of the Presidency.* Ithaca: Cornell University Press, 1968.
Armbruster, Maxim Ethan. *The Presidents of the United States: A New Appraisal*. New York: Horizon, 1960.
Armstrong, William H. *Major McKinley: McKinley and the Civil War*. Kent, OH: Kent State University Press, 2000.
Barry, David S. *Forty Years in Washington*. Boston: Little, Brown, 1924.
Bauer, K. Jack. *Zachary Taylor: Soldier, Planter, Statesman of the Old Southwest*. Baton Rouge: Louisiana State University Press, 1985.
Beard, Patricia. *After the Ball*. New York: HarperCollins, 2003.
Beer, Thomas. *Hanna*. New York: Knopf, 1929.
Benson, Lee. *The Concept of Jacksonian Democracy*. Princeton: Princeton University Press, 1961.
Brands, W. H. *The Man Who Saved the Union: Ulysses S. Grant in War and Peace*. New York: Doubleday, 2012.
Brenner, Arron, and Benjamin Day. *The Encyclopedia of Strikes in American History*. New York: Routledge, 2009.
Bunting, Josiah, III. *Ulysses S. Grant*. New York: Henry Holt, 2004.
Busbey, L. White. *Uncle Joe Cannon: The Story of a Pioneer American*. New York: Henry Holt, 1927.

Cain, Peter. *Free Trade and Protectionism: Key Nineteenth Century Journal Summaries*. London: Routledge, 1996.
Campbell, Bruce, and Richard J. Trilling. *Realignment in American Politics: Toward a Theory*. Austin: University of Texas Press, 2014.
Cash, James. *Unsung Heroes*. Wilmington, OH: Orange Frazer, 1998.
Coben, Stanley. "Northeastern Business and Radical Reconstruction: A Re-Examination." *Mississippi Valley Historical Review* 46, no. 1 (June 1959): 67–90.
Coletta, Paolo Enrico. *The Presidency of William Howard Taft*. Lawrence: University Press of Kansas, 1973.
Crichton, Judy. *1900*. New York: Henry Holt, 1965.
Croly, Herbert. *Marcus Alonzo Hanna*. New York: Macmillan, 1912.
Curry, Richard O. "The Union As It Was: A Critique of Recent Interpretations of the 'Copperheads.'" *Civil War History* 13, no. 1 (1967): 25–39.
Dawes, Charles. *Journal of the McKinley Years*. Chicago: Lakeside, 1950.
Depew, Chauncey. *My Memories of 80 Years*. New York: Charles Scribner & Sons, 1924.
Downes, Randolph. *The Rise of Warren Gamaliel Harding 1865–1920*. Columbus: Ohio State University Press, 1964.
Ebinger, Eric. *100 Days in the Life of Rutherford Hayes*. Wilmington, OH: Orange Frazer, 2016.
Everett, Marshall. *Complete Life of William McKinley*. Marshall Everett, 1901.
Fallows, Samuel. *Life of William McKinley—Our Martyred President*. Chicago: Regan, 1901.
Fitch, John A. *The Steel Workers*. 1910. Reprint. Pittsburgh: University of Pittsburgh Press, 1989.
Frank, A. G. *Capitalism and Underdevelopment in Latin America*. New York: Monthly Review Press, 1967.
Frolik, Joe. "How Ohio Made a President: Mark Hanna of Cleveland Created Modern Politics in 1896." *Plain Dealer* (Cleveland, OH), October 16, 2012.
Gage, Beverly. *The Day Wall Street Exploded*. Oxford: Oxford University Press, 2009.
Gerstle, Gary, and John Milton Cooper, Jr., eds. *Reconsidering Woodrow Wilson: Progressivism, Internationalism, War, and Peace*. Washington, D.C.: Woodrow Wilson International Center for Scholars, 2008.
Glad, Paul W. *McKinley, Bryan and People*. Chicago: Ivan R. Dee, 1991.
Goodwin, Doris Kearns. *The Bully Pulpit: Theodore Roosevelt, William Taft, and the Golden Age of Journalism*. New York: Simon & Schuster, 2013.
Goodwin, Lawrence. *The Populist Moment*. Oxford: Oxford University Press, 1978.
Graff, Henry. *Grover Cleveland: The American Presidents Series: The 22nd and 24th President, 1885–1889 and 1893–1897*. New York: Henry Holt, 2002.
Grant, U. S. *Personal Memoirs of U. S. Grant*. 1885. Reprint. New York: Acheron, 2010.
Gregg, Richard. "The National War Labor Board." *Harvard Law Review* 33, no. 1 (November 1919): 39–63.
Halstead, Musat. *The Life and Distinguished Services of William McKinley*. McKinley Memorial Association, 1901.
Hamilton, Alexander. *Report on Manufactures*. January 15, 1790. New York: Kessinger, 2010.
Harrison, Benjamin. *Speeches of Benjamin Harrison—Twenty-Third President of the United States*. New York: Leopold Classic Library, 2015.
Harvey, George. *Henry Clay Frick*. Privately printed, 1936.
Heckscher, August. *Woodrow Wilson*. New York: Easton, 1991.
Heffner, Richard D., and Alexander Heffner. *A Documentary History of the United States (Updated & Expanded)*. New York: Penguin, 2013.
Heidler, David, and Jeanne Heidler. *Henry Clay: Essential American*. New York: Random Press, 2010.
Hesseltine, William. *U. S. Grant, Politician*. New York: Dodd, Mead, 1935.
Hessen, Robert. "Charles Schwab and the Shipbuilding Crisis of 1918." *Pennsylvania History: A Journal of Mid-Atlantic Studies* 38, no. 4 (October 1971): 389–399.
Hill, John E. *Democracy, Equality, and Justice: John Adams, Adam Smith, and Political Economy*. New York: Lexington Books, 2007.
Hirsch, Susan. *After the Strike: A Century of Labor Struggle at Pullman*. Urbana: University of Illinois, 2003.

Holt, Michael. *The Rise and Fall of the American Whig Party: Jacksonian Politics and the Onset of the Civil War.* Oxford: Oxford University Press, 1999.

Hopkins, James, and Mary Hargreaves, eds. *Papers of Henry Clay.* Vols. 1–11. Lexington: University of Kentucky Press, 1959–1992.

Hoover, Herbert. *The Memoirs of Herbert Hoover: The Cabinet and the Presidency, 1920–1933.* New York: Macmillan, 1952.

Horner, William. *Ohio's Kingmaker: Mark Hanna, Man, and Myth.* Athens: Ohio University Press, 2010.

Jennings, William. *Transylvania: Pioneer University of the West.* New York: Pageant, 1955.

Jensen, Richard. *The Winning of the Midwest: Social and Political Conflict, 1888–1896.* Chicago: University of Chicago Press, 1971.

Jones, Stanley. *The Presidential Election of 1896.* Madison: University of Wisconsin Press, 1964.

Kasson, John. *Civilizing the Machine.* New York: Hill & Wang, 1977.

Kerr, Winfield. *John Sherman: His Life and Public Services.* Vol. 2. Boston: Sherman, French, 1908.

Kohlsaat, H. *From McKinley to Harding: Personal Recollections of Our Presidents.* New York: Charles Scribner's Sons, 1923.

Krause, Paul. *The Battle for Homestead 1880–1892.* Pittsburgh: University of Pittsburgh Press, 1992.

Leech, Margaret. *In the Days of McKinley.* New York: Harper & Brothers, 1959.

Lindsay, Almont. *The Pullman Strike: The Story of a Unique Experiment and of a Great Labor Upheaval.* Chicago: University of Chicago Press, 1943.

Link, Arthur. *Wilson: The Road to the White House.* Princeton: Princeton University Press, 1947.

Linkon, Sherry Lee, and John Russo. *SteelTown U.S.A.* Lawrence: University of Kansas Press, 2002.

Lorant, Stefan. *Pittsburgh: The Story of an American City.* Lenox, Mass.: Donnelley & Sons, 1964.

Lundberg, Ferdinand. *America's Sixty Families.* New York: Citadel Press, 1938.

McCartney, Leton. *The Teapot Dome Scandal: How Big Oil Bought the Harding White House and Tried to Steal the Country.* New York: Random House, 2006.

McClure, Alexander, and Charles Morris. *The Authentic Life of William McKinley: Our Third Martyr President.* U.S. Congress, 1901.

McFeely, William. *Grant: A Biography.* New York: W. W. Norton, 1981.

McKinley, William. "The Value of Protection." *North American Review* 150, no. 403 (June 1890): 740–748.

McKinley Memorial Addresses. Cleveland: Tippecanoe Club, 1913.

Merrill, Horace Samuel. *Bourbon Leader: Grover Cleveland and the Democratic Party.* Boston: Little, Brown, 1957.

Millard, Candice. *Destiny of the Republic: A Tale of Madness, Medicine, and the Murder of a President.* New York: Anchor Books, 2011.

Morgan, Wayne. *From Hayes to McKinley: National Party Politics, 1872–1896.* Syracuse: Syracuse University Press, 1969.

Moye, William. "End of the Twelve Hour Day in the Steel Industry." *Monthly Labor Review* 100, no. 9 (September 1977): 21–26.

Nevins, Allan. *Grover Cleveland—A Study in Courage.* 5th ed. New York: Dodd, Mead, 1933.

Niven, John. *Salmon P. Chase: A Biography.* Oxford: Oxford University Press, 1995.

Ogilvie, John, ed. *Life and Speeches of William McKinley.* 1896. Reprint. New York: Kessinger, 2010.

Okrent, Daniel. *Last Call: Rise and Fall of Prohibition.* New York: Scribner's, 2010.

Pafford, John. *The Forgotten Conservative: Rediscovering Grover Cleveland.* New York: Regnery History, 2013.

Papke, Ray. *The Pullman Case: The Clash of Labor and Capital in Industrial America.* Lawrence: University of Kansas Press, 1999.

Perret, Geoffrey. *Ulysses S. Grant: Soldier & President.* New York: Random House, 1997.

Perry, James. *Touched with Fire: Five Presidents and the Civil War Battles That Made Them.* New York: Public Affairs, 2003.

Peskin, Allan. *Garfield.* Kent, OH: Kent State University Press, 1978.

———. "Who Were the Stalwarts? Who Were Their Rivals? Republican Factions in the Gilded Age." *Political Science Quarterly* 99, no. 4 (1984): 703–716.

Platt, Thomas. *Autobiography of Thomas Collier*. New York: Dodge, 1910.
Rees, Albert. *Real Wages in Manufacturing 1890–1914*. Princeton: Princeton University Press, 1961.
Reitano, Joanne. *The Tariff Question in the Gilded Age: The Great Debate of 1888*. University Park: Pennsylvania State University Press, 1994.
Remini, Robert. *Henry Clay: Statesman of the Union*. New York: W. W. Norton, 1991.
Robinson, Edgar Eugene. *Presidential Vote, 1896–1932*. Stanford: Stanford University Press, 1934.
Roosevelt, Theodore. *The Autobiography of Theodore Roosevelt*. 1913. Reprint. New York: Charles Scribner's Sons, 1958.
Roseboom, Eugene. *The Civil War Era: 1850–1873*. Columbus: Ohio Historical Society, 1944.
Rubino, Rich. "Trump Was Not The First to Use 'America First.'" *Huffington Post*, April 17, 2017. https://www.huffingtonpost.com/entry/the-etymology-of-america-first_us_5889767de4b0628ad613de3f.
Safire, William. *Safire's New Political Dictionary*. Oxford: Oxford University Press, 1993.
Skrabec, Quentin. *The Pig Iron Aristocracy: The Triumph of American Protectionism*. Westminster, MD: Heritage Books, 2008.
Smith, Page. *The Rise of Industrial America*. New York: Penguin Books, 1984.
Smith, Theodore Clarke. *The Life and Letters of James Abram Garfield*. Hamden, CT: Archon Books, 1968.
Smith, William Henry, and Charles Richard Williams. *The Life of Rutherford Birchard Hayes: Nineteenth President of the United States*. Vols. 1–3. University of Michigan Library, January 1, 1914. Digital copy via Amazon.
Stewart, James. *Joshua R. Giddings and the Tactics of Radical Politics*. Cleveland: Press of Case Western Reserve, 1970.
Strouse, Jean. *Morgan: American Financier*. New York: HarperPerennial, 2000.
Summers, Mark. *Party Games*. Chapel Hill: University of North Carolina Press, 2004.
Thelen, David. *Robert M. La Follette and the Insurgent Spirit*. Madison: University of Wisconsin Press, 1986.
Tucker, Spencer C., ed. *World War I: The Definitive Encyclopedia and Document Collection*. 2nd ed. Santa Barbara: ABC-CLIO, 2014.
Valelly, Richard. *The Two Reconstructions: The Struggle for Black Enfranchisement*. Chicago: University of Chicago Press, 2009.
Walters, Everett. *Joseph Benson Foraker: An Uncompromising Republican*. Columbus: Ohio History Press, 1948.
Wayne, Morgan. *William McKinley and His America*. Syracuse: Syracuse University Press, 1963.
Weisenburger, Francis. *The Passing of the Frontier: 1825–1850*. Vol. 3. Columbus: Ohio Historical Society, 1941.
Wheeler, John. *Pierpont Morgan and Friends: The Anatomy of a Myth*. Englewood Cliffs, N.J.: Prentice-Hall, 1973.
Winkler, John. *Morgan the Magnificent*. Babson Park, MA: Spear & Staff, 1950.
Wolraich, Michael. "The Original Tea Partiers: How GOP Insurgents Invented Progressivism." *Atlantic's Politics & Policy Daily*, July 22, 2014. https://www.theatlantic.com/politics/archive/2014/07/the-original-tea-partiers-how-gop-insurgents-invented-progressivism/374557/.

Index

Abolition 3, 6, 34–36, 43, 60, 82
Adams, John 139–140
Akron (Ohio) 84, 135
Alger, Russell 140
Allegheny County (Pa.) 23, 26, 55
Alliance (Ohio) 27
Allison, William 140–142
Amalgamated Association of Iron and Steel Workers 106, 108–110
American Federation of Labor (AFL) 184–185, 192
American Socialist Party 138, 184
American system 32, 34, 50–52, 56, 116–119, 139–140, 153–158
Anarchists 136–138
Anthracite Coal Strike 163–164
Antietam, Battle of 53–54
Anti-Mason Party 32–33
Arthur, Chester A. 87–88, 91–94, 119

Beecher, Catherine 37–42
Beecher, Harriet 39
Beecher, Lyman 37–42
Bell, Alexander 91–92
Bimetallism 105, 114, 117, 121–123, 129, 140–143, 151
Blaine, James G. 72–75, 78–79, 96, 104, 121–127, 129
Bourbon Democrats 97–98
Braddock (Pa.) 24–25
Bryan, William Jennings 145–148
Buchanan, James 56
Buffalo 11–15

Calhoun, John 50–51
Campbell, James 132
Cannon, Joseph 175–177

Canton (Ohio) 17–18, 24–26, 118, 121–122, 131–133
Capitalism 15–20, 24, 28, 122–125, 139–140, 181–182, 202–203
Carey, Henry C. 56–57
Carlisle, John 106
Carnegie, Andrew 96–99, 105, 122, 138, 141–144, 196–197
Carnegie Steel 108–111, 122
Case Western Reserve University 75
Chase, Salmon 48
Chicago 14, 76, 110, 137–138
Chinese migrant workers 77–78, 85, 117
Cincinnati 14, 26, 32, 37, 54, 71–72, 124
Cincinnati College 37–38
Cincinnati Literary Society 42–43, 75–76
Civil Rights 6, 65–74, 81–83, 155–158
Civil Rights Act of 1875 68–69, 72–74
Civil War 27, 49–57
Clay, Henry 9, 13, 23, 27, 32–33, 35, 55, 113–115, 139–141
Cleveland 14, 55, 135
Cleveland, Grover 2, 92–97, 103–105, 122–123, 132–138; tariffs 94–97, 102–103, 132–138; views on the economy 96–97, 100–103, 132–138
Coal miners 23–24, 134–136
College of Teachers 37–42, 46, 74–75, 172
Columbiana County 94–95, 116, 203–204
Columbus (Ohio) 51
Compromise of 1877 73–74
Congressional election of 1888 105–107
Conkling, Roscoe 72
Constitution: 14th Amendment 67–68; 15th Amendment 67–68
Copperheads 67–70
Coxey, Jacob Sechler 134–136

219

Coxey's March 134–136
Cuyahoga County 81
Czolgosz, Leon 15–18, 124

Dawes, Charles 142–144
Debs, Eugene 20, 136–138, 184–185
Delaware (Ohio) 70–71
Democratic Party 33, 61–64, 67–72, 84–85, 181–186, 202–205
Dinner Pail Republicanism 29
Drake, Daniel 37–41

Edison, Thomas 7, 203
Eight-hour day 18, 20, 96–97, 100–102, 121–122, 201

Farm vote 73–75, 85–88, 131–138
Farmers' Revolt (1890 midterms) 131–138
Federal Reserve Act of 1913 187–189
Findlay (Ohio) 133
Ford, Henry 7, 204
42nd Ohio Infantry Regiment 82
Free Silver Movement 86
Free Soil Party 44–45
Free trade 18–19, 63–64, 84–88, 109–110
Fremont (Ohio) 47
Fremont, John C. 47, 71
Frick, Henry Clay 25, 105, 113–114, 138, 141–144, 196–199

Garfield, James 1, 11–13, 48–57, 67–69, 76–89, 91–93; civil rights 48–57; tariffs 77–78, 84–88; technology 91; views on education 80–81; views on the economy 84–88
Garfield, Lucretia 85–86
German farmers 73–75, 85–88, 131–138
German immigrants 101–102
Giddings, Joshua 32–33, 46–47
Glass industry and tariffs 133
Gold standard 83–85, 97, 104, 116–117, 122–123, 129, 138, 140
Gompers, Samuel 18, 137
Grange 86, 117–119, 122–123, 130–131
Grant, Ulysses S. 1, 9, 16, 45, 57–69; civil rights 49–57, 58–61, 67–69; tariffs 57, 62–64; technology 58–59; views on education 60–61; views on the economy 57–59
Great Awakening 39–40
Great Railroad Strike of 1877 19, 76–78
Greeley, Horace 62–63
Greenback Labor Party 87, 117, 131
Greenback Party 69, 107

Half-Breeds (Republicans) 72–73
Hamilton, Alexander 8–9, 43, 52, 84

Hanna, Mark 45, 51, 89–91, 116–120, 131–133, 136–143, 166–168
Harding, Warren 1, 16, 45, 193–205; civil rights 1, 16, 45; tariffs 203–204; technology 204; views on education 193; views on the economy 194–199
Harrison, Benjamin 1, 19, 45, 99–110, 129–129, 130–138; tariffs 100–102, 126–130; 131–135; views on the economy 126–129, 131–135
Harrison, William 1, 31, 33, 45, 48–57; civil rights 34–35, 48–56; tariffs 100–101; views on the economy 33
Hayes, Lucy 54–55, 75
Hayes, Rutherford 1, 11, 15, 19, 40–42, 45, 48–57, 64–78, 112, 114; civil rights 48–57, 70–74; tariffs 84; technology 7, 65–66; views on education 40–42, 54, 74–75; views on the economy 64–66
Haymarket Riot 101–103, 124
Heinz, H. J. 20
Holmes County 129–131
Homestead (Pa.) 25–26
Homestead Strike of 1892 108–112
Hoover, Herbert 199–200
Hurd, Frank 106
Hyde, James 167–168

Income taxes 64–65, 179–180, 187–188
Internationalism 80–89
Interstate Commerce Act of 1887 100
Irish workers 28, 74, 76–77
Iron Whigs 54, 57

Jackson, Andrew 16, 32–33, 35, 50
Jim Crow Laws 185
Johnson, Andrew 60–62
Jones, Bill 122

Kelly, William, "Pig Iron" 84–85, 112, 114
Kenton College 54, 70
Knights of Labor 101–102, 106–107
Knox, Philander 25, 164–166, 196
Ku Klux Klan Act 68

Labor Party 107
Labor vote 105–110, 115–120
La Follette, Robert 174–176, 199–200
Laissez-faire capitalism 97–98
League of Nations 196–197
Liberal Republican Party 63–64, 67–68, 71–74
Liberty Party 45
Lincoln, Abraham 9, 23, 24–25, 43, 46, 48, 51, 58–59, 61, 71
Lodge, Henry Cabot 17, 143–144, 154
Ludlow Strike 188–189

Mahoning Valley 134–135, 202–203
Manifest Destiny 6
Marx, Karl 18
Massillon (Ohio) 134–136
Maumee (Ohio) 133
McGuffey, William 30, 36–41, 74–75
McGuffey Readers 6, 37–38, 39–41, 60, 82, 103, 172, 194
McKinley, Ida 118, 123, 144
McKinley, William 1, 5, 11–20, 48, 92–98, 112–124, 135–158; civil rights 155–161; Civil War 21–23, 48–57; death 21–25; tariffs 15–20, 25–26, 93–97, 115–120; technology 7, 15, 139–140; Veteran relations 21–23, 159–160; views on the economy 15–18, 28, 93–97, 115–120, 124, 133–135; women rights 22
McKinley Tariff Act of 1890 103–104, 126–127, 129–132
Mellow, Andrew 25, 196–198
Miami College (University) 37–41, 104
Mills, Roger 125–126
Mills Act 125–126
Moral values 2–6, 16
Morgan, J. P. 16, 53, 57, 96–97, 122–124, 132–138, 140–143, 160–166
Morrison Tariff Bill 95–97, 123–124
Morton, Levi 140
Mugwumps 122
Mulligan letters 97–98

National Capitalism 80–89, 113–116, 139–140, 202–204
National Republican Party 32–33, 61–63, 120
National Road 51
National Union Party 59–62
National War Labor Board 192–194
Niagara Falls 15, 140
Niles (Ohio) 25–27, 204
Nullification Crisis 50–51

Oberlin College 37, 40
Ohio Canal 6, 8, 11–12, 32–33, 81–82
Ohio Republicanism 1–4, 7, 8–10, 14, 21, 29, 31–41, 49, 56–78, 83–88, 90–97, 112–120, 129–135, 137, 139–150, 171–180, 187–194
Ohio State University 75
Owen, Robert 38

Panama Canal 6, 11–12, 59, 65–66, 104, 173
Panic of 1872 68–69, 75–76
Panic of 1893 132–137
Panic of 1907 159, 167–170, 187–189
Payne-Aldrich Tariff Act 178–179
Pendleton Act of 1883 92–93

Pennsylvania Railroad 76–78
People's Party 69–70
Pig Iron Aristocrats 51–52, 55
Pittsburgh 23–25, 55, 76–77, 132
Platt, Thomas 140–144
Point Pleasant (Ohio) 60
Poland (Ohio) 51
Polk, James K. 44–45
Populist Party 132–135
Presidential Election of 1876 73–74
Progressive Party 183
Progressivism 159–170
Prohibition 194–196
Protectionism 5–6, 9–10, 29, 43, 56, 63–64, 77–79, 84–88, 95–97, 114–120
Public School System 37–40
Pujo Committee 187–189
Pullman, George 136–138
Pullman Strike 136–138
Purell, Archbishop of Cincinnati 38–39
Puritan 7

Quay, Matthew 105, 140

Radical Republicans 48–49, 58–63, 67–68, 71–73, 78
Railroad safety 127–128
Railroad Safety Act 127–128
Reed, Thomas 140, 143
Republican Party 1–2, 8, 31–32, 35, 43–51, 55, 75–79, 126, 129, 140–143, 172–175, 181–184
Republicanism (defined) 2–4
Rockefeller, John D. 188–189
Roosevelt, Theodore 17–18, 25, 29, 145–150, 154, 159–170
Rosecrans, William 51
Rubber industry tariffs 177–178

Schwab, Charles 192–193
Scientific Tariffs 52, 59–60, 65–66, 77–79, 80–81, 85–88
Scots-Irish 36–37, 55
Second Great Awakening 38–39
Sherman, John 48, 51, 56, 72–73, 76–79, 95, 114–117, 121–122, 126
Sherman Anti-Trust Act 154
Sherman Silver Act 107–108, 127, 129–130, 152–155
Silver currency 103–107, 113–114, 116–118, 142–145
Skilled labor 108–111
Slavery 58–65, 68–69, 81–82, 159–160
Socialism 17–21, 28, 38–39, 124–125, 159–160, 183–186
Socialists 109–111, 135–138
Spanish-American War 146–148

Stalwart Republicans 71–73, 77–78, 83, 91
Stark County 115–116, 129–130
Sugar tariff 130–131

Taft, Alphonso 47
Taft, William 1, 5, 29, 171–186 civil rights; tariffs 181–186; technology 7, 176–177; views on the economy 182–186
Tariff Act of 1828 50
Tariff Act of 1833 50–51
Tariff Act (Morrill Act) of 1861 67
Tariff Act of 1862 51
Tariff Act (Underwood Act) of 1913 67
Tariff Commission 9, 94–95, 120
Tariffs 5–6, 9–10, 12–13, 25–26, 48–57, 56–57, 62–66, 68–70, 76–79, 85–88, 91–103, 109–112, 114–116, 123–127, 131–138, 177–180, 187–189
Tariffs for Revenue 56, 63–65, 85–86, 114
Taylor, Zachary 44–46
Teapot Dome Scandal 198–200
Temperance 3, 35–36, 39–40, 74–75, 80–81, 119, 179–180, 194–195
Tilden, Samuel 73
Toledo 106, 117
Trade dumping 10
Trade reciprocity 9–10, 13–14, 77–79, 104, 157–158
Transylvania 30–35, 60, 81, 105, 133–134, 172, 180, 203
Transylvania College 36–37
Trumbull County 203
Trump election 202–206
Trusts 153–155
23rd Ohio Infantry Regiment 51–53

Union Party 70–71, 107

Van Buren, Martin 44–46
Vincennes University 33–34
Volstead Act 194–195

Washburne, Elihu B. 61–62
Western Reserve (Ohio) 7, 33, 45–47, 74, 80–84
Westinghouse, George 15–16, 20, 23–25, 118–120, 125–127, 168–170
Whig Party 1, 8–9, 23, 26, 29, 32–35, 39, 41–46, 49–51, 61–63, 90, 134, 159–160, 203
Whiskey Rebellion of 1794 36–37
Wilmerding (Pa.) 24
Wilson, William 137–138
Wilson, Woodrow 183–186
Wilson-Gorman Tariff 138
Window Glass Workers 106
Workingman's Tariff Club 106
Workingmen's Party 163–164
World Fair 1876 (Philadelphia) 6
World Fair 1896 (Chicago) 6
World Fair 1901 (Buffalo) 11–12
World Fair 1904 (St. Louis) 6
World War I 189–192

YMCA 24, 118
Youngstown 10, 203–205

Zoar (Ohio) 38–39

www.ingramcontent.com/pod-product-compliance
Lightning Source LLC
Chambersburg PA
CBHW032052300426
44116CB00007B/703